MIRACLES IN MOTION

JANET DIANE MOURGLIA-SWERDLOW

Expansions Publishing Company, Inc.
Saint Joseph, Michigan
USA

Copyright © 2021 Expansions Publishing Company, Inc.

Published by: Expansions Publishing Company, Inc.
                P.O. Box 12
                Saint Joseph Michigan 49085 USA
                269-519-8036
                Skype: eventsatexpansions
                customersupport@expansions.com
                www.expansions.com

ISBN: 978-1-7349281-4-3

Cover Photo by Jonathan J. Swerdlow
www.jonathanswerdlow.com

All rights reserved. Printed in the United States of America. No parts of this book may be used or reproduced in any manner whatsoever without written permission except in the case of brief quotations embodied in critical articles and reviews.

MEDICAL DISCLAIMER

The information provided in this publication is not an attempt to attempt to practice medicine or provide specific medical advice, nor is it a substitute for medical care.

We always recommend consulting with a healthcare professional before starting any diet, exercise, supplementation, or medication program.

You assume full responsibility for using any information provided and agree that we are not responsible or liable for any claim resulting from its use by you or any user.

Dedication

To
Mamie Lou McCormick Lane
December 1938 – March 2020

For her ability to look at the Soul with
Chakhmah/Wisdom and Binah/Understanding.
and
For Her Unconditional Love and Acceptance of
Me Exactly as I AM.

Books by Stewart A. Swerdlow & Janet Diane Mourglia-Swerdlow

13-Cubed: Case Studies in Mind-Control & Programming
13-Cubed Squared: More Case Studies in Mind-Control & Programming
1099 Daily Affirmations for Self-Change
Alternative Medical Apocrypha: Body-Mind Correlations
Blue Blood, True Blood: Conflict & Creation
Dark to Light: Ancient Codes of Torah, Kabbalah & Zohar
Decoding Your Life: An Experiential Course in Self-Reintegration
Healer's Handbook: A Journey Into Hyperspace

Healing Archetypes and Symbols
Heights of Deprogramming
Heights of Health
Heights of Relationships
Heights of Spirituality
Heights of Wealth

Hyperspace Helper
Hyperspace Plus
King Bee, Queen Bee
Little Fluff's Children's Series
Miracles in Motion
Montauk: Alien Connection
Revelations of Time & Space, History and God
Stewart Says…
Template of God-Mind
True Reality of Sexuality
True World History: Humanity's Saga
White Owl Legends: An Archetypal Story of Creation

Contents

Introduction 11
Crossing Your Own Reed Sea 13
    AFFIRMATIONS—Courageous Communication 44
Introduction to the 72 Names of God 49
    NAME FREQUENCIES
    #1: Time Travel 57
    #2: Recapturing the Sparks 65
    #3: Miracle Making 71
    #4: Eliminating Negative Thoughts 81
    #5: Healing 85
    #6: Dream State 89
    #7: Soul-Personality Mind-Patterns 93
    #8: Neutralizing Negative Energy 99
    #9: Proper Angelic Frequencies 103
    #10: Protection From Negative Projections 107
    #11: Cleansing Evil 111
    #12: Unconditional Love 115
    #13: Personal Transformation 119
    #14: Neutralizing Conflict 123
    #15: Clear Vision 129

#16: Releasing Depression 133
#17: Animal Mind Control 135
#18: Fertility 137
#19: Conscious Source Connection 141
#20: Releasing Addictions 145
#21: Root Causes 149
#22: Filtering Negativity 153
#23: Dark to Light 157
#24: Releasing Jealousy 161
#25: Giving & Receiving Truth 165
#26: Order from Unrecognized Patterns 169
#27: Tithing 173
#28: Soul Mates 177
#29: Releasing Hatred 181
#30: Building Bridges 185
#31: Completion 187
#32: Memory 191
#33: Confronting Darkness 195
#34: Balancing Ego 199
#35: Sexual Energy 203
#36: Fearlessness 207
#37: Big Picture 211
#38: Growing by Flowing 215
#39: Transformation 219
#40: Speaking Correctly 223
#41: Self-Value 227

#42: Revealing the Hidden 231
#43: Mind Over Matter 235
#44: Eliminating Judgment 239
#45: Prosperity & Wealth 243
#46: Absolute Certainty 247
#47: World Peace & Global Transformation 251
#48: Unity 255
#49: Happiness 261
#50: Limitlessness 263
#51: Repentance 267
#52: Passion 271
#53: Unconditional Sharing 275
#54: Correct Death 279
#55: Actualize Ideas 283
#56: Releasing Anger 287
#57: Soul Connection 291
#58: Letting Go 293
#59: Feeling Safe 297
#60: Freedom 299
#61: Emotions 303
#62: Living Example 307
#63: Appreciation 311
#64: Appropriate Influences 315
#65: Acute Observation 319
#66: Self-Responsibility 323
#67: Eternal Now 327

#68: Contacting the Departed 331
#69: Spiritual Direction 335
#70: Finding Direction & Movement 337
#71: Simultaneity 341
#72: Spiritual Cleansing 345
AFFIRMATIONS—FREQUENCY 347
Kabbalah 353
AFFIRMATIONS—Multidimensional Questing 391
Book of Formation 397
AFFIRMATIONS—Healing Past Spirituality 465
AFFIRMATIONS—Creating By Breathing 471
APPENDICES
The 10 Sefirot 478
The 10 Sefirot Correlated to Hyperspace 479
The Ana Beko'ach Prayer 480
I AM that I AM 482
What is a Mezuzah? 483
Glossary 485
Index 495

Introduction

Stewart and I have been studying **Kabbalah, Torah, and Zohar** for several years in a variety of ways from a variety of sources. Interestingly enough, we both started studying the **72 Names of God** in more depth after the completion of our *Spirituality Book Bundle:*

King Bee, Queen Bee

Template of God-Mind

Revelations of Time & Space, History and God

Heights of Spirituality

What is even more interesting is that my devout Southern Baptist Aunt Mamie Lou had a favorite book called *The Red Sea Rules*. I was unaware of this book until after her passing when a cousin mentioned it to me. I share with you in the first chapter how my Aunt sent this book to me from the Beyond.

Amazingly, it turns out that *The Red Sea Rules* is a perfect segue into the **72 Names of God**. This means that my Aunt was also studying the **72 Names of God** in her own way. To me, this is beyond coincidence; this is part of the Divine Plan. This in turn inspired me to write the first chapter of this book, followed by increasingly important information and essential words of wisdom that lead you deeper into your Multidimensional Self.

I have blended this information with Hyperspace/Oversoul tools and techniques to help you put your life together in a way that uplifts and elevates. Always remember that **Kabbalah**, **Torah**, and **Zohar** are not meant to be a religion. They are Ancient Codes of Existence meant for all of Humanity as instructions for living.

The Eternal Existence of Your Soul is fascinating!

Always remember what I told you in **Decoding Your Life**:

You are the Most Fascinating Person You Know!

The deeper you go, the more you know all of this to be true!

Crossing Your Own Reed Sea

Yes, I meant to write *Reed Sea* and not *Red Sea* as I shall explain. But first, I want to tell you the sequence of events that led me to write this chapter. A few months ago, I lost my most favorite aunt. It was a horrible blow to my Animal Mind that wants her *here* and not *there*. My Spiritual Mind knows that she is where she wants to be and she is happy. And I know that she is still watching over me. After she passed, because of the plannedemic, only a small graveside service was allowed. My cousin subsequently told me that the pastor read from her favorite book called *The Red Sea Rules*. I had never heard of the book, but wanted to read it so I could feel closer to my aunt.

    I had a difficult time finding even a used copy but eventually found one online. Every time I checked my online account, the book was marked not shipped, so imagine my surprise when one day a copy showed up with a blank gift card enclosed. I thought my cousin must have sent it, so in one text I alluded to the gift book, but he ignored the comment. My online account still said the book had not shipped. Since I had a gift copy I asked for a refund. The seller immediately responded saying that the book had been sent, could not explain why the book was marked not shipped (even to this day) and the gift card must have been enclosed in error. Now I know my aunt caused the blank gift card to be enclosed. It was her gift to me. My aunt was extremely spiritual and intuitive. I feel /see her guiding hand in the sequence of events that followed my receipt of this book. Here is a synopsis of the book from the Amazon website:

The Red Sea Rules

Ten rules of dealing with dilemmas and discouragements – a divine protocol for handling life. Red Sea Rules has been updated with new study questions.

> Life is hard, especially for Christians. It is certain that we will face difficulties, and that God will allow them, as He allowed the Israelites to become trapped between Pharaoh's rushing armies and the uncrossable Red Sea. But just as certain is the fact that the same God who led us in will lead us out. As The Red Sea Rules makes comfortingly clear, He is in control.
>
> Using the Israelites' story in Exodus 14 as an example, Robert Morgan offers ten sound strategies for moving from fear to faith. Just as Moses and the Israelites found themselves caught between *"the devil and the deep Red Sea,"* so are we sometimes overwhelmed by life's problems. The Red Sea Rules reveals that even in the midst of seemingly impossible situations God promises to make a way for us. His loving guidance will protect us through danger, illness, marital strife, financial problems, or whatever challenges Satan places in our path.
>
> https://www.amazon.com/Red-Sea-Rules-God-Given-Strategies/dp/0529104407

Many English translations refer to the sea that the Israelites cross in Exodus as the *Red Sea*. The English follow the Greek Septuagint and Latin Vulgate, which both have "Red Sea" (ἐρυθρὰν θάλασσαν; Mare Erythrae). In Hebrew, though, the body of water is called *"Yam Suf"* (יַם סוּף), which literally means, *"Sea of Reeds"*.

When the baby Moses escaped from Pharaoh, his mother put him in a basket and *"placed it among the reeds (קָנֶה) by the riverbank"* (Exod 2:3). Moses' first escape from Pharaoh through the *"reeds"* foreshadows Israel's escape from Pharaoh through a sea of *"reeds"*. Moses' experience among the reeds in his infancy anticipates his ultimate calling to lead God's people to freedom.

https://weekly.israelbiblecenter.com/red-sea-reed-sea/

So even though my aunt is not physically here, she is still helping me cross through my own inner *Reed Sea*, gifting me with instructions through symbolism to help me find my path. Thus, I will share with you some tools to help you find your way through your own inner *Reed Sea*.

- Do you have an inner *Reed Sea*?
- What happens if you put the words *Reed Sea* at your Pineal Gland?
- What happens if you put the words *Red Sea* at your Pineal Gland?
- Do you think *Reed Sea* was purposely mistranslated to *Red Sea*?
- If so, why?
- What is the positive function of the color Red?
- What does "Sea" refer to with regard to Self?
- What is the symbolism of a reed?
- Do you think Moses' experience in the reeds was setting the frequency to lead the Israelites to freedom?
- Do you have childhood events that set the frequency for your adult life?
- Do you feel certain that *the same God who led you in will lead you out*?

- Do you sometimes feel caught between *the devil and the deep Reed Sea*?
- Do you think that in the midst of seemingly impossible situations God promises to make a way for you?
- Do you feel protected through all your challenges?
- Have you had gifts of wisdom given to you by those who have passed on?
- Do you have a cheering squad on the other side?
- Do you have events that upset your Animal Mind even though your Spiritual Mind knows that all is as it is supposed to be?

72 Names of God

Synchronistically, the *72 Names of God*, which was already published in **Revelations of Time & Space, History and God** was based on the same 3 **Bible** verses that I received from my aunt in *The Red Sea Rules*. So, while I was studying and reading about **Kabbalah**, so was she! In fact, when she first began having serious health issues, I sent her a YHVH card along with various Internet explanations so she wouldn't be frightened of the information or think it was something nefarious.

My great-grandmother, her grandmother, was full-blooded Cherokee which meant that my aunt had a lot of Hebrew genetics that were active. My aunt was extremely connected to her Source and always just knew whatever she needed to know. For example, when my brother passed away, a gardenia plant that had never bloomed before, suddenly bloomed out of season. Gardenias were my brother's favorite flower. When the flower bloomed, she knew my brother was telling her goodbye, so when I phoned to tell her my brother was gone, she told me she already knew.

It is extremely interesting to me that without even mentioning the *72 Names of God*, that this book focuses on these 3 verses in the

Bible. Review the information in Stewart's ***Revelations*** book on pages 196-197, as well as the information on the Sefirot which tells you that Chesed is Kindness, Gevurah is Strength and Tiferet is Beauty, and then read the following article:

72 'Names' of G-d

The 3 verses of 24 letters each refer in sequence to the divine attributes of chesed, gevura, and tiferet. The 72 triplets become 72 "names" of Gd.

The three consecutive verses from Exodus 14:19-21 each contain 72 letters, an obviously rare phenomenon. The letters of these three verses can be arranged as 72 triplets of letters. But we are taught in Kabbala that if we reverse the order of the letters in the middle set, the 72 triplets become 72 "names" of Gd. In the story of the exodus from Egypt, three consecutive verses describe Gd's power as manifest just before He split the Sea of Reeds, which the Jewish people passed through on dry land while the Egyptians were drowned:

"And the angel of Gd who had been going ahead of the camp of Israel now moved and went behind them, and the pillar of cloud went from in front of them and stood behind them. Thus [the pillar of cloud] came between the camp of Egypt and the camp of Israel, making it cloud and darkness [to the Egyptians], but it gave light by night [to the Jews], so that the one came not near the other all the night. Then Moses stretched out his hand over the sea, and Gd drove the sea back with a strong east wind all that night, and made the sea dry land; thus the waters were divided." (Exodus 14:14)

A name is a means by which one is made known to others.

In Hebrew, these three verses each contain 72 letters. In the Zohar (II:51b) it is stated that these three verses refer in sequence to the divine attributes of chesed, gevura, and tiferet.

The harmonious blending of these three principle emotive attributes forms the basic paradigm of how Gd relates to the world. Thus, they together form a composite name of Gd, since a name is a means by which one is made known to others, i.e. manifests his attributes.

The fact that each verse contains 72 letters means that they can be aligned in parallel, forming 72 triplets of letters. In this configuration, the Zohar states, the first verse is to be written in its proper order, since it represents Gd's loving-kindness, or a direct revelation of Gd's goodness. The second verse is to be written in reverse order, from the last letter to the first, since it represents Gd's severity, which is an indirect revelation of His goodness. Although tiferet is a blend of both chesed and gevura, the third verse is not to be written half in the proper order and half in reverse order, as one might expect. There are two reasons for this: (1) in tiferet, chesed dominates over gevura, and (2) as the ideal blend of chesed and gevura, tiferet is a direct revelation of Gd's goodness and glory rather than an indirect one.

(This array may be seen inter alia in the standard editions of the Zohar, volume 2, p. 270a.)

כהת	אכא	ללה	מהש	עלם	סיט	ילי	והו
הקם	הרי	מבה	יזל	ההע	לאו	אלד	הזי
חהו	מלה	ייי	נלך	פהל	לוו	כלי	לאו
ושר	לכב	אום	ריי	שאה	ירת	האא	נתה
ייז	רהע	חעם	אני	מנד	כוק	להח	יחו
מיה	עשל	ערי	סאל	ילה	וול	מיכ	ההה
פוי	מבה	נית	ננא	עמם	החש	דני	והו
מחי	ענו	יהה	ומב	מצר	הרח	ייל	נמם
מום	היי	יבמ	ראה	חבו	איע	מנק	דמב

https://www.chabad.org/kabbalah/article_cdo/aid/1388270/jewish/72-Names-of-G-d.htm

The **72 Names of God** is another layer of the information that was gifted to me by my aunt in **The Red Sea Rules**. When it is time for you to have information, it finds its way to you. So, I have been studying these three **Bible** verses as well as the **72 Names of God**. I need help crossing my own *Reed Sea*. The more I study these verses the more layers of information open up that are pertinent and specific to me. When I first looked at all the information on the writings of **Kabbalah**, my Animal Mind felt discouraged when I started to think about all that I don't know. Then, my Spiritual Mind kicked in to remind me of how much I do know. For starters, I have very active Hebrew genetics, and so do you or you would not be interested in this information.

One of the first thoughts that came to me was to use the Hebrew letters Aleph (א) in the right brain, Bet (ב) in the left brain, and Gimmel (ג) at the Pineal Gland as Stewart wrote about in **Healer's Handbook**.

Focusing on these letters helps to activate what is already within and pull out even more Self-information on deeper layers.

- Have you used this visualization?
- When you use it now, what comes before your inner eye?
- Does your Animal Mind step forward to tell you what you can't do before your Spiritual Mind kicks in?

- Do you get discouraged thinking about how much you do not know?
- Do you feel like you need deeper information now to help you cross your own *Reed Sea*?
- Can it be difficult to formulate exactly where you need help?
- Can reaching deeper inside help activate positive tools for Self-information?
- Does this mean that your programming might kick in to try to stop you?
- Are these Hebrew Alphabet Aleph/Bet Archetypes powerful enough to override your programming?
- Do your genetics contain Hebrew genetics?
- What happens when you work on the deeper inner layers of your mind?
- Does more muck get stirred up?
- Can things fall apart before they get better?
- Does more inner strength activate to get you through the challenging times?
- Have you studied the *Sefirot* in the **Template of God-Mind** on page 40?
- If so, does this touch into deeper layers of your Soul?

The Reed Sea Story

In the story of the *Reed Sea*, 600,000 Israelites were stranded on its shores while the Pharaoh's Egyptian army pursued them. They had two choices: enter the sea or be captured and placed back into slavery.

They cried out to God, but God's answer was *why are you calling out to me?*

Then, God told them to *Go jump in the water.*

According to the teachings of **Kabbalah**, this was a code from God to activate the *72 Names of God* that would part the *Reed Sea*. The Israelites then went into the sea, up to their necks before the water parted so they could cross. In the same way, you have to activate your own internal connection by jumping into your metaphorical waters up to your neck while focusing on your inner knowing that Source is there to get you safely across to the other side. When you cry to God for help, you have to remember to do something. You must act upon what you know. And, the more you know, the more responsibility you have for using what you know.

Red Sea Rule #1 from my aunt's book is:

Realize that God means for you to be where you are.

The author quotes a South African pastor who says:

I am here

1. By God's appointment

2. In His keeping

3. Under His training

4 For His time.

...there's no better place to be.

An older commentary of Exodus 14 said,

When God fixes our position for us, we may rest assured that tis a wise and salutary one; and even when we foolishly and willfully choose a position for ourselves, He most graciously overrules our folly and causes the influences of our self-chosen circumstances to work for our spiritual benefit.

All of this work is extremely synchronistic because it has to do with reaching into deeper levels of your Self vs. the outer work. Outer work is better than nothing and can get things moving, but ultimately, it is the inner levels that have to move first before the outer levels can act. One of your goals is to learn to be proactive rather than reactive. The deeper you go, the more you control with your mind which then controls your outer world. When I hear stories of the challenging times of others, I have compassion, but I know that you are exactly where you are supposed to be, just like me and just like the Israelites. The secret to survival is to jump in and know Source. To know Source, you have to get past the outer world into the Building Blocks of your Soul. This is where you are going as you cross your *Reed Sea*.

- Are you always ready to help anyone who is ready to be helped?
- Do you put one hand out behind you to help others and one hand in front so you can be helped?
- Do we all help where we are allowed?
- Are you willing to take the hand of your Creator when it is offered?
- Do you realize that God means for you to be where you are?
- Do you know that your Source will show you the way out?
- Does God speak to you in code/metaphors/layers?
- Do you know how to interpret what you are told?
- Do you reject the answer when it is not what you want to hear?
- Can bad get worse?
- Can good get better?
- When the outer methodologies do not work, do you resort to inner methodologies?
- Should inner methodologies be first?
- Does doing mental work make you a mentalist?
- Can you do mental work without knowing that you are doing mental work?

- Is every thought produced a form of mental work?
- Does every thought produced create something?
- Do you want to live your life in a proactive or reactive state?
- Do you want to reach into the Building Blocks of your Soul?
- Are you content to dig around in the surface layers?
- Or do you only want to dig deeper in your way vs. God's way?

Reeds represent phallic symbols. Phallic symbols are a representation of strength. Sea is a large body of emotions that are semi-contained. You need strength to cross your contained or semi-contained emotions. This is why I am directing you to move using ancient, infallible tools. You are finding your own strength by jumping in your own sea of emotions up to your neck, just like the ancient Israelites. Then you know without a doubt, with utmost faith, that you are where you are supposed to be and that your Source is taking care of you.

Red Sea Rule #2

Be more concerned for God's glory than for your relief.

Interestingly enough, the page following this rule says,

Asking the Right Question

and follows with:

Sometimes we can't find the answers to our dilemmas because we're asking the wrong questions.

This is exactly what I teach you in **Decoding Your Life**.

In Exodus 14:3-4, God says that He will harden Pharaoh's heart so that he will pursue the children of Israel. In this way, He used the occasion to help push the Israelites into deeper faith and knowing that they were being watched over, protected, and cared for. The book continues on to say that:

> ***The Lord is in the business of delivering His people, in His own way, in His own time, for His own glory.***

All of this is exactly what you are learning in your Hyperspace/Oversoul work. Even if it is phrased a different way, it all means the same thing. The outer world is stirring up the sea of emotions within, and as you are finding out, usually without a lot of logic. It is taking courage on your part to deal with the outer world, even with what you know. It is taking courage to know when to say what to whom and when to keep your mouth closed. This is why you need to work with the building blocks of your Soul. DNA is the building blocks of your body which are built via your mind-pattern. But even deeper is the mind-pattern of your Soul, which is why I am giving you the visualizations of the Aleph/right brain, Bet/left brain, Gimmel/Pineal Gland. These are primordial archetypes that help to waken the sleeping parts of your Soul that you now need.

- Do you know the difference between the building blocks of your body and the building blocks of your Soul?
- Do you know the difference between your physical body/vessel/container and your Soul?
- Do you feel like you need even deeper tools to help you understand and cope?
- If the world is in chaos, is it easy to fall into the chaotic soup?
- Do you think the outer chaos is purposely allowed by the Creator to force people to make choices?
- Is the Creator behind the show?
- Will God deliver His people, in His own way, in His own time, for His own glory?
- Are you asking the right questions or the wrong questions?
- Do you need the correct questions to get the correct answers?

- What do you get when you put the words *Reed Sea* at your Pineal Gland?
- How does what you get pertain to you?
- What happens when you put the words *Red Sea* at your Pineal Gland?
- Is *Reed Sea* purposely mistranslated to *Red Sea*?

Red Sea Rule #3

Acknowledge your enemy but keep your eyes on the Lord.

The Egyptians, with all the king's horses, chariot drivers, and army, chased the Israelites. They caught up with them while they were camped by the Red Sea. Exodus 14:9

The Red Sea Rules book goes on to say:

Have you ever felt pursued? Oppressed? Sensed the devil nipping at your heels? Ever wondered if your simultaneous troubles were orchestrated by a fiendish, invisible hand? Suspected that your depression or anger stemmed from a malevolent source?

In Exodus, Pharaoh could threaten all he wanted but he was powerless to harm the Israelites as long as they stood steadfast in their faith in God. This chapter of ***The Red Sea Rules*** concludes with:

When things are going badly, when you feel trapped between sword and sea, when you're under assault, acknowledge the devil but keep your eyes on the Lord.

All of this is what is happening on the Earth right now. The forces of darkness are doing their best to unsettle you and make you feel like you have no choice. But as long as you stand in your center, anchor into Source, and do not be so foolish as to underestimate your enemy, then you are safe. Know that everything you need comes from within, from your Source. Ultimately it is the same Source behind your tormentor;

your tormentor exists for a reason. Whatever your torment, there is always a solution already in existence. Another reason to trust the process.

- Is life a series of tests?
- When you take a test, do you feel tormented?
- If you feel tormented, does it thus follow that your mind-pattern attracts more tormentors?
- Have you been in these types of situations where you felt pushed upon until you eventually said, "Enough!" and then life was able to change?
- Have you ever underestimated your enemy?
- What can be an enemy other than a person?
- Does everything ultimately come from One Source?
- What is the point of Self-tests?
- Can forces of darkness intimidate you when you stand in the strength of your Source?
- Do feelings of intimidation come from the Animal Mind, fight or flight?
- Do you have to surpass the physical body and reach into your Spiritual Mind to surpass feelings of intimidation?
- Is this why fear comes up first?
- Is fear a warning sign that the Animal Mind sends out when it feels threatened?
- Are you continuing to use the Aleph/right-brain, Bet/left-brain, and Gimmel/Pineal Gland?

Red Sea Rule #4

Pray

> When Pharaoh drew near, the children of Israel lifted their eyes and behold, the Egyptians marched after them. So they were very afraid, and the children of Israel cried out to the Lord. Exodus 14:10

The author of the book says that often situations seem to leave him with two choices, to panic or pray. As you know, panic comes from the Animal Mind fight or flight while praying comes from the higher Spiritual Mind.

> Because there were no graves in Egypt, have you taken us away to die in the wilderness? Exodus 14:10-11

This means that they did not actually expect God to answer their prayers. The author says:

> When you face impossible odds, pray urgently, unfeignedly, unitedly. Trust the great prayer-answering God who grants mercy and imparts grace to help in time of need.

Prayer takes many forms and means many different things to every person. Ultimately prayer is about aligning Self, Oversoul and God-Mind so that everything you do, every thought you think, and every breath you breathe is in alignment with your Source.

This reminds me of the story told to our group in Suriname by the grandson of a slave. He said his grandmother told him that the Dutch owners told the slaves to hide in the jungle so that when the tax collectors came they would not know how many slaves the owners had. The slaves took the opportunity to escape through the jungle without anything but each other and clothes on their backs. They prayed and an Angel appeared that gave them a seed. The Angel said to plant it each night so that each morning when they awoke they would have enough food to get them through the jungle each day until they were eventually met and saved by the Amerindians.

Deep prayer can take you into many interesting places inside of Self. Sometimes, you need the *urgency of emergency* to push you to go deeper. When your prayers are answered, you experience *Red Sea Rule #2*.

Be more concerned for God's glory than for your relief.

This means that you now have a testament to the power of God. Without the *urgency of emergency* you would not have prayed fervently enough to cause anything to stir. Always keep in mind that thought is powerful and yes, can and does move much more than you sometimes consciously acknowledge.

- Do you remember when you do your mental work that this is work, not imagination?
- Do you know without a doubt that with your mind, you are moving mountains within Self so you can align with your Creator?
- Do you think about the energetic layers of Self that must be crossed to get deeper into your own Reed Sea?
- Are you using the tools that you already have?
- Do you realize that each individual letters printed on this page are each an archetype?
- Are these letters energetic tools that come together in a specific way to create changes within?
- Has an *urgency of emergency* pushed you to pray deeper?
- Did you get results that convinced you without a doubt that a Higher Power was involved?
- Have you received information/answers when you least expected it?
- Do you think sometimes you have to relax and let go so that information can surface into your conscious mind?

- Can you try too hard?
- Do all efforts count?
- Is it sometimes easy to panic first before you remember to pray?
- Even when you pray, can focusing on negative make the negative feel bigger than it may be?

Red Sea Rule #5

Stay calm and confident and give God time to work.

The author says to commit your Red Sea situations to God in prayer, then trust God as well as wait for God to do His work. Recognize that there is only so much you can do; you have to wait for God to part the waters. Sometimes we must choose an attitude that is contrary to the way we feel. He goes on to say that this is the point of Exodus 14:

> The children of Israel had every reason for utter terror...There was no human escape. Although there were good reasons to be afraid, there were even better reasons for remaining confident. They had an Ally who sent lightning and locusts and other plagues to the Egyptians, who billowed up as a pillar of cloud and fire. The Ally was saying 'Get a grip on yourself. Reel in these runaway emotions. Bring yourself under control. Work your way from fear to faith. Trust Me, for I'm going to take care of this. I'm going to fight for you.

When you wait for God, a way will open for you. Today I found out that my youngest son must take one of those invasive up-the-nose Covid tests before returning to university. I was so upset! He is resigned to taking the test because he wants to go to school; he only has 1 year left before he graduates. I obviously don't want him to have to take this for a variety of reasons. I told Stewart that I want to send the school some of my news article links by experts, but he said what I already knew; he doubted the school would take what I have to say into account and we don't want them to label our son a troublemaker, perhaps telling him not to come at all. Emotionally, there is so much I want to say and do. But I know it is not my place. Therefore I have to wait for God to part the waters. I have to have faith and trust the plan, knowing that my son will be okay and in the *Eternal Now* he is already okay. I have to step back and let God Work in His way/Its way, not my way.

- Are you challenged to give God time to work?
- Do you want to jump in the middle and fix things your way in your timing?
- Do you rise above your fear into the *Eternal Now* where all is done?
- Or do you allow the panic of the Animal Mind to control you?
- Can it be challenging to trust the process once the Animal Mind's fear and panic with a little terror thrown in, rise up within you?
- Are these opportunities to allow fear, panic and terror to just keep rising until they are all the way up into your Oversoul and God-Mind?
- Is there a reason for any situation to exist that is not humanly possible to resolve?
- How often do you turn to God first before the Animal Mind?
- How challenged can you be to gain control over the Animal Mind once it starts to get out of control?
- Can you use your logical mind to gain control over your emotions?

Red Sea Rule #6

When unsure, just take the next logical step by faith.

The Lord said to Moses, *Why do you cry to Me? Tell the children of Israel to go forward.* Exodus 14:15

On the shores of the *Red Sea*, the Israelites could not see what was in the distance. They could not even see the opposite shore, yet God still told them to go forward. Some believe that the *Red Sea* did not divide all at once, but instead opened progressively as the Israelites moved forward. The author goes on to say:

> When you don't know what to do next, cast out fear and seek light for the next step. Trust God for guidance in small increments; and if you can't see what lies dimly in the distance, do what lies clearly at hand....At the moment of the Israelites' greatest perplexity, the Red Sea divided before them and they took their first hesitant steps into the midst of the piled-up waters, timidly testing the seafloor and finding it a highway of hope—one that had to be traveled step-by-step, moment by moment. We mustn't doubt in the darkness what God has shown in the light. We mustn't collapse when faced with adversity. The One who knows the faraway future reveals each close-at-hand-step as needed. Take things moment by moment and when you don't know what to do, just do what comes next. Trust God to lead you a step at a time.

When you go to bed at night you do not know what you are going to be told or read or discover when you wake up the next morning. When everything is out of your control, you can either fall apart or deal with what is in front of you, trusting the plan of Source. Source knows the outcome. In True Reality, it is already done. However, because people are creatures of habit, having your world upended causes distress for many reasons on many levels. I have been dealing with my own negative emotions that pop up from day to day. I have always taught you to take one step at a time, so that is what I am doing. Some days I feel like I am not accomplishing what I want to accomplish, but my motivation for certain tasks just isn't happening. So, I am focusing on what I can do to keep my Self going in the most positive and productive way. Because frequency/tone is what I love, I found a really fascinating book called *Energy of Hebrew Letters*. To my chagrin, while I love the book, it is a little energetically thick for me to get through. I can only read a little at a time, meaning only a few paragraphs.

I am not used to reading like this. I am an extremely fast reader and usually, it is easy for me to pull out of a book what I want/need. Not so with this book, yet I just love it. At first, I felt so discouraged but realized I had to release my discouragement. This is why I went back to the Aleph/right brain; Bet/left brain and Gimmel/Pineal Gland in my visualization work. To keep you going, one step at a time, simply take the first letter of your first name and put that at your Pineal Gland. See what comes to you.

- What is the first letter of your first name?
- What does it mean in Hyperspace/Oversoul work?
- What happens when you put this letter/archetype at your Pineal Gland?
- What happens if you turn the letter upside down, backward, float it in the air, let it sink down to the ground, become multidimensional?
- Do you keep in mind that all letters are *Hyperspace Archetypes*?
- When you do not know what to do, does doing something different shake up the energy so you are more open and receptive to whatever step you are supposed to take next?
- Do you have to do something big to shake Self up?

- Or, can something seemingly small create something seemingly big inside?
- Are all alphabets archetypes?
- Are you challenged to take one step at a time?
- Or slow down from your normal life pace?
- Are you challenged to adjust to all the new changes/rules/regulations every time you turn around?
- Or how about all the crazy news stories that get crazier?
- Are you being forced to take one step at a time?
- Are you challenged to stay positive?
- Are you determined to make the best of whatever the world is dishing out right now?

Red Sea Rule #7 and **#8** are based on Exodus 19, 20, and 21. What is so interesting about these rules is that the *72 Names of God* come from Exodus 19, 20, and 21. Remember that *The Red Sea Rules* book was a gift from my aunt at the same time I was studying the *72 Names of God*. Once we are through the 10 Red Sea rules, I will tell you more about the *72 Names of God*. For now, keep in mind that whatever work you do always has layers upon layers within layers, which is why I find this work so fascinating. Before I received the book from my aunt, I did not realize that the *72 Names of God* come from this story. Obviously, my mind-pattern was/is drawing this particular body of work to me for a reason. When things like this happen, you definitely must pay attention.

Red Sea Rule #7

Envision God's enveloping presence.

The Angel of God, who went before the camp of Israel, moved and went behind them; and the pillar of cloud went from before them and stood behind them. So it came between the camp of the Egyptians and the camp of Israel. Thus it was a cloud and darkness to the one, and it gave light by night to the other, so that the one did not come near the other all night. Exodus 14:19-20

The Red Sea Rules book says that:

God gives light to those who trust him and darkness to those who reject him. He comforts one and confounds the other; Savior to one and judge to the other. For His children, he is both Guard and Guide. He both precedes and protects us. He is simultaneously our Shepherd and Shield. He is Alpha and Omega, the first and the last, the One who goes before, guiding into the future, and the One who goes behind, gathering up our debris, our failures, and our poor attempts at ministry, blessing us and leaving a blessing behind for others.

You have Hyperspace/Oversoul Protection Techniques that you can mentally create. When you do not trust that you are protected, you keep doing all of these techniques, enforcing them as you go. But, when you know on all levels without a doubt that you are protected, your mind-pattern automatically emanates whatever protection you need on whatever level. This reminds me of the **Masters of the Far East** series. The Master simply walked through the forest fire without any harm. The fire did not, could not touch them. Mind-pattern creates this within you. When you can do this, you have moved beyond any doubt and into total understanding and knowing. Fear stops this from happening in most people. Trust is not there that you will be protected. The Animal Mind speaks constantly. The world situation throws out one fear after another to keep you off balance and put you in the Animal Mind. It takes all you have not to give in to the Animal Mind.

- Do you feel like some days you are doing better than other days?
- Or some days you think you have a handle on your Animal Mind fears but then the media throws something different at you?
- Do you think that the law enforcement officers who are at the front lines feel fear when met with demonic activity?
- Or, do they feel empowered by their mission to eradicate the wrongs of society?
- Are the law enforcement officers who are standing up to say they will not arrest or issue fines risking their jobs?
- Do the law enforcement officers who are quitting or retiring have faith that they are protected and guided?
- If your Animal Mind does not control you, can the Animal Mind of another harm or hurt you?
- Must the sexual deviants come out of hiding because the Animal Minds are being driven out in full force?
- Are the evil ones driving the global agenda and world control sacrificing their own to save themselves?
- Do you think they know that they are in a death fight?
- Is the media bad, or is it a way to test the masses?
- Do you think that for some people, this is judgment day?
- Do you have compassion for those unknowingly caught up in the outer world drama?
- Do you have compassion for the perpetrators of these crimes against humanity?
- Should one have compassion for demonic forces?
- Does what you give out come back to you?

Red Sea Rule # 8

Trust God to deliver in His own unique way.

The author continues:

> The waves rose forming translucent walls that became an avenue for the Israelites and an ambush for their enemies; a gateway to the one and a graveyard to the other.
>
> My thoughts are not your thoughts nor are your ways My ways. Isaiah 55:8
>
> God will deliver His children from every evil work, from every peril and problem, from tribulation, even death itself. God doesn't have standardized, same-size-fits-all solutions to our various problems. He treats every situation as singular and special, and He designs a unique, tailor-made deliverance to every trial and trouble.

The author gives the example of a couple in Chicago with a ministry for the homeless. They could not pay their bills and were 24 hours away from losing the lease on their home. The couple prayed throughout the night. At daybreak, they looked out their window to see their yard blanketed in white. Their lawn was covered with high-quality rare mushrooms even though it was not mushroom season. They were able to gather and sell the crop to chefs for enough money to pay their rent. Apparently, no mushrooms were ever seen there before or since.

God helps His people in ordinary, providential ways rather than in overtly supernatural ways. This is why it is important to pay attention to the accidents, misfortunes and coincidences that befall you. As you already know, this is only an ordering by an unseen hand that guides, guards, arranges and rearranges circumstances. Life seldom works out the way you want it to work out. My dad, for example, prepared last fall for his first Michigan winter. He began stocking up his freezer and pantry with extra supplies so if he could not get out, he would have what he needed. Interestingly enough, we had a mild winter so my dad did not need his extra supplies. He was able to get out and get what he needed. However, when our state was shut down in mid-March due to the plannedemic, all of his extra supplies came in handy to get him through the spring and well into summer. He thought he was preparing for winter, but God had other plans!

When my oldest son went to Houston to start his PHD in physics we were all very excited for him. But instantly he knew this was not his path. However, he kept at it because he reasoned that maybe with all the changes he could not give in to his first impressions. As the year progressed he became increasingly convinced that this was not his path and decided to quit the program. It was an extremely agonizing decision for him. We were all disappointed as we thought he would be settled for several years. So that summer I flew to Houston to help him, his wife, and 2 cats move to Tennessee to another university that they felt would be more suitable to meet their goals. They are much happier, life was going along well and then the plannedemic hit. Rioting is rampant all over the country. His colleagues from that PHD program are not getting the education they had planned on. I am extremely grateful that they are out of Houston. So often you think you are planning for one thing because you are not privy to the linear future. But you are being guided, watched over, and protected so that you are given exactly what you need in the way you need it when and where you need it.

- Have you prepared for one thing, but something totally unexpected happened instead?
- Does this make you stop and count your blessings?
- Do these kinds of events confirm that there is a bigger hand guiding the bigger picture?
- Do you have small, ordinary-appearing events in your life that prove meaningful to your overall life experience?
- Is it easy to miss these smaller, significant details when you are only waiting for larger miracles to take place?

- Is it always important to appreciate each and every moment as an answer to your prayers?
- Do you have to like the way your prayers are answered?
- Do God-Mind and your Oversoul create what appears to be chaos in your life, but ultimately only proves to be a reordering for your ultimate benefit?
- Is it too easy to fall into a state of judgment vs. observation?
- Does everything have a time and place, or it could not exist?
- Does everything have a function, even demonic entities?
- Is a function good or bad, correct and beneficial, and/or necessary?
- Do the mind-patterns of the people have to match that of the demonic entities for the demonic entities to be present?
- Are all demonic entities Souls?

Red Sea Rule #9

View your current crisis as a faith builder for the future.

The Red Sea Rules author writes:

> Trials and troubles are dumbbells and treadmills for the soul. They develop strength and stamina.

Because of their experiences, the faith of the Israelites increased. In the same way, you learn Spiritual Laws and then you are given the opportunity to practice what you learned. Passing the test gives you strength for the next test. Your trust in the Spiritual Law, and thus in your Oversoul and God-Mind, grows each time you pass a test and move forward into the next one. Each test is the opportunity you need to increase your faith in Self, your process, and your inner guidance.

This is why I always tell you to greet your challenges rather than run from them. I often think of how many challenges I have run from and how much I could have learned if I had stayed put. But, this is part of my process so rather than bemoan what I didn't do at the time, I am grateful that I stopped running away and started running toward that which I need to grow. Without the challenges and tests, you really do not know what you can do. You can have a lot of knowledge, but to make it work, you actually have to use and apply it. When you walk into a dark room, you just can't stand there. You have to walk over and turn the light switch on to change the dark from light. You must act upon what you know.

- Do you have faith that what you know will carry you through your personal Self-tests?
- Do you want to keep passing the same tests repeatedly, or do you want your faith to grow stronger?
- Are you willing to take the tests that build faith in Self, Oversoul and God-Mind?
- Is it easy to talk about what you know but to practice what you preach is another thing?
- Is this why it is easier to solve the issues of someone else before your own?
- Is it easier for you to greet your challenges now?
- Have you stopped running away?
- Do you run to your challenges?
- Is your faith growing?

Red Sea Rule #10

Don't forget to praise him.

The celebration of the Israelites turned to song when they realized that they were saved and their enemy was drowned. Exodus 15 is the first recorded song in the ***Bible***. Interesting that now in California, the governor has ordered churchgoers not to sing. This tells you how powerful your voice is. This is why the masking; is a symbolic silencing of the lambs about to be lead to slaughter. Whether you believe in the plannedemic or not is actually irrelevant when it comes to mask-wearing. Science says that masks do not stop the virus. The mask also says that you trust the mask more than you trust your Creator to protect you. No matter who you are or what you do or do not believe in when it is your time to have an experience of any kind, it is going to come to you. I often cite the example of people afraid to fly because the plane might crash. However, there are many recorded incidents of airplanes crashing into people's homes and killing them. When it is your time and your way, you cannot escape.

When it is not your time and not your way, nothing can touch you. My example for this is the destruction of your neighbor's home but not yours during a tornado or hurricane. Your house stands yet the neighbor's home falls. You can change or mitigate some future linear events by your actions in the present moment. One way is to always focus on the Power that is behind everything. It is always important to be thankful for what God has done, is doing, and is going to do, according to the author. I agree!

He goes on to say:

> Whether you are on the upper side or the underside of the storm, whether you are on the east bank or the west bank of the Red Sea, God will make a way. And as He does, don't forget to praise Him.

- Do you remember to be thankful for your challenges?
- Do you know that your challenges are getting you to your correct path?
- Do you remember to be thankful for the challenging people who make you stop and think about your choices?
- Are you thankful that *the same God who led you in will lead you out?*

The same God who led you in will lead you out.

Current events are definitely forcing you into your own *Reed Sea*, whatever that means to you, personally. As much as you are doing your best to not participate, sometimes you are given certain situations where you have no choice but to participate. When this happens, this means that there are lessons to be had.

For example, the Italian webmaster who stole my website tried to blackmail me with it and took me to the Italian court for slander. Because I was not versed in Italian law and did not initially understand my rights, the final outcome after 3 years in the process was that I had to plea bargain to not say I was wrong but to allow the judge to give me a fine. It was a long stressful process which means I will not forget those lessons. The primary lesson was that I studied my definition of judgment since I was being judged. It was ludicrous but nevertheless, I had no choice but to participate. If I was being judged then this meant that I was judging. I do not hate the Italian webmaster or wish him any harm. He had a role to fulfill and he fulfilled it. What he gave out will come back to him. What I give out will come back to me. As long as I give truth and honesty, I will be okay. If I give anything other than truth and honestly, it will all come home to harm me. No thank you; in that, I refuse to participate. I have control over my thoughts, emotions, actions and reactions. In the same way, you are being baited to give out something negative to whomever you view is standing in your way of living your life the way you want to live it. Your choices are not being taken away by an opponent; your choices are narrowed now by *the same God that led you in who will lead you out.*

I found the best thing that I could do was to send Unconditional Love via the Oversoul level to the webmaster. It was up to him to receive or reject, but what I give out comes back to me. It was my mind-pattern that pulled this person to me for the lessons that I needed. If I gave hate and resentment, then that would come back to me. If he could get me to abandon my principles and stoop to his level, he would be the true victor. Thus, in the Game of Souls, he would be declared the winner.

In the same way, it is your mind-pattern that pulls in the people with lessons that you would not consciously choose, but is what you need. You can vilify people or you can change your mind-pattern and rise above the situation. As you know, this all sounds good on paper, but in practice, it isn't so easy. I told you it upsets me that my son might have to take the up-the-nose Covid test. That first reaction is the Animal Mind reacting. I have to go into the Spiritual Mind to know that he will be okay. If I can't change it then I have to change me. There is a reason why my Oversoul wants me here, experiencing what I am experiencing. In the *Eternal Now*, all of this is already decided and resolved. In this Present Moment, you have to know that *the same God who led you in will lead you out.*

- Do the Spiritual Laws make sense on paper, but yet when you are put to the test none of it makes sense?
- When you read about other people, do life complications seem far off and distant?
- When the same situation happens to you, are your emotional reactions a surprise?
- Are there times when you are resigned to your fate because your choices become fewer and fewer?
- Even with fewer choices do you always have a choice, even when you do not like the choice?
- When you do not like the choice are you more inclined to get into some serious discussions with your Oversoul and God-Mind?
- Do your prayers then become deeper, more intense, and more prolonged?

- Does this force you to focus more on the Spiritual Mind rather than the Animal Mind?
- Are the looters, rioters and their controllers focusing on the Animal Mind?
- Will there be retributions for these people?
- Do you want to see the retributions?
- Is wanting to see the retribution a function of the Animal Mind?
- Does the Spiritual Mind want to see the retributions?
- Do you remember your most challenging lessons longer than you do less challenging lessons?
- Do more challenging lessons force more Soul-growth?
- Have you asked for Soul-growth?
- Do you only want your Soul to grow in the ways you want it to grow?
- Are you *letting go and letting God*?
- Is *letting go and letting God*, easier said than done?
- Are you focusing on doing the correct thing for the correct reason at the correct timing?
- Are you maintaining your attitude of gratitude?

AFFIRMATIONS—COURAGEOUS COMMUNICATION

Gather your Courage as you plunge into the depths of Self, because the deeper you go you never know what you are going to stir up. Embrace the Totality of Your Soul with humility and grace, knowing that everything you find is an important link to All That Exists.

I dig into the building blocks of the creation of my Soul.
I courageously agree to observe my inner life.

I release my preconceived ideas of what I contain within.
I recognize that I AM layers upon layers within layers.

I release the need to avoid the deeper layers that might disturb me.
I allow my inner sanctum to unlock.

I release the need for my status quo.
I allow Source to guide me.

I see into the building blocks of my Soul.
My color, tone, and archetypes reveal themselves.

The building blocks of my Soul upgrade and elevate my current circumstances.
I am open to knowing who and what I AM.

The building blocks of my Soul emanate throughout my Soul-personality.
I AM upgraded and elevated.

I release the need to hide from my Self.
All that is within is important to my Soul-growth.

I AM in a place of constant understanding.
Source explains my choices.

Source expands my options.
I consider all options that present themselves.

Unlocking knowledge creates movement.
I AM flexible.

I give my desire to control to Source.
I agree to my Greater Soul Plan.

I follow my Source wherever It leads me.
I courageously trust my Inner Guidance.

I release preconceived and programmed ideas of who and what I AM.
I listen only to Source.

I have no judgment of Self.
I AM an observer.

Logically, I understand.
Emotionally, I know.

All That Exists within is part of my Creator.
I exist for experience.

I release the need to numb any experience.
All experience is valid.

I delve deeper into the Emanations of Creation with my Soul.
The Emanations of Creation greet me.

I courageously face the Magnificence of My Being.
The Magnificence of My Being is multi-faceted.

The Magnificence of My Being encompasses positive, negative and beyond.
I courageously face the beyond of My Being.

I AM deeper than I can consciously imagine.
I follow the path of Source to take me beyond my imagination.

The path of Source unlocks deep levels of my Soul.
Soul-unlocking means Soul-personality-growth.

My Soul is constant.
The expression of my Soul in this lifeline is my Soul-personality.

My Soul is ageless.
My Soul-personality reflects the agelessness of my Soul.

My Soul knows all.
My Soul-personality knows what it needs to know in this timeline.

My Soul has a purpose for my Soul-personality.
My Soul-personality accomplishes its purpose and mission.

My Soul knows True Reality.
My Soul-personality knows physical reality.

My Soul feeds my Soul-personality exactly what it needs.
My Soul is fed by my Oversoul.

My Oversoul is fed by God-Mind.
God-Mind is fed by Absolute.

Absolute is fed by All That Is.

I Embrace the Totality of My Soul with humility and grace, knowing that everything I AM is a part of All That Exists.

Introduction to the 72 Names of God

The three consecutive verses from Exodus 14:19-21 each contain 72 letters, an obviously rare phenomenon. The letters of these three verses can be arranged as 72 triplets of letters. But we are taught in Kabbala that if we reverse the order of the letters in the middle set, the 72 triplets become 72 "names" of Gd.

¹⁹ Then the angel of God, who had been going in front of the Israelite camp, moved and went behind them, and the pillar of cloud moved away from in front of them and stood behind them.

יט וַיִּסַּע מַלְאַךְ הָאֱלֹהִים הַהֹלֵךְ לִפְנֵי מַחֲנֵה יִשְׂרָאֵל וַיֵּלֶךְ מֵאַחֲרֵיהֶם וַיִּסַּע עַמּוּד הֶעָנָן מִפְּנֵיהֶם וַיַּעֲמֹד מֵאַחֲרֵיהֶם:

²⁰ And he came between the camp of Egypt and the camp of Israel, and there were the cloud and the darkness, and it illuminated the night, and one did not draw near the other all night long.

כ וַיָּבֹא בֵּין | מַחֲנֵה מִצְרַיִם וּבֵין מַחֲנֵה יִשְׂרָאֵל וַיְהִי הֶעָנָן וְהַחֹשֶׁךְ וַיָּאֶר אֶת־הַלָּיְלָה וְלֹא־קָרַב זֶה אֶל־זֶה כָּל־הַלָּיְלָה:

²¹ And Moses stretched out his hand over the sea, and the Lord led the sea with the strong east wind all night, and He made the sea into dry land and the waters split.

כא וַיֵּט מֹשֶׁה אֶת־יָדוֹ עַל־הַיָּם וַיּוֹלֶךְ יְהֹוָה | אֶת־הַיָּם
בְּרוּחַ קָדִים עַזָּה כָּל־הַלַּיְלָה וַיָּשֶׂם אֶת־הַיָּם לֶחָרָבָה וַיִּבָּקְעוּ
הַמָּיִם:

https://www.chabad.org/kabbalah/article_cdo/
aid/1388270/jewish/72-Names-of-G-d.htm

There is generally information that is lost in translation, just as the Sea in Hebrew is *Reed*, not *Red*. Mistranslation hides information from people. However, even with the mistranslation, you can "sea/see" that the author of **Red Sea Rules** still found information that is compelling and helpful. Now, as you step back deeper into the original *Reed Sea* story as told in Hebrew, another layer of information is revealed. These verses, in Hebrew, all have 72 letters. When the verses are laid out parallel to one another, a hidden code reveals itself, as is described in the previous article.

Here, you see the **72 Names of God** chart which are derived from these 3 **Bible** verses. In Hebrew, remember that you read from right to left. Keep in mind that each box is numbered beginning with the first box on the right as #1 and the very last box is #72 on the bottom row, left hand side.

כהת	אכא	ללה	מהש	עלם	סיט	ילי	והו
הקם	הרי	מבה	יזל	ההע	לאו	אלד	הזי
חהו	מלה	ייי	נלך	פהל	לוו	כלי	לאו
ושר	לכב	אום	ריי	שאה	ירת	האא	נתה
ייז	רהע	חעם	אני	מנד	כוק	להח	יחו
מיה	עשל	ערי	סאל	ילה	וול	מיכ	ההה
פוי	מבה	נית	ננא	עמם	החש	דני	והו
מחי	ענו	יהה	ומב	מצר	הרח	ייל	נמם
מום	היי	יבמ	ראה	חבו	איע	מנק	דמב

Each of these boxes represents a specific frequency of the God-Mind. You do not need to know the Hebrew AlephBet to use the table. The *Name Frequencies* are not meant to be pronounced because they are not words. You can simply look at the Hebrew letters and hold the image of the letters in white at your Pineal Gland. However, if you feel like you must say the frequencies to help you focus and concentrate, these are transliterated for you.

In Ancient Hebrew the "V" is pronounced like a "W".

B in Bet without a dot/dagesh is pronounced like a "V".

Ch and Kh are pronounced like the "CH" in Loch and Achtung in German.

Because I have been compiling my blogs into books, I have the opportunity to review my progress through the years. They are like a diary of sorts, so I hope that you are keeping notebooks of your own responses so you can go back and then realize how far you have come.

Enough grains of sand will fill a glass. You have to do your part and be the best grain of sand that you possibly can. Combined grains of sand are an incredibly powerful force. Having farmed in the high mountain desert of Eastern Washington State I can attest to the power of sand.

These *Name Frequencies* are multidimensional so in True Reality, the order you use the *Name Frequencies* is not as important as using them. Remember that the letters you see are 2 dimensional representations of something that is multidimensional. For this reason, you can put each Hebrew letter at your Pineal Gland to understand more about the Frequency that animates it. In the same way, you can put each *Name Frequency* at your Pineal Gland to see what comes up for you. They are multidimensional and yes, you can use them in any order that you wish.

In fact, I will tell you a secret. Simply having the *Name Frequencies* in your presence activates them within you. You can print out the **72 Names of God** chart and keep it in your presence or hide it away. It does not matter. The energy is there with you. You can use the fingertips of your hand to scan the chart, beginning at the top right and scanning right to left, top to bottom. By specifically focusing and concentrating you are aligning the frequencies on the chart with what is already within you. You could focus on one letter, one *Name Frequency* for a lifetime. They are infinitely deep.

- When you scan the **72 Names of God**, how many people do you think worldwide are doing the same?
- When you focus on one *Name Frequency*, how many people do you think worldwide are doing the same?
- When you focus on one Hebrew letter, how many people do you think worldwide are doing the same?
- When many people do the same thing at the same time, does this help align the frequency on the nonphysical and the physical as well?
- What happens when everyone in the world focuses at a different time on the same Frequency?
- How much difference does your one grain of sand make to the overall prayer?
- Collectively, how much difference do our combined grains of sand make to the overall prayer?
- When we pray together, what happens to each individual within the group?
- How powerful is prayer?
- How powerful is the pray-er?
- How much potential power do you have to bring forth from the nonphysical into the physical?

- Do you want to feel powerless or powerful?
- Do you do your Source injustice when you Self-oppress your own power?
- Is your purpose to Self-oppress?
- Do you keep a notebook of your responses so you can review where you were and where you are?
- Does using the *Name Frequencies* help to activate your power within?
- Do you discount your internal power?
- Do you give credit to Source for your internal power?
- Why do you not want to acknowledge who and what you are?
- Why do you feel unworthy?
- Does not acknowledging Self mean not acknowledging Source?

Judaism has religious rules and laws for everything and everyone. Through the years I have sporadically researched and read much about this topic, but I know that I have barely scratched the surface. To some people, religious rules and laws can seem quite restrictive and limiting. Some people leave Judaism to find freedom in the secular world.

I was not born into Judaism for a reason. Those born into Judaism have a mission and purpose in life different from mine. Their lives revolve around keeping religious law. This means, for example, that many people are saying the same prayers at the same time for the same reason. So if you use a specific prayer, or *Name Frequency*, at the same time someone else does, let's say *Name Frequency* #47 World Peace/Global Transformation, then the strength of the prayer intensifies.

The ***Torah*** is said to be the complete *Name of God*. If Jews all around the world are reading the same ***Torah*** passages on the same day, there is a lot of powerful energy focused on whatever formula is being spoken that day. A true ***Torah*** reading is actually sung/toned, not read.

Muslims pray 5 times per day. All of this thought and spoken energy is creating something. The more people doing this at the same time, the more strength inherent in the prayers. There are many religions that give the pre-written Sunday sermon to the pastors to be read with the congregations answering specific passages at specific times, with the same hymns sung at the same points in the sermon in every church of that religion worldwide. This is a ritual of some kind with some kind of desired result by that church's hierarchy.

One of the first things to be banned in the global lockdown was going to church. Even gathering in individual cars in church parking lots was forbidden. In California, people are banned from singing or chanting in church. This tells you that group singing and chanting are powerful. Yet, looters and rioters can yell, scream, screech, sing and chant. This is why when you are focusing on a specific *Name Frequency* or on the ***72 Names of God***, you are adding your voice/energy/prayers to the collective who are doing the same or who have done the same.

Like attracts like.

You are Never A-Lone.

We are All-One.

- When you work with the *Name Frequencies*, do you remember to send all your work up to your Oversoul?
- Do you allow your Oversoul to take what you give it and do with it as is most correct and beneficial?
- Do you allow your Oversoul to instruct you on your next steps during your inner level work?
- Does silencing the singing and chanting of churchgoers allow the singing and chanting of rioters and looters to take precedence in the nonphysical world?

- Does the singing and chanting of the rioters and looters coalesce with like minds globally with the same singing/chanting/screaming/screeching/yelling?
- Do you think the verbal noise of the rioters and looters are going to pull in lower level frequencies vs. the churchgoers pulling in higher level frequencies?
- What kinds of rituals do congregants engage in who attend churches whose pastors globally give the same sermon with the same hymns and same responses?
- Are the rules of all religions restrictive?
- How does one decide Spiritual Law vs. human-made religious law?
- If you are born into a specific religion, is it to maintain it, change it, leave it, all of these or something else?

Name Frequency #1

Time Travel

Vav Hey Vav
Read Hebrew Letters Right to Left
Name Frequency Pronunciation
Wah Heh Wah

This frequency is used for Time Travel. Place this *Name Frequency* at your Pineal Gland to help clean up your past so that your linear future is brighter. This *Name Frequency* helps pull up old memories and experiences that are contributing to your current life circumstances that you most likely have forgotten. Yes, good deeds can be buried right along with the not-so-wonderful deeds. What may appear to you as random events most likely began a long linear time ago. Even old deep-seated ideas can be pulled out by their roots and released, thus freeing you to move on.

- What happens when you place this *Name Frequency* at your Pineal Gland?
- If you want to uproot deep-seated thoughts, ideas and actions do you think just working with it one time is sufficient?
- Is "deep" a subjective term?
- When you say that you want to go deep inside, do you really know what you are saying?
- Can you reach a deep place inside of Self and then think that you are done?
- Is it easy to forget that deep can get deeper?
- When you disturb deep seeds planted in deep soil, what is going to happen to surface events?
- Do you think that current events may be happening in the outer world because you, and others like you, are reaching into deep inner soil?
- Are geological catastrophes really catastrophes, or a shaking up of people so they can release their past and move forward?
- Is it challenging to watch others suffer even though you know that this is exactly what their Soul wants for them?
- Is it challenging to watch your Self suffer knowing that this is exactly what your Soul wants for you?
- Are you able to find Compassion for all, including Self?

Exploring Your Layers

Everything I write helps you reveal Self layer by layer in a way that you can handle. This is why every time you read one of my books or articles you get something new and different from it. This is the same way the **Bible** was written. The True **Bible** originally given to Moses is known as the **Torah**. This is why there is one layer of ***The Red Sea*** written about in the translated **Bible** vs. *the Reed Sea* as originally written about in the Hebrew **Bible/Torah**. The **Torah** is called the five books of Moses. *The Red Sea* is a layer of the *Reed Sea* information. The Hebrew **Bible/Torah** is a code for life, not a religion.

The *Torah* was given/revealed/transmitted to Moses approximately 3600 years ago. The **Sefer Yetzirah**, also known as the **Book of Formation/Creation** was given/revealed/transmitted to Abraham approximately 4000 years ago. The oral **Zohar/Book of Splendor** was revealed to a Rabbi approximately 2000 years ago and is said to be the Soul of the **Bible/Torah**. Without going into the history, it is purported to have been found in Spain approximately 700 years ago and has only recently been shared with the public.

As you go within you are digging up your own inner soil. The deeper you go, the more you disturb/disrupt the surface layers. Your work is proactive. Interestingly enough, one of the books that I recently read called *The Power of Kabbalah* is about the 13 Principles of **Kabbalah**. Number 4 reads as follows:

> ***The purpose of life is spiritual transformation from a reactive Being to a proactive Being.***

This is exactly what I wrote about in **Decoding Your Life** almost 40 years ago without any conscious knowledge of **Kabbalah**. While you are proactively disturbing your inner soil, most of the outer world is having its inner soil reactively disturbed. I am currently editing my **Heights of Wealth** book and going through one of the chapters called "Stress or No Stress". In this chapter, I discuss unexpected stress (such as world events) vs. planned stress (such as a career change, moving house). All of this is another layer of proactive/reactive.

My information comes to me orally. My Oversoul shows me the frequency, gives me the words to describe it, and I write it down. Thus, there are 2 versions of my books: oral and written. Before I wrote **Decoding Your Life** I taught classes to a select few individuals for several years. This was the oral version. When I wrote **Decoding Your Life**, I thought I was done. I thought people could read it, practice the

Spiritual Law contained therein, and they would have no need for me. Because I was only 25 years old, I was really shocked that it did not work this way. People still wanted me to tell them what to do vs. just reading the book.

When I taught **Decoding Your Life** in my **Self-Healing Webinars** it took us 3 years to get through it! Those who completed the course truly transformed in verifiable ways. This is another demonstration of how everything is multi-layered and coded. It is up to you to be open and receptive to the multilayers and codes. If you cannot deal with the simplest codes that are most obvious, you are not going to get the deeper codes. Letters are archetypes and each archetype has multiple meanings. Each word is an archetype sentence with multiple meanings. Yet, when put together correctly, you unlock multiverses within Self.

- Are you recognizing the layers of your lessons?
- Do you remember that letters are archetypes?
- And with archetypes come color and sound?
- Have you become so engrossed in a book that you no longer see words, but instead the story comes alive in your head like you are watching a motion picture?
- Are people who enjoy reading more apt to see a movie unfold than merely see words on a page?
- Do the word arrangements on a page literally paint a picture or movie?
- Do the letter arrangements within words create a specific picture or movie?
- How does one transform moving pictures in such a way that they can be given from one person to another?
- Do all people looking at the same moving picture see the same thing?

- Can everyone see something different while looking at the same moving picture and all be accurate?
- How does one ensure the accuracy of information when sharing a moving picture?
- Are words and the letters that comprise the words attached to moving pictures of some kind?
- Do words and letters provide focus to your experiences?
- Do all written works have an oral version?
- Are the oral versions hidden behind the written versions?
- Can you tap into the oral version by focusing on the written version?
- Even though you choose proactive learning, can the results still be disturbing?

Because the global population has been avoiding their proactive Self-exploration they are being forced to reactively make some tough choices. I expect it to get worse before it gets better and the tide will only begin to turn as we get closer to the elections. Whether you do or do not like Trump, the Hebrew prophecies are predicting a win. There are a lot of books written around this. I have not read them although I have read a lot of news articles about this. It is always in your favor to be informed. This is a fight between dark and light to give people the opportunity to choose.

Even when you are proactive, there are always situations that force you to move in a reactive way. Some months ago my hair stylist closed shop before anything in Michigan was closed down. I was in Tennessee when I got a text asking if I could come in the next afternoon instead of the following morning at 9am because they were closing the salon. She knew I was in Tennessee and she knew I couldn't come in. Apparently, she felt safe doing my hair at 3pm one day but the next day at 9am she did not feel safe doing my hair. I texted the salon owner who also would not help me. My initial plan was to come home that evening, get my hair done the next morning and go to an afternoon appointment followed by an important meeting the next day.

I was undecided about how to react to her treatment after having been a good customer for almost a decade. She is a good stylist and up until this time I had always liked and appreciated her. My first appointment with her after the salons were allowed to open was awkward. I thought perhaps she would apologize but that didn't happen. She acted normal and I made it a point to not speak too much. I had a second appointment with her, the same situation. I eventually told the salon pedicurist that I was looking for a new pedicurist for my dad, so she broke the news to my stylist who then sent me a curt text asking if I wanted to cancel my appointments. I just said, "yes, thank you." Now I have an appointment at a new salon and I feel such a relief to be done with the old one. End of story.

My first upset was when my stylist kind of forced me to change salons without any notice 4 years ago. I didn't like that. This current salon owner and my stylist made secret plans to open their own salon behind the back of their salon owner. I wasn't told until the day before, that my appointment was now at a new location, about a 30 minute drive from where I live. I was torn because I had no issue with that salon owner, liked her and it made me feel disloyal to her. My deeper level work reminded me of this. Perhaps at that time, I should not have gone with the stylist because that business started under "bad energy" but I went with it anyway. My excuse was that I was given 1 day's notice. I justified it because parking was better vs. at the other place sometimes in the middle of my appointment, even in snow, I had to move my car 2-3 blocks away, which I didn't really like doing. Now, that buried bad energy rose up. When I really needed that appointment, again with only 1 day's notice, the appointment was taken away. I was again in a reactive position, even though I took my time to make my decision as I wanted to make the correct choice for the correct reason. I am cleaning up what perhaps I should have done 4 years ago.

And our handyman found 7 wasp nests around our house and a 7 foot long rat snake. Those wasp nests were big and didn't start yesterday. There is always so much deep cleaning to be done, it is amazing how it comes out.

- Are you working with *Name Frequency #1*?
- Are you planting the energy to see what comes up for you?
- Is your still soil getting disturbed?
- Is the only way to deep clean to disturb the deep soil?
- Have you had something that you started many years ago that you weren't quite okay with eventually come back for you to face in unexpected ways?
- As much as you try to be proactive with what you know, do you still get caught in the reactive position?
- Are you careful to do the correct action for the correct reason and the correct timing?
- Do you find that the closer you are to balance the more challenging it is to know which side of the fence you are on?
- Do you sometimes take what you perceive as the safe way because it is what you know?
- Sometimes, do you need to take risks as a leap of faith?
- Do leaps of faith always mean a positive outcome?
- Can a positive outcome be uncomfortable?
- Do leaps of faith always mean what is most correct and beneficial to help you narrow your focus and find your way?
- Does having faith that *the same God that led you in will lead you out* mean that the way out is easy?

The Name of God Frequency #1 stirs things up. When you place this *Name Frequency* at your Pineal Gland, you really are placing this inside of Self. Then, you let go and you let this *Name Frequency* do its work. As with any mental work, you may get something immediately, but normally this stirs up the process already underway. Things happen when the deeper inner soil gets disturbed. For example, one person may be led to research the meaning of her name, another person may remember forgotten childhood memories and another person may have clients who reveal his/her hidden issues. You are learning to know your audience, not take things personally, not make your Self a target yet be true to your Self while doing your best to be proactive instead of reactive. You are also learning that when you plant a seed you do not always get immediate conscious and visible results. This does not mean that something is not happening. You have more patience with your process knowing that all is in Divine Order; chaos is only order not yet understood. You are on your way to understanding all your life in its intricacies.

Think of what is in an apple seed, but by looking at it you would not guess that a huge tree is contained therein. You have to plant the seed, then wait for that seed to reveal its magnificence in its timing. You wanting it to grow faster does not make it happen.

Name Frequency #2

Recapturing the Sparks

Yud Lamed Yud
Read Hebrew Letters Right to Left
Name Frequency Pronunciation
Yuh Lah Yuh

Yehuda Berg, in his book ***The 72 Names of God*** says that according to ***Kabbalah***, "spiritual light contains all the colors of fulfillment that a human being seeks throughout existence…Negative thoughts create negative forces that rob you of your Light. These dark entities have no life of their own; they subsist off your energy… as their power grows stronger, your life grows progressively darker."

By focusing on the Hebrew letters in *Name Frequency #2*, "shards of Light are drawn out of the destructive entities that reside within your being. Their life force is cut off and you are replenished with Divine Energy. Life grows brighter each and every day as billions of sacred sparks return to their source, your soul."

Use *Name Frequency #2* when you feel low, empty, and like your life force is slowly slipping away. When you are filled with Divine Energy, you are no longer tired, bored and lethargic. When you focus on this *Name Frequency* and its personal implications within Self, you better understand how others have fallen into the entrapment of dark entities that sap their life force until there is nothing left for the person. You see that there is a body, but no one in his/her human mind would do the things that some of these people are doing. What you are seeing now did not just happen overnight. People have been giving up parts of themselves for a long time in order for the disarray and chaos that is going on in the world today to happen. The best that you can do is to stop feeding the negativity and fill your Self with Divine Light. The more people that *Recapture the Sparks* of Light, the less power evil has. This is another reason why when your Light shines outer forces try to attack. They can make a lot of noise, but as long as you are anchored in Source, they cannot touch you.

- What happens when you use *Name Frequency #2*?
- Do you feel like you need to *Recapture the Sparks* of Light Force?
- Are you challenged to feel positive and uplifted in the midst of all that is going on?
- Are you finding places in your life that need to be illuminated so you can make decisions about what stays and what goes?
- Do you see photos of people or read about their actions and think that these people are not even as good as animals?
- Do you have compassion that these people have fallen into the entrapments?
- Are the entrapments tests that people have not passed?
- Is it important to have faith that "this too, shall pass"?
- Is it challenging to pray for others or for the world, knowing that there are a lot of tests going on right now?

- Is it important to allow others' their tests in the way they need to be tested?
- Is it important to not judge, but only observe?
- What kinds of global prayers are needed right now?

It is always challenging to know exactly what you need, much less what others need. You may know what you want without a doubt. When most people don't get what they want they often try to run away but eventually *wherever you go, there you are.* This means their mind-pattern pulls the same experience but with different people. And yes, it can always be worse.

This is why I tell you to stay where you are and do your best to correct your mind-pattern. Running from place to place doesn't ever change the scenario. When I was married to my first husband, we had terrible fights. We moved quite a few times. I always viewed it as a fresh start and we always pledged that "it wouldn't happen again" but it always did. He was never happy wherever we lived and spent his time searching for real estate. I eventually realized that he would never be happy and he was taking me down with him. I kept working on my Self only because I was afraid to leave until eventually, Stewart appeared in my life.

Yes, we have had plenty of issues, but we did not run from them. We both came with baggage and as challenging as it is, by staying together we have grown and gotten better. Not "perfect" but better. Good can always get better. I had spent my life running but with Stewart, the running stopped. When you run and never get anywhere, you get discouraged. You do lose the Sparks of Light/life to darker forces that tempt you into a perpetual state of Self-pity. When I feel my Self going downhill emotionally, I turn my attention to something that makes me happy—my dogs and cats; even Instagram—I love the dog and cat pictures there; I admire the creativity of the people who cook and do crafts. Anything that uplifts me and makes me smile.

This does not change me but I get a respite from whatever is bothering me so that instead of sinking to (-1000) maybe I get pulled up to +500. Then, when I go back to my issues maybe I only fall down to (-100) which is manageable and I can look at my issues instead of feeling overwhelmed by them. I was very depressed about not being able to travel this summer. These few days away are really the only major thing that I do for my Self as a fantastic re-set from my every day routine. I still work when I am away, but it shakes me up in ways that cannot happen here. I wanted to travel! But apparently, I needed to be home. I have made the best use of my time that I can. The days I was supposed to be away were the most challenging. Every time I was tempted to be depressed I did something to uplift my Self. I even started studying my Italian again during this time period when I would have been in Italy actually speaking it.

It is easy to lose your Sparks of Light little by little until you don't know how you got there or how to get out. Daily maintenance work is extremely important. This is what my new pet groomer told me about my animals. Excellent advice for all of life!

- Do you do your daily maintenance work to uplift and elevate Self?
- Do you recognize the difference between what you want and what you need?
- When all doors close to what you want, are you challenged to stay put and take inventory of what you need?
- Is what you need as fun and inviting as what you want?
- When you don't get what you want are you tempted to lose some of your Sparks of Light via the negative emotions that call you to engage with them?
- Do demonic forces that cannot directly get to you indirectly push your outer world so you negatively react?

- If the demonic forces cannot get to you, do they get to others that can get to you?
- Are demonic forces designed to test you?
- Should you fear demonic forces?
- Does fear give your power to demonic forces?
- How do you rise above demonic forces?
- Do demonic forces need your Sparks of Light for strength?
- Are your specific Sparks of Light embedded in you?
- Can you give them away?
- Or can they only be borrowed because they are embedded in you?
- Is this similar to the cords of psychic energy that go from you to others and others to you as discussed in **Decoding Your Life**?
- Should you pray that demonic forces not tempt anyone or that anyone tempted by demonic forces have the inner strength to withstand the temptations?
- Should you pray that demonic forces not tempt the world or that the world finds its strength to say no?
- Should your energy go into banning demonic forces or into Sparks of Light so bright that Brightness blinds the evil forces?
- How important are your Sparks of Light in the overall scheme of existence?

Name Frequency #3

Miracle Making

Samech Yud Tet
Read Hebrew Letters Right to Left
Name Frequency Pronunciation
Sah Yuh Teh

To ignite the power of this *Name Frequency*, you must free your Self of negative temptations. This means do your best to do the correct action for the correct reason in the correct timing. Remember that you have to do your part. Having information without using it cannot ignite anything. This is why you have to put what you know to the test.

In the last couple of days, I have had a couple of interesting little miracles happen. The first is regarding a friend who I have not heard from for a long time. I got an email from her about 6 months ago, to which I replied and then nothing. She has been in my thoughts on and off so finally I wrote about 6 weeks ago. Still nothing. Yesterday I wrote again and at the same time, she was writing to me. Our emails crossed in cyberspace! Apparently, her husband had been quite ill and is now recovering which then precipitated some other life changes. Obviously, we had a meeting of the minds on the inner levels.

Then, 2 days ago I suddenly thought about potato chip cookies that a friend of mine used to make for me. I see her on occasion and coincidentally she was coming to see me today. I decided that when she came I would tell her that sometime if she could make those cookies for me again I would really appreciate it. I didn't want to ask in advance of her visit because I didn't want her to feel pressured to make them for me on such short notice. Well, guess what! She had made a big batch of the cookies a couple of days ago at the same time they popped into my head. She gave the extra to the guests because she didn't want to keep the extras for her Self. If I had asked her to bring me some, it would not have been a problem because apparently, she was well-stocked. I had the information and in the first case, I applied it. I had the information in the second case but did not ask enough questions to bring those cookies to me even though they were already baked and needing a home.

It is important that you recognize the miracles that happen in your life, no matter the size. Miracles usually happen in ways that cannot be foreseen at the time. My son getting out of Houston in advance of the global Covid-19 crisis to me is a miracle. My dogs from Russia are a miracle. I look at them and ask them if they knew before they were born that they were destined to travel here to the US to bring happiness and joy into a time of my life when I really needed that. Stewart is a big miracle that I never expected to happen, yet he saved my life. Some miraculous change had to happen inside of me for all of these things to happen. The more I reject negative temptations, the more room I have for positive experiences to come into my life. The inner work has to be reflected in the outer world.

- Do you allow miracles to happen in your life?
- Does *Name Frequency #1* dig into your inner soil?
- Does digging into your inner soil allow *Name Frequency #2* to work?
- Can you easier reclaim your Sparks of Light/Life because you are digging?
- Is the reclamation of your Sparks of Light an inner transformation?
- Does the reclamation of your Sparks of Light allow for more miracles to enter your life?
- Do miracles have to be big?
- Can small miracles have profound effects on your life?
- Is any miracle small?
- Is being able to connect with friends and family on the inner levels a miracle?
- Do you have any bleak and hopeless looking situations in your life right now?
- What happens if you think about that situation at your Pineal Gland and then visualize this *Name Frequency* on top of it?
- Regardless of results, does this plant the seed for something miraculous to happen in that situation?
- If so, does this mean that the situation will resolve the way you want or the way you need?
- Do you remember what an apple seed contains?

Often, people think that miracles happen overnight. But usually, this is not the case. You have to plant the seed/energy/frequency to get the miracle in motion. For example, a family was looking for old gas cans because the new ones did not fit their needs. They discussed, researched and discussed some more. The frequency that they needed those old gas cans grew stronger in their mind-patterns.

Need is a Self-fulfilling prophecy. Once you have a need, it has to be fulfilled.

On their walk, they just happened upon exactly what they needed in their neighbors' trash that he had set out for the garbage collectors. I wonder how long that neighbor had those cans lying around. And suddenly, it came to him to put them out for the trash person. This means on the inner levels because we are All One, the need of this family reached out and touched the neighbor causing him to need to release the cans. On the inner levels the neighbor had to tell the family to walk past his house at a specific time on a specific day so they could have what they need. The seed for this miracle to happen was planted when the family realized what they needed.

Stewart finding me was a miracle. If you read our story in his autobiography **Montauk: Alien Connection** you know that he labeled the chapter of our meeting "Paradise Found". Years later we discovered that *Janet* means *Paradise* in Arabic. Not a coincidence but a meeting of the minds on the deep inner levels. We both needed each other and when the time was correct, we found each other.

What appears to be a miracle does not happen overnight. You have to trace this moment back to the original moment when the miracle began. This is the miracle of working with the **72 Names of God Frequencies**. Specific frequencies are stirring up something primordial within you. Primordial is the specific word that my Oversoul gives me to give to you. Primordial means since the beginning. You need something primordial to stir up that which is hidden deep within. Regardless of when you found **Expansions'** work, we had to have a meeting of the minds when the seed of **Expansions** was planted in my mind when I was only 25 years old.

- Where were you in 1980, when I was 25 years old and first stepping out of my metaphysical closet?

- Is it a miracle that **Expansions** exists in its current form bringing all kinds of interesting information to you?
- Or, did you already know this and **Expansions** work simply reminds you of what you already know?
- Where were you in 1956 when I agreed to be born and bring this information into the public eye?
- Do you think we had a meeting of the minds way back then, or even before?
- In the *Eternal Now*, are our minds in constant contact?
- What pulls you to study the **72 Names of God**?
- Is there something primordial within you that needs to come forward at this time?
- Is it a miracle that your mind-pattern pulled this body of **Expansions'** work to you?
- Is it a miracle that I, along with Stewart, survived our ordeals to be able to put this material out?
- Do you think on some level, that you have always supported our journey so that we would be here for you when it was time?
- Do you understand the depth of your True Inner Connection and why your inner level work is the most important work that you can do?
- Was it a coincidence or a miracle that the family found those old style gas cans?
- What do you think the old gas cans symbolized to the neighbor?
- What do the old gas cans symbolize to the family who received them?
- Do miracles happen suddenly or must they be set in motion?

- Can miracles be explained?
- Is need a Self-fulfilling prophecy?

Last night I spent quite a bit of time contemplating *Name Frequency* #3 and all of the miracles that I would like to happen in my life. I was actually surprised that I had such a long list! The long list brought up a lot of intersecting subjects, so I was awake until almost 4am this morning. By the time I was in a nice deep sleep, the alarm was going off at 6:20am! So, that is how my day started. This afternoon I had an appointment with my dad and after I had a couple of things to pick up at the local supermarket. I had not been there since the governor decided that the stores could no longer assume that maskless people have a medical issue. Now, the stores here in Michigan have to ask us to wear a mask and we have to state one of the governor's 10 exemptions if we are not wearing a mask. The onus is on the business which does put them in a precarious spot.

With this said, I had an issue at checkout which I decided to follow up with a letter to my State Senator as well as the store owner. This is part of not being silent. I am publishing the letter below so if you have any issues you can use this as a basis to create your own letter which I highly recommend you send not only to the store owner/management but also let your State Senator know what is going on.

There was a lot more said at checkout but I wanted to keep this as succinct as possible.

> Hello Roger,
>
> I have just returned home from a very unpleasant experience in your store. I entered your store, wandered around shopping, spoke to store employees without any problem while not wearing a mask. Upon checkout the cashier, who was courteous, said that she was not allowed to check me out unless I was wearing a mask.

I politely explained that I am medically unable to tolerate a mask. She called a supervisor, who was one of the people who helped me while I was mask-less and shopping. He was very nice when I asked him about the frozen stir fry. There did not seem to be a problem. However, when I told him that I was medically unable to wear a mask at checkout, he became quite agitated and upset, at first telling me to leave the store without purchasing my items.

I told him that under ADA I cannot medically tolerate a face mask. He didn't seem to know anything about this. I told him the Governor's orders have 10 exemptions from wearing a face mask, one of which is if you are medically unable to tolerate one. I told him that he and his staff need to be educated because there are others like me, including a friend who came through that morning with the same issue and was also given a hard time. I showed him my ADA paperwork and he yelled that I should hurry up and then leave as he stormed off. As you know, fines for violating ADA are quite steep from $75,000 to $150,000.00. This was a violation

Of course, all the customers within hearing range were staring at me and a man on his way out the door yelled at me repeatedly "Selfish lady". Then, when I was outside putting my groceries into my car, this man drove around my vehicle while continuing to repeatedly scream at the top of his lungs 'Selfish lady". Needless to say, I did not feel safe in your store or in your parking lot. It is up to you to know that these orders are not laws and that these orders have exemptions. I should not have to educate you or your staff. These may be trying times but the goal is still to help; each other and not promote a violent or unsafe atmosphere.

My father who is 94 and cannot medically tolerate a mask will not even go in your store and was waiting for me in the car the whole time the man driving the car was verbally assaulting me.

How would you feel if either of us made the news because the angered customer did more than verbally assault me?

I am not the first person to enter your store and I will not be the last who cannot medically tolerate a mask. I know for a fact that there are people who cannot medically tolerate a mask but do it anyway because of these kinds of incidences.

Again, these people are at risk for wearing a mask. I understand your store is also in a challenging position, but our goal should still remain to help each other. I have lived in this community for 20 years and I want to be able to shop in your supermarket without harassment.

I appreciate a reply although I do understand that you are on vacation.

Thank you for taking the time to educate yourself and your staff, I am copying the Senators because they need to make sure that business owners are educated so they are not put in these trying positions.

If you live in the US, I suggest you find the orders for your own state to determine state exemptions, but ADA which is Federal still applies. Not being able to medically tolerate a mask means mental, emotional and/or physical. You do not have to answer any medical questions under the HIPAA laws for medical privacy. If anyone tries to make you answer any questions they are in violation of ADA laws and may be subject to fines between $75,000.00 and $150,000.00. The only thing you have to tell them is that you cannot medically tolerate a mask. With that said, always remember to know your audience and do your best to not make your Self a target.

My miracle today is that I stood up for my Self and my beliefs as well as educate and be an example. I am proud of the letter I wrote to the Senator and proud to be able to share it here in case you need to use it or something similar. Enough people need to step up with conviction to say no to fear, anger and mind-control.

I am going to keep working with the first 3 *Name Frequencies* because they are stirring up something deep within me that needs to rise to the surface in a balanced way.

I received a phone call from my Senator regarding my mask experience at the supermarket yesterday. She said that either she or her staff will phone the supermarket to help them understand what the ADA is as well as the fact that the governor's orders are not laws, and inform them about the exemptions. She said she would not have been as calm as I was and was very understanding about all of it. I have not heard from the supermarket.

- What kinds of miracles do you need in your life?
- When you stop to think about it, is your list longer than you first realized?
- Have you thought more about what a miracle is vs. what you are told that it is?
- Have you lost sleep because of your mental work?
- Or not been able to stay awake because of your mental work?
- Is your mental work affecting your dreams?
- Is it challenging to say no to fear, anger and mind-control?
- Is it important that you know your audience?
- Do you remember to do all your protection work every day and every night?
- If you are in the position of having to wear a mask, can you do it without negative emotion?
- Which is worse, wearing a mask or the internal negative emotion that it evokes?

All of these **72 Names of God** take time to work. You may find favorites, ones that you are particularly drawn to or you may find that some do not resonate with you at all. If you are challenged to use a *Name Frequency*, then either you need more or less of it. Just like with a food, for example. If you do not like a food, either you really need it or you really don't need it. I was always challenged to eat bitter foods. I totally rejected them. But, over time I came to understand that instead of rejecting my bitter experiences I needed to learn to assimilate them. Now, I can eat bitter foods and enjoy them. You can spend a lot of time with just one *Name Frequency* when you are diligently working on your inner issues.

- Why are you drawn to stay with one *Name Frequency*?
- Even if you do not see immediate results, why do you still choose to stay that one *Name Frequency*?
- Do you think part of your mission and purpose is to educate?
- Do you have to open your mouth to educate?
- Is being an example leading by example?
- Can doing your mental work re-arrange your energy field so your frequency is in a more correct alignment with your Source?
- Do these frequencies disrupt and dismantle your programming?
- Which of the 3 Names discussed so far are you using and why?

Name Frequency #4

Eliminating Negative Thoughts

Ayin Lamed Mem
Read Hebrew Letters Right to Left
Name Frequency Pronunciation
Aye Lah Meh

Name Frequency #4 is used for eliminating negative thoughts. Everything that is stirring up needs someplace to go. As much as you may want to release them up to your Oversoul and into God-Mind, negative emotions can become obsessive and take over your mind. Programming is also stirred up and mixed with this negative morass as it tries to take hold. All of this inner stirring bring forth color, tone, and archetypes that resonate with the negativity in the outer world, making all more challenging to resist.

This *Name Frequency* gives you that extra boost to boot all this negativity right back up to Source. It also helps you gain insight, understanding, and clarity as to why all of this is inside you in the first place. This Name can fill the empty space that these exiting negative emotions leave. In addition, you can use Medium Green for emotional healing as well as Pale Pink for Unconditional Love and Acceptance, or anything else that your Oversoul may give you. The important thing is to fill in the empty space so you do not allow the negativity back in.

Today, I went to the dentist for a cleaning. Nothing was said about wearing a mask but when I got to the door there was a sign saying to wait outside until your appointment time and be sure to have your mask. My hygienist let me in and asked me to use their hand sanitizer. I have known her forever, so I told her that hand sanitizer is poison but I would be happy to wash my hands in soap and water where she could watch me. She said I could do that at her station. Then, she told me I needed to put my mask on. I told her I was medically unable to tolerate a mask, so she asked me if I could hold up a mask in front of my face to walk the few steps down the hall to her chair. So this I did. No negative feelings on my part, doing what I needed to do in that moment.

She is a huge Civil War fan, so she was extremely upset over what she is seeing happen in the world. After some talk, I asked her if she knew about Q, which she did not. I told her I had some videos that may be of interest to her and let it go at that. After paying my bill, she came up to me with her phone number and asked that I text her the videos.

Teaching by example as led by my inner voice. This is what I am telling you to do. Know your audience as best as you can. Release your own inner negative emotions so you do not taint your message. You can be passionate while being true to your Self and teaching by example. The goal is not to fuel your own negative emotions nor fuel the negative emotions of your audience. The goal is to challenge-resolve in the most peaceful, positive, proactive way possible.

Miracles happen on the inner level first before they can manifest in the outer levels.

One step at a time.

- Do you find it interesting how one *Name Frequency* seems to dovetail with the next *Name Frequency*?
- Are you being Spiritually taken care of every step of the way while working with these *Name Frequencies*?
- Is everyone a teacher?
- Are most people aware that they teach others?
- Is teaching by example the most important form of teaching?
- Is it challenging to know your audience?
- Do you agree that a good teacher can teach to every level?
- Does a good teacher know it all?
- Is a good teacher always learning?
- Is it challenging the depth of your own negative emotions some times?
- Can negative emotions overwhelm and pull you under?
- Do you need to tread lightly when dealing with negative emotions?
- Do suppressed negative emotions sometimes unleash in a torrent?
- When this happens, is this a Self-test to see if you are proactive or reactive?
- Is it okay if you are reactive?
- Can you observe when you are being reactive so you know what to do the next time?
- Does the next time always come, usually when you are least prepared?

- Does it take one step at a time to change from reactive to proactive?
- Are you better than you were?
- Do you judge Self or evaluate Self?
- What is the difference?

Name Frequency #5

Healing

Mem Hey Shin
Read Hebrew Letters Right to Left
Name Frequency Pronunciation
Meh Heh Shih

It is interesting that the *Name Frequency* for Healing is #5 because you already know that in Hyperspace the #5 represents healing. Put this *Name Frequency* at your Pineal Gland to see what happens. While doing this create a mental list of everything in your life that needs healing. This can be mental, emotional, physical and spiritual. This can also be finances, career, organization, relationships and pets. You can ask that this *Name Frequency* be put into others via the *Oversoul* level. You can even add in the Earth and all planetary and universes healing. Allow everything in your life that you would like healed to focus into this *Name Frequency* and observe. Just as you made a list with Miracle Making, allow this list to grow.

- Does sending Healing to others help you heal?
- Do you get back what you give out?
- Are you able to receive what comes to you?
- Are you able to receive healing?
- Do you feel worthy of receiving healing?
- Do you feel that you should suffer and be punished?
- Do you feel guilty when positive things happen?
- Do you worry about others when you receive positive and others do not?
- Do others you know easily receive?
- Can you receive negative but not the positive?
- Does using *Name Frequency #4*, Eliminating Negative Thoughts, help you to receive healing?
- Do you think your Oversoul is doing its best to cheer you on?
- How long is the list of what needs to be healed in your life?

Working with these *Name Frequencies* stirs up much. As you are noticing, this work is not a quick fix, but rather it is about stirring up the deeper primordial layers where consciously you fear to tread. As much as everyone says he/she wants healing, it is challenging to let go of those parts that need to be healed the most. These are the parts upon which you have built your life and identity.

When I reached my 50th birthday I was so excited because 50 is the decade of healing. I don't know why but I definitely associate the word "healing" with "positive". Of course, healing is positive but healing does not mean easy, and positive does not mean easy. That decade of my life was one of the most challenging; it definitely was not fun or easy, but the outcome eventually I could call positive. It is truly challenging to break through preconceived ideas. Just like me looking forward to my 50s, I am always amazed at my conscious expectations vs. the reality of what happens. I have let go of what I want. I do my best to focus on what I need. I am doing my best to be flexible in what I get. My left brain logic spends a lot of time explaining to my right brain/emotion so I can balance at my Pineal Gland to maintain my sanity.

The *72 Names of God Frequencies* are definitely helping me which is why I am taking the time to slow you down to focus on them. You could spend forever on just one *Name Frequency*. But studying them in this way allows you to take the time to sample them, just like food on a smorgasbord. You can take a small taste of each one. Then when you go back, you can pick and choose, or you can use them all. But the time you spend now starts another layer of your foundational mind-pattern that supports you in the deeper layers and levels.

- Have you let go of what you want?
- Do you do your best to focus on what you need?
- Are you flexible in what you get?
- Does your left brain/logic spend time explaining to your right brain/emotions?
- Is it imperative to find balance at the Pineal Gland?
- Do you remember to put Bet in the left brain, Aleph in the right brain, and Gimmel at the Pineal Gland to help maintain your balance?
- Do your conscious expectations get in your way of acknowledging the reality of what actually happens?
- When you think "healing" do you think "easy" and "positive"?
- Can your inner wounds heal if they have a protective scab on the top but inside they are festering?
- How challenging is it to open up the protective scab to get to the festering inside?
- Is cleaning out wounds a painful process?
- Is cleaning out old wounds an important part of healing?

- Is cleaning out old wounds a positive?
- Is cleaning out old wounds easy?
- Is cleaning out old wounds healing?
- How many old wounds do you still have festering inside?
- When you use the *Name Frequency #5* at your Pineal Gland, how many old wounds do you see with scabs that are still festering inside?
- Is humanity healing differently than you would like to see humanity healing?
- Can healing encompass some very rough stuff?
- Do the victims need the oppressors to teach them whatever it is they need to know?
- What kinds of mind-patterns do the victims have to attract horrific physical lessons?
- Does someone have to play the part of the oppressor?
- Do you have compassion for all?
- Do you have compassion for all parts of Self?

Name Frequency #6

Dream State

Lamed Lamed Hey
Read Hebrew Letters Right to Left
Name Frequency Pronunciation
Lah Lah Heh

*N*ame Frequency #6 helps align you with your Dream State. By focusing on this *Name Frequency* you are more likely to pass through programming dreams into Oversoul dreams. If you do have programming dreams, you will be more likely to remember them so you can correct them upon waking. You may be able to correct them while you are dreaming. Remember that programming dreams generally involve human-made structures such as buildings, airplanes, elevators and escalators.

Oversoul dreams generally involve more Nature-made objects such as wood, stone, water, soil, plants and animals. The more you record your dreams, the more you begin to understand the symbolism.

Remember that there is a dream dictionary in the back of **Healer's Handbook**. In general, most dreams are about you. Some people do receive prophetic dreams, but generally, these dreams are about you and are influenced by what is going on around you. Some people communicate with loved ones and even pets who have passed on while in the dream state. Continue to do your Hyperspace/Oversoul protection work while working with the *Name Frequencies*.

Many people report better sleep patterns as a result of working with these *Name Frequencies*. Others say that they are more disturbed at night because the *Name Frequencies* are stirring things up and they feel agitated. Everyone is different and there is no right or wrong. You may wish for pleasant Oversoul dreams but instead, get intense programming dreams. This is not wrong but what you need at this time.

I highly suggest focusing on the *10 Sefirot* in **Template of God-Mind** page 40 to help heal and align the body. This is the original energetic template, which we have laid out for you according to the chakra system.

- Do the *Name Frequencies* help you sleep or agitate you?
- Are you remembering your dreams better?
- Are you having Oversoul or programming dreams?
- How do you know which is which?
- Do you have a tendency to judge your dreams?
- Do you study your dreams without judgment?
- Do you keep a dream journal?
- Does working with your dreams help you interpret symbolism?
- How important is symbolism?
- Is the code in the **Torah** based on symbolism?
- Are the **72 Names of God** based on symbolism?

- Are all alphabets archetypes?
- Can you find codes in everything that exists?
- Technically, is *All That Exists* the *Name of God*?
- Does *All That Exists* come from the nonphysical into the physical using the 22 Hebrew Letters as explained in the **Torah**?
- If so, would your Soul have had to enter the physical as a result of a code within the **Torah**?
- And if this is so, do you have to study this for lifetimes, or is it already embedded within?
- Are you using these Hebrew letters to unlock what is already within in the most correct and beneficial way for you?

Name Frequency #7

Soul-Personality Mind-Patterns

Aleph Khaf Aleph
Read Hebrew Letters Right to Left
Name Frequency Pronunciation
Ah Khah Ah

This *Name Frequency* helps you find order amidst the chaos by connecting deep within your Soul so you can see what is vs. what you perceive exists. If you think of the in-breath of God, that is where you are headed so you can see clearly from a more objective vantage point. You know how challenging it can be when you are in the middle of the forest. Your understanding of the forest is greater if you look at it from above rather than standing in the midst of it. Usually, it is much easier to explain and understand something after it happens more so than when you are in the middle of any event. Obviously, the plannedemic was planned some time ago.

- Are we in a game of Good Cop, Bad Cop where everyone is on the same side?
- Even if these people are all related does it mean that they are on the same side?
- If you create order out of your own chaos, does that help clean up the outer world?
- Does your world feel like it is in chaos and you want it to stop?
- How do you feel when you walk out your door and see masks on everyone, including children?
- Or have to fuel your vehicle and half the pumps are covered to maintain social-distancing?
- Are the billionaires laughing all the way to the bank?
- Do you feel like you need to create more order in your external world, such as your home?
- Are you challenged to organize your home?
- Do you think the global handlers are using these powerful Hebrew tools against humanity?
- If the *Name Frequencies* are formulas, can anyone use them?
- If there is a formula to quell chaos, do you think there is a formula to create chaos?

When I organize my living space, I always feel like I can breathe. Clutter/chaos gives me claustrophobia. Sometimes, the outer world is so cluttered and chaotic that you want to hide. Many movies have the plot of chaos caused by the bad guys prompting the good guys to intervene, usually after a long fight. The bad guys are always extremely smart and cunning, often outsmarting the good guys until the very last moment. Bad guys and good guys think differently. The bad guys rely on the gullibility of the good guys.

Even in Waldensian history, there is the story of the Easter Massacre of 1655. The Catholics convinced the Waldensians to give up their arms and take the Catholic soldiers into their homes as a gesture of goodwill. In the middle of the night, the soldiers slaughtered all the Waldensians who were defenseless. Estimates of the Waldensians killed range from 1,000 to 6,000 innocent people.

Chaos brings out the worst in people as you are witnessing throughout the globe. But, it can also bring out the best in them as you are witnessing many people standing up and saying that they have had enough. There are always villains eager to create chaos. It is your duty to not react to the chaos. To hold steadfast to your values, morals and beliefs is always your goal. I often wonder about the people who join forces with domestic terrorists thinking that they are doing something good. When they are hurt and/or arrested, I wonder if this wakes them up to the reality of their choices. Programming, as well as demonic/astral attachments, can also take hold telling them to do something that they ordinarily would not do.

Chaos will try to suck you in. Some Kabbalists work for those who are determined to rule the world. Just as you are learning to create order, these Kabbalists are using what they know to create chaos. You are fortunate to have your tools and protection techniques. Use *Name Frequency #7* to create order out of your own internal and perhaps external chaos.

- Is it challenging to think like a criminal?
- Why is it easy for a criminal to spot a victim, yet much more challenging for a potential victim to spot a criminal?
- Do you remember that the *Name Frequencies* are formulas that anyone can use?
- Does it make sense that there are formulas to create chaos?
- Is there ever a positive reason to create chaos?

- Does using *Name Frequency #1* to dig deep within your inner soil create chaos?
- Is it welcome chaos?
- Do you think there are a lot of good people who are now being sucked into the world chaos?
- Do you think there are some people doing things they ordinarily would not do?
- Can you discern by looking at people if they are reacting to programming, demonic possession and/or astral attachments?
- Do you want to see this?
- Is it sometimes easier to not know?
- Does not knowing simplify or complicate life?
- Have you seen the outer world chaos bring out the best in people?
- Have you noticed that most movies have some sort of chaos that happens and then has to be sorted out before the movie concludes?
- Does organizing your living environment chaos make you feel more internally organized?
- What prevents you from organizing your living environment?

Because you are so focused on creating positive it is challenging to realize that there are many people focused on creating negative. Most likely in your sphere of influence, you do not interact with such people. In my world, I have come across truly evil people who tried several times to destroy me. Unless you have lived through such things, it is challenging to imagine. For this reason, I am grateful to them for teaching me about pure evil. I learned a lot from my experiences, including never underestimate the enemy, even if the enemy is your Self.

By studying them, I know a lot about the evil frequencies and how to identify them. I also know a lot about how to stand in my center, anchor into Source, feel my power and hold my ground. The stronger the attack, the deeper the opportunity to grow, if you survive.

When people have access to power, they are often tempted to use the power for themselves. They have a recipe that is neutral and can be used for either good or evil. Those who use it for evil call it a good day when evil is successful and a bad day when good is successful. All the Hyperspace/Oversoul work you are learning can be used for good or for evil. A baseball bat can be used to play a fun game or to seriously harm someone. If I give you a bat, I expect you to use it to play a fun game. I teach you the rules of the game and how to play fair. If you choose to use the bat in a negative way instead, there will be consequences.

The next 4 *Name Frequencies* all are various aspects of Protection. You can protect something that is negative. Just like those who are purposefully creating chaos. Their goal is to protect the chaos. They can use these same tools to protect the chaos, but their energy comes from dark forces. Their goal is to tempt you to fall into the chaos and embrace it. Your goal is to stand steadfast in your center, anchored in your Oversoul and God-Mind while allowing the power of the Absolute, God-Mind, and Oversoul to flood your Being. No one can do anything to you unless you allow it on some level. Your goal is also to protect the positive, including order and organization. At the same time, you cannot take away the lessons of others. They must be tempted so they can make choices. You can lay out the path, but you cannot walk the path for them. You can set them up for success, but they must ultimately choose between good and evil.

Name Frequency #8

Neutralizing Negative Energy

Khaf Hey Tav
Read Hebrew Letters Right to Left
Name Frequency Pronunciation
Khah Heh Tah

This *Name Frequency* emanates a frequency which negativity and evil cannot tolerate. This gives you space to work on your mind-pattern to permanently eliminate the negativity within that no longer serves a purpose.

- Are there people in your life who emanate negativity?
- Do you have to accept their negative emanations?
- Do these people provide opportunities to stand in your center and anchor into Source, without allowing them to disturb the calm peace of your Soul?

- Can you use this *Name Frequency* to neutralize your own negative thoughts when you realize that they no longer serve a purpose?
- Does some part of you want to hold onto your own negativity?
- Can you use this *Name Frequency* to help you let go?
- Can you use this *Name Frequency* to help clean up your energetic space, neutralizing any evil or dark forces they may want to cause you chaos?
- Is it challenging to think of people who want to protect their negative creations?
- When you do not want to part with negative mind-patterns are you protecting your own negative creations?
- Do you keep in mind that Spiritual Law is neutral and available to all regardless of intent?
- Are you set up, for example, to hate the banking system so that the banking system self-perpetuates by all those who pour hate into it?
- If you hate the banking system does hate come back to you?
- Does this make hate a negative creation that you protect by continuing to hate?
- What negative creations do you protect?
- How many ways do you protect them?
- If you know the Spiritual Law that says what you give out comes back to you, are you using Spiritual Law in a negative way?
- Do you always remember to never underestimate the enemy, even if the enemy is your Self?

Working with these *Name Frequencies* does not usually bring immediate results because you are just getting to know them.

Whenever change comes too fast you can be thrown out of balance in such a way as to disturb your overall work-in-process. However, you may begin to notice some subtle differences that something is happening. Sometimes, you may not be able to articulate exactly what that is, but you feel something.

Not too long ago I was doing my evening stretching exercises in front of my bathroom mirror when all of a sudden a giant Gimmel appeared the length of my body in front of me. I was not thinking of anything in particular other than going through my nightly routine in preparation for bed. So, I was a bit surprised to see this Gimmel show up. A bit puzzled, I gave it to my Oversoul and didn't think too much about it beyond that. Fast forward a couple of weeks later. While out walking the dogs, thinking of nothing in particular again, a Gimmel appeared at my Pineal Gland, this time with a dot in it, called a dagesh. While studying the Mother Letters of Hebrew, I learned about Doubles, which are 7 Hebrew letters that have 2 sounds when a dot/dagesh is used. Modern spoken Hebrew only uses 3 Doubles, and the Gimmel is not one of them.

A Gimmel with a dagesh is pronounced like a soft g, as in "gelatin". Well, guess what, a j as in "Janet" has the same sound as a soft g. I was shown that to write my name in Hebrew, I needed to begin with a Gimmel with a dagesh. Then I remembered the body-length Gimmel from some days prior. Now I know why it appeared. Consciously, I would never have thought about using a Gimmel. In addition, I realized that when doing my stretching exercises, the one I was doing actually formed a Gimmel. My feet were about 18 inches apart, left arm at my side, right arm raised over my head as I stretched my raised right arm to the left. I became a Gimmel!

These are the kinds of things that can happen as you open up your inner resources. It would have been interesting if someone would have told me this, but it is extremely interesting when you get to experience this for your Self. In the overall scheme of life, this information is not too Earthshaking. But it is these small clues that can be the missing piece to complete puzzles that are Earthshaking. And, I can also easily verify that this is true because I have the book that says a Gimmel with a dagesh sounds like a soft g which I know sounds like a j.

Most Hebrew speakers, if asked how to spell my name in Hebrew would start it with a Yud, which makes the y sound as in yellow. I was shown the most correct way to spell my name. Also, remember that each letter has a numerical value. A Yud has a value of 10 while a Gimmel has a value of 3. In addition, the sound is completely different. Sound is important in the Creation of the universe as well as your own Soul-Personality. My True Sound came to me via the pull of my mind-pattern. This is why it is important to keep going even if it seems like nothing is happening. You never know what is being stirred up deep within until something happens that catches your attention long enough to verify your own inner process.

Name Frequency #9

Proper Angelic Frequencies

Hey Zayin Yud
Read Hebrew Letters Right to Left
Name Frequency Pronunciation
Heh Zye Yuh

Most people think of Angels only as positives. But remember, Lucifer is an Angel, and Lucifer has an Angelic Army. So yes, there are negative Angels that may try to negatively influence you. Use this *Name Frequency* to attract positive Angels that help guide and protect while dispelling negative Angels and their influences.

- Is it easy to forget that not all Angels are positive?
- Can forgetting this allow Angels of negative influence to slip in?
- Do you think Angels must work within certain Spiritual Laws, just like you do?

- If they break Spiritual Law, will they also have consequences?
- Does this remind you to always question whatever is around you?
- When you are anchored and centered in Source, do you have the power within to withstand whatever negativity comes your way?
- Does learning about Self bring personal satisfaction?
- When your information comes from within vs. without, do you get an even greater sense of accomplishment?
- Is there a part of you that is impatient and wants to know yesterday?
- Do you know that you already know?
- Can you accept that what you need to know will reveal itself when you need to know?
- Can it be challenging to keep up an attitude of gratitude?
- Is finding the correct question to ask a breakthrough?
- How important is it to correctly interpret the data that comes to you?
- Does your Oversoul always explain whatever information it gives you?

You must always keep in mind the power of your voice. The words you speak are really a projection of sound that disturbs the air and in so doing, create. All of your positive, uplifting work that you, personally do, adds to the upliftment of humanity. By sending everything up to your Oversoul, you allow your Oversoul to organize and keep you in order which in turn adds to the order of the collective unconscious of humanity. Think about how many people speak but do not send their words up to their Oversouls. This means that their words are floating around in the air, kind of like undirected radio waves.

Like attract like.

If there are Kabbalist's intent on creating chaos, it would make their work a lot easier if all these undirected words were not out disturbing the air. By masking and muffling people, the words do not have the same force when spoken. Plus, people are not as comfortable speaking, so they speak less. Singing is not allowed in churches. I'm wondering if this will be extrapolated to schools because usually elementary school age and under children sing a lot in classrooms. Choirs start forming in the upper grades, so these may also be banned. Wind instruments are banned. Sounds are being silenced one by one, except for those produced by rioters and those causing chaos. Sounds of chaos are welcome because the negative Kabbalists can direct these energetic sounds into more negativity.

Like attracts like.

In Kabbalah, chaos is said to be the root of evil.

Name Frequency #10

Protection From Negative Projections

Aleph Lamed Dalet
Read Hebrew Letters Right to Left
Name Frequency Pronunciation
Ah Lah Dah

I always tell you that it only takes letting your guard down for less than a nanosecond for something to enter your energy field. This can happen if you are tired, depressed, upset, angry; any negative emotion weakens your field. I also tell you that if the negative projection cannot get to you, it gets to those around you or even your environment.

For example, we had our water distiller cleaned. In doing so, the process of cleaning found a weak spot that broke through the side of the water distiller filling our basement with steam. This meant we needed a new water distiller so the plumber was going to give us a quote. The plumber tried for 2 weeks to get a quote from their normal source but could not get answers. In the meantime, I found one online. The plumbers were so exasperated that they told me to order it. The wait was 2 weeks. It finally came, they installed it and the next morning when Stewart checked, it was buzzing and bouncing around. We had to have the plumbers back out to stabilize it.

Then our water filtration system which replaced the one that failed only a few months previously had an alarm going off the following morning. The plumber came back, fixed it, and the next morning the same thing happened. The plumber came back and said the UV light was burned out. He ordered a new one which would take another two weeks.

I told you that my youngest son was supposed to get the up-the-nose Covid test for school which had me so upset. I kept praying that things would change. Finally, I wrote to the school to see if they could just screen students and only do this test if the students exhibited Covid symptoms. I was told they have already contracted a lab to come to the university and give the invasive tests but they would accept a saliva test! Yay!

The issue is my son is healthy and does not have a primary care doctor. I called the university medical clinic and they do not order Covid tests. I called the Covid hotline, explained my situation and they set up a phone screening at night by an unknown medical person who would phone us. Somehow, the call went directly into our voice mail and we never got the call. There was no callback number so I had to call the hotline again, reschedule, and this time I was told the person could call 20 minutes before the appointment time to 20 minutes after the appointment time. We got the call, got the labs. The woman on the other end of the phone line would not give her name, a confirmation number, or any other information except that his labs would be in the system when he was ready to schedule. When I phoned to schedule, they could not find his labs or any record of the phone appointment! So, I called the Covid hotline again, explained the situation, the woman spent a long time looking and found that there were 2 labs in the system for him but not visible to the schedulers. This meant I had to call the schedulers again but this woman said she would transfer me to the schedulers. Somehow, after being on hold for another 20 minutes, I got the same woman again who does not know how she transferred me back to herself! Finally, I got to the scheduler, she found the labs and he was good to go.

The interesting side note is that the person who wrote the lab orders said they do not give the saliva test, but there is a new Covid test, that has only been out for one week, that goes just slightly inside the nostril and he does it to himself! Hallelujah! If I had phoned one week earlier I would have been trying to find a lab that does the saliva test, so amidst the chaos, my son was still protected. I wanted to contact the school earlier but I was consistently told not to by my Oversoul. Then one day, I was granted permission and I went for it.

Once again, even with all your protection work, the chaos is still around you and will do its best to wreak havoc in your life. It is up to you to stay centered and anchored in Source so that no matter what comes at you, you move through it with Grace and Dignity. Use *Name Frequency #10* to aid in whatever negativity, chaos and evil that comes at you.

- Does a Bright Light attract many bugs?
- Are you a Bright Light?
- Is your Bright Light plugged into and powered by Source?
- Have you noticed that if chaos cannot get to you that it will get to those around you?
- Can chaos wreak havoc in your life by attacking things or even people who are trying to help you?
- Can chaos even wreak havoc with the people who are trying to help you?

- Can you use these *Name Frequencies* via the Oversoul level to reach beyond your immediate locale into all necessary people, places, and things to restore Divine Order?
- Do you find your Self in positions where you think something will take 5 minutes, but instead takes hours and even weeks?
- Do you think that what is chaos to you might have a very well understood order to the person who is causing the chaos?
- If I told you to create chaos in one of your closets, would you know how to do it?
- Could you explain to anyone how you disorganized/created the chaos in your closet?
- Would there be a methodology for the creation of the closet chaos?
- If you created enough chaos in enough closets, could you become an expert at creating closet chaos?
- If I told you to put everything back in order, could you do it?
- If you know how to take something apart, does this mean you know how to put it back together?
- If you know how to put something together, can you then discern how to take it apart?
- If society is organized, could someone then have a methodology to take it apart in ways the ordinary person would not understand?
- Does Sound create?
- Can Sound destroy?
- Does the sound of a high-powered blast destroy?
- Does chaos have a sound?
- Does silencing what you consider organized sound allow room for more sound of chaos to emanate and destroy?
- Is chaos the root of all evil?

Name Frequency #11

Cleansing Evil

Lamed Aleph Vav
Read Hebrew Letters Right to Left
Name Frequency Pronunciation
Lah Ah Wah

You know a lot about psychic energy, specifically as detailed in ***Decoding Your Life***. You know that most people leave their psychic energy lying around long after the physical body has left the room. You know the mental work to release psychic cords from you to others and from others to you. You know how to clean up your space so that when you leave an area it feels like you were never there. You know a lot about protection using Color, Tone and Archetypes.

Name Frequency #11 is another tool that cleanses your environment of psychic energy, astral forces, and malevolent entities and beings. Do your preliminaries, do what you already know to do, and add this in as another layer of cleaning, releasing and protection. Always remember that everything that comes to you, comes for a reason. There is a part of you that is attracting something negative, even if consciously you do not want it. This *Name Frequency* helps bring this information into your conscious mind. It helps give you the boost to release this negativity from your own mind-pattern, giving it back to your Oversoul and God-Mind.

This also means that it can help you push through your programming, breaking the programming apart so that it is no longer effective. As you clear the negativity life may appear to get worse before it gets better. When you see life getting worse, know that you are doing something correctly. The negativity tries to suck you back in and take hold, but your inner strength is growing and expanding so that this can no longer happen. Evil forces are everywhere. Use this *Name Frequency* to send them away from you. Stay clean and clear no matter where you are. Keep your nonphysical environment clean and clear. You know that even when you send something away, that without mind-pattern correction it will come back to you again. Keep working on Self first as you incorporate this powerful mind-pattern booster.

- When you are diligently doing your inner level work, do you usually find life getting worse before it gets better?
- Is it easy to get discouraged?
- Does it take fortitude to recognize that you are doing something correct?
- Does the upheaval tempt you to stop?
- Is upheaval always a part of the process?
- Does your Bright Light tempt evil to do its best to thwart you?
- Can you increase your Bright Light enough so that it blinds evil?

- Which tools do you use for protection and nonphysical energy clearing?
- Do you have standard "go to" tools or do they change depending on what is going on in your life?
- Does this *Name Frequency* bring up any hidden negative mind-patterns, thoughts or experiences?
- Have you reviewed the material in **Decoding Your Life** on psychic energy?
- Do you know what psychic energy is through personal experience?
- Is reading about it the first step to bringing conscious awareness?
- Is the next step to observe and ask questions?
- What is your first awareness of psychic energy vs. Universal Energy?

Name Frequency #12

Unconditional Love

Hey Hey Ayin
Read Hebrew Letters Right to Left
Name Frequency Pronunciation
Heh Heh Aye

Until you have Unconditional Love for your Self, it is challenging to have this for others. In fact, most people do not know what Love is, much less Unconditional Love. I wrote about this extensively in **Decoding Your Life**, so please review this section of the book. Growing up, I thought I knew what Love was, but in retrospect, I can honestly say that I did not. I had a lot of confused feelings about a lot of things, and Love was definitely in that mixture. I have also written about this extensively in **Heights of Relationships** so be sure to read this book for another layer of understanding.

Until you begin to understand what Love is, it is challenging to Love anyone, including Self. This *Name Frequency* begins to open you to understanding what Unconditional Love actually means. When you send Unconditional Love via the Oversoul level, this means that Unconditional Love Frequency can come back to you. The most challenging thing to do for most people is to Unconditionally Love everyone and everything. Ultimately, because everyone comes from One Source, loving others is loving Self. Loving others is loving the Source.

Unconditional Love can be tough love. You have to love others enough to allow them to be who and what they are in the way they want to be who and what they are or think they are. Sometimes, the most loving thing you can do for another may not feel good to the recipient. For example, if your teenager wants to go somewhere or do something that you consider dangerous the most loving thing you can do is be a parent who says no. This means not relinquishing your decision no matter how much the teen screams, begs, pleads, threatens and cries.

Maybe a relative needs to borrow your car to go to work, but you know that he/she is not a careful driver. You do not want the relative, your car or another person to be injured, so the most loving thing you can do is to refuse. Unconditional Love in many cases does not feel good to the recipient. Sometimes, it does not feel good to you, either, even when you know you are making the correct decisions for the correct reasons. An unpopular decision may be an expression of Unconditional Love. This all means that Life may be in Divine Order and filled with Unconditional Love, but it still may not feel good.

People think that Love always feels good, but this is not the case. Your Oversoul, the True Parent of Your Soul, may have to make some tough Love decisions to get you to focus on your correct path. You may want a specific job, but your Oversoul sees that this is not where you need to be for the lessons that you need. Perhaps the job might be dangerous. Think of the people who were in the World Trade Towers when it was destroyed. Maybe your dream job was in that building but you did not get the job. Your Oversoul let you suffer in silence until the day the building went down. Then, you were grateful that you did not get the job that would have literally turned you into a dream!

These are all only small samplings of Unconditional Love. So, like everything you do, proceed with caution. Consciously you may want Unconditional Love. Unconsciously you may already be getting Unconditional Love that you cannot yet recognize. It is easy to focus on the positive aspects of what you think Unconditional Love is, so when the negative/not so comfortable aspects of Unconditional Love come knocking at your door, you may think that you are doing something wrong or that there is something wrong with you. Unconditional Love Frequency is a spectrum, like all Frequencies. Proceed with caution.

- Is it challenging to think of Unconditional Love in any terms but something that feels good?
- When you objectively observe and study Unconditional Love, can you see this frequency more present in your life than you first thought?
- Is Unconditional Love tough Love?
- Does tough Love always feel good to the recipient or the giver?
- Have you been the recipient of tough Love?
- Does tough Love feel like Unconditional Love?
- Have you been the giver of tough Love?
- Does being the giver of tough Love feel good?
- Does tough Love have the potential to build character in both recipient and giver?
- Can you Unconditionally Love someone enough to let them go?

- Is it sometimes your job to pick up others who fall, no matter how many times he/she falls?
- Is it always the job of your Oversoul to pick you up when you fall, no matter how many times you fall?
- Do you know what Love is?
- Do you know what Unconditional Love is?
- Do you always have Unconditional Love for Self, no matter what?
- Is knowing Love and Unconditional Love a process for most people?
- Can Love and Unconditional Love only be understood/known through a process?
- Is it strange to consider using a *Name Frequency* for Unconditional Love "with caution"?

Name Frequency #13

Personal Transformation

Yud Zayin Lamed
Read Hebrew Letters Right to Left
Name Frequency Pronunciation
Yuh Zye Lah

Global transformation can only happen in accordance with personal transformation. Personal transformation can be positive or negative. Personal transformation can even be horizontal as you exchange one mind-pattern for a similar mind-pattern. Yes, you are transforming but not really going anywhere. However, movement is still movement and is better than stagnation.

The reason the world is in such a state is because of the choices that people have made. I always tell you that you live your past. Whatever you thought or did yesterday determines what happens today. Today, I read about a 22 year old woman who gouged out her own eyes while using a hallucinogenic drug. The decision to take the drugs cost her dearly. What is now her past created her future. If you had a lot of negative yesterdays, then you have a tough load to carry as you work on turning your boat around. Yes, life can feel very discouraging. Sometimes you need to take a timeout; sometimes your life gives you no opportunities for timeouts. Your choice is to keep going because there is no turning back. Do your best to not be upset about what you did in the past because negative emotions only feed and drag out whatever you are in process of cleaning up.

Do your forgiveness work on Self and any others who you feel were involved, but ultimately, you made choices that you have to live with. The negative is a fantastic teacher; you remember these lessons well. You are always in the process of personal transformation; it is up to you what that personal transformation is. No one can make you do anything. You always have choices, even when you do not like the choices. Global transformation is a process that happens based upon each person. Use this *Name Frequency* to uplift and elevate so you can bring positive Global Transformation sooner rather than later via your own Personal Transformation. Look at all the millions of dollars that are funding the riots and the energy that the rioters and looters are expending. Think of how much positive could be done if those funds were used to help build rather than destroy.

- Global Transformation is happening, but what is it transforming into?
- Is destruction Global Transformation?
- Whose lives are being elevated and uplifted by rioting, looting and violence?
- How do good people get sucked into such negative activity?
- Will they have to pay a price for their actions?
- Is there a Spiritual price along with a societal price?
- Have you made choices that transformed you negatively?
- Were you aware of this at the time?

- Did you think at the time that what you were doing was positive?
- Is it easy to exchange one mind-pattern for another without ever really going anywhere?
- Is any movement better than stagnation?
- What happens if you stagnate?
- Are some choices irreversible in this lifeline?
- Are you conscious that what you do and think today creates your tomorrow?
- Are these *Name Frequencies* adding another layer of Personal Transformation to your inner work?
- Does Personal Transformation ultimately mean more work?
- Are you okay, knowing that you are stirring up your deeper levels?

Name Frequency #14

Neutralizing Conflict

Mem Bet Hey
Read Hebrew Letters Right to Left
Name Frequency Pronunciation
Meh Veh Heh

Stop the Conflict. I just finished scrolling through social media and a few news sources that I read regularly. Our power and Internet connection went out yesterday so I needed to catch up on the news. More Conflict. Those who are against the system, those who are for the system, those who want to Save The Children. Everyone is fighting with someone about something. Stop the Conflict is a beautiful idea, but there is a lot more conflict amongst people than you realize at first glance.

I have studied many schools of thought, cultures, and religions through the years. There is a lot of infighting about what is appropriate and what is not. I was recently reading on a Jewish site about what constitutes work on the Sabbath. There was a whole page written about whether or not mixing bread dough is work; when it is and when it is not and how to differentiate between the two. I thought to my Self, "This is not the way it is supposed to be!"

I am enjoying my study of the **72 Names of God**. I am exploring, learning, and sharing with you. I take nothing at face value. Just because you read it in a book does not make it true. You are reading someone else's interpretation. You must read through the Oversoul level. You must ask a billion questions. You must continue to explore according to the wishes of your Oversoul and the needs of your Soul. The study takes you into experiential learning so you know by experience, not by parroting back someone else's information. You are trained and programmed to parrot back the work of others. If you have ever done a research paper, you are encouraged to cite reference after reference after reference. I am not opposed to crediting sources because we can spark ideas off of each other. But at some point, you are your own reference point. You know because you experienced; you know because you know. Try putting that on a research paper and see how much credibility you are given!

I told you about my experience with the Gimmel which I found fascinating because it happened to me. I cannot prove to you that it happened, I can only share my experience and you can do with it what you will. In some of my classes, I have taught people to use the Latin Alphabet to understand that each letter is a two-dimensional representation of something that is very multidimensional. The easiest way to understand this is to write the letter, then look at it backward, upside down, from above, below, the side, and keep going. The Letter is infinitely deep with infinitely different colors and even tone/sound. Sometimes, we have even disregarded the Letters and looked only at the background, which fits right in with the **Sefer Yetzirah/Book of Formation** which talks about "engraving" the Letters.

You are so accustomed to the Latin Alphabet that you do not normally see what it is; you look right through the letters even though each letter that comprises your name says something extremely unique about your frequency. I could probably sit with you for a week just teaching you to explore the archetypes/Latin letters of your name and we would still not finish, that is how much information your name contains.

Focusing on the Hebrew AlephBet shakes up your thought process a bit, which takes you back to *Name Frequency #1* Time Travel, going back to shake things up and dig around in your dirt. You need to use a different alphabet to take you to another level so you can get another layer of information. Our work together sparks something inside so you can get your own information, whatever that turns out to be. Whatever you get has meaning on many layers. This is what you explore. You can stay with one Hebrew letter, one *Name Frequency* or you can try them all out as you go along.

The important thing is that you acknowledge what you get even if you do not completely understand it. I have learned through the years that my understanding deepens over time. Every level has a meaning. Each level of meaning that you attain adds to the richness of the previous meaning and level. I always suggest that you read the **Golden Compass** book by Philip Pullman to get an understanding of how you learn to read frequency, search for the correct ones and then put that together in a meaningful way to meet the needs of your specific Soul.

In this book, you are moving through these *Name Frequencies* relatively quickly. You are getting a taste of something different to give you another perspective and set of tools to Self-explore. Do your best not to fight how you feel. Do your best to let the information and observations flow. In my opinion, you have better things to do with your time than to debate whether mixing bread on the Sabbath is work or not. This is the nit-picky details that people lose sleep over.

Stop the conflict within. Stop the conflict without. Relax and let go. Use this *Name Frequency* to neutralize your inner conflict. Letting go allows what needs to come forward in your life to come forward. There may be a time for conflict and if so, then your Oversoul will tell you. But generally speaking, if you give out conflict you get conflict back. That is a Universal Law that you already know. Neutralizing inner conflict allows outer conflict to neutralize, dissolve and dissipate.

- How much inner conflict do you have?
- Can you easily name 10 things that you are in conflict with within Self?
- Is it challenging to step back and let life work itself out?
- If you untie your inner knots do the outer reflections have to change?
- Have you found your knowledge and information deepening over time?
- Is there a difference between knowledge and information?
- Does knowledge come from within?
- Does information come from without?
- Do you need wisdom to deal with both?
- Do you discount what you already know?
- Do you give precedence to what you read in a book vs. what you know from within?
- Are you your own best researcher?
- Is it challenging to state what you know to others?
- Do others often want proof?
- Have you been programmed to give credit to others but not to Self?
- Have you explored the archetypes of the Latin Alphabet as extensively as you are doing the Hebrew AlephBet?

- Does it matter which Alphabet/archetypes you use?
- Will you eventually get to the same place?
- Do you think it is important to delineate every single minute detail of every day such as what is or is not work on the Sabbath?
- Can people take religious laws too far?
- How do you discern what is or is not a Spiritual Law?
- How do you get to the state of knowing what it is without the debate of what is right or wrong?
- Can the state of knowing be spoken in words or is knowing nonphysical and unspoken?
- How can you explain to another if he/she is "on frequency" vs. way off base?
- Are all of these questions a reason for some people to fight with one another?
- What is your definition of fighting?
- Would others agree with your definition?

Name Frequency #15

Clear Vision

Hey Resh Yud
Read Hebrew Letters Right to Left
Name Frequency Pronunciation
Heh Reh Yuh

When you want to see something clearly, it is challenging to become the objective observer so you can see what is vs. what you want to be. Even when you have a nagging feeling that something is not what it presents itself to be, but you want the situation to be what you want it to be, you may move forward anyway. Eventually, that nagging feeling that you tried to suppress a long time ago can stay suppressed no longer.

When I decided to remodel my kitchen, I found a designer that I really liked. I told her what I did and did not want. I told her I did not want a tile floor because I don't like standing on tile while I cook. I told her my budget and she said most kitchens cost twice as much as my budget but she would proceed to see what she could do. We had a few meetings over the summer months. I kept telling her I did not want a tile floor and she kept telling me why I did. I finally gave up telling her, waiting until I saw the final design and budget. I also told her that I wanted to be able to at least seat 6 people but she kept coming up with a seating plan that sat 3 people. I told her that I wanted to see my family while I cooked, but she came up with a plan that had my back to everyone. And so it went.

I started the process, I paid her the money and I had to keep moving forward even though she wasn't listening to me. I finally chose a design so I could get a price out of her, which turned out to be over 2x what I told her my budget was. The price was ridiculous and still not what I wanted. Even if I had the money I could buy a new house for what she wanted. Stewart said to tell her I couldn't afford it but I told him it had nothing to do with the money. I didn't want to do it. I didn't like it and no amount of money in the world would make me want to go along with her plan. I think I was supposed to fall in love with the design so much that I would stretch my budget to fit her proposal. She made the proposal knowing that it was way over my budget. By working with her I learned what I definitely did not want and it made me more flexible in what I was willing to accept.

I needed the process. I wanted to use that designer and I wanted her designs to work. I felt when I gave her my budget that she would create something that was within my budget, or perhaps slightly over. No matter how much I wanted this to work, no matter how many times I told her what I didn't want, there was no connection between my words and her final proposal. I had that nagging feeling the further we got into the planning stages that this wasn't happening the way I wanted, but I wanted to see her final proposal before I made my final decision.

She was so confident that I was going to meet her budget that she told me that she told her staff when they passed by my house for another job, that my house was their next project. I think she needs to use this *Name Frequency*! Whenever you are in the position that you want what you want, use this *Name Frequency* to help you see beyond your wants. Sometimes you need to physically go through the process as I did; sometimes you do not. One step at a time.

- Even when you objectively observe, do you sometimes need to physically go through a process?
- Can you mentally and emotionally go through a process without having to go through the physical process?
- Because you are in physical reality, is it sometimes more important to have the physical experience rather than just mental/emotional experience?
- Could this *Name Frequency* be useful when you have nagging feelings about proceeding with something?
- When it looks like life isn't working out the way you want, is it easy to get discouraged?
- Is it always initially exciting to get what you want?
- When what you want does not work out, do you sometimes feel like you fell off a cliff?
- Are there times when you do not want to see clearly, you simply want what you want when you want it?
- Is it enjoyable when you are forced to look at the facts vs. your perceptions?
- Is it always a positive to see reality vs. what you want?
- How challenging is it to change your attitude when you have pretty lies in your head and then reality dumps on you?
- Is this always an opportunity for growth?
- Do you need the bucket of cold water in your face sometimes to wake you up to the reality of your life?

- Does this make you get honest with your Self about what you will and will not accept?
- Does this force you to reevaluate your boundaries and become more flexible or more rigid, depending upon what is necessary?
- Is being honest not always enjoyable and/or appreciated even if it is necessary?

Name Frequency #16

Releasing Depression

Hey Kuf Mem
Read Hebrew Letters Right to Left
Name Frequency Pronunciation
Heh Kuh Meh

This *Name Frequency* was particularly helpful to me this summer when I realized all my summer plans were getting canceled. Logically, you know that you are always where you are supposed to be. Emotionally, life can be challenging. Today I was reading about one of my favorite restaurants in another town. To eat there, you have to get your temperature taken, wear your mask to the table and keep your mask on until you are served your food. I guess this means you are not allowed to drink your water or any other beverage until your meal arrives. Oh, and you are not allowed to have more than 4 people at your table. It all sounds like a fun time!

Now that summer is coming to a close once again I find my Self thinking about everything I planned to do that did not happen. I'm loving all the photos my cousin posts on social media of her family hikes and explorations in the Cottian Alps, but of course, I wish I was there and it makes me miss her very much. I also think about what I would normally do but most likely won't during all this political unrest. I am doing my best to not get sucked into the drama because negativity adds to a frequency that the world needs to be lifted out of right now. Each person must do his/her part to uplift and elevate even when you least feel like doing this. Take one day at a time and use this *Name Frequency* as a Beacon of Light to pull you out of any depression that tries to pull you down and under.

- Does the change of seasons affect you?
- Do you think of your life in terms of Summer, Fall, Winter, Spring?
- Is it challenging to think beyond the current season when you are depressed?
- Can it be depressing to watch those you love and care about fall for the plannedemic?
- Or moving farther toward the left not realizing that they are headed toward a cliff?
- Does depression help anyone?
- Does your depression add to exactly what the world does not need right now?
- Are you forcing your Self to have an uplifting and elevating attitude?
- Can you use this *Name Frequency* as a Beacon of Light to pull you out of depression?
- Is depression part of programming activations and triggers?

Name Frequency #17

Animal Mind Control

Lamed Aleph Vav
Read Hebrew Letters Right to Left
Name Frequency Pronunciation
Lah Ah Wah

This *Name Frequency* helps you free your Self from the control of your Animal Mind. It is the Animal Mind of the physical body that tells you that everything is finite, limited and you need to get yours first before there is nothing left. The Animal Mind obeys human-made time restraints and succumbs to specific and genetic programming. Animal Mind makes you feel trapped with no way out like you have to fight if you cannot flight. Use this *Name Frequency* to help you gain control of your Animal Mind so you control it and it does not control you. Once it is under your control you can align it with the nonphysical so it can elevate right along with you.

- When you feel stressed or depressed, is it easier to go back to what you know than to keep moving forward into something new?
- Sometimes, do you get tired and feel like giving up?
- How challenging is it when you know you cannot go backward, you do not have the strength to go forward, yet you know that stagnation/doing nothing definitely is not the answer?
- Do you sometimes have control over the Animal Mind and sometimes not?
- Do you sometimes give in to the Animal Mind because part of you just doesn't care?
- If so, what do you allow the Animal Mind to do that you wouldn't if your Spiritual Mind was in control?
- Do you eat or drink excessively?
- Do you allow programming to be triggered and activate?
- Do you give in to negative emotions?
- Do you get upset with your Self when this happens?
- Or do you forgive your Self knowing that this happens to many people and you are not alone?

Name Frequency #18

Fertility

Khaf Lamed Yud
Read Hebrew Letters Right to Left
Name Frequency Pronunciation
Khah Lah Yuh

Many people associate fertility with having children. Yes, if you want children this is an excellent *Name Frequency* to focus on, especially if both partners use this *Name Frequency*. In addition, you have the Pale Orange Archetype of Fertility that you can place in the Pale Orange Chakra Band for the female. The male can place the Fertility Archetype in the Pale Red color in the Pale Red Chakra Band. Children always represent new ideas.

Similarly, new ideas are like children that need to be birthed, With this in mind, you can also place this *Name Frequency* in the appropriate Chakra Bands depending upon your gender to see what comes into your conscious mind. You can combine both the Hyperspace

Archetype and the *Name Frequency* in the appropriate Chakra Bands. You can work with various combinations to see where and what is most effective for you.

Most people have visions of something positive in conjunction with the word fertility. You must also keep in mind that you can also be fertile with negative ideas and programming. Be mindful of your thoughts and always, always ask your Oversoul and God-Mind to bring you what is most correct and beneficial for you.

You can use these tools to push for what the Animal Mind wants or preferably to align with Source so you receive what your Spiritual Mind needs for Soul Growth. As you already know, this may not be pleasant, but Growth is not always pleasant. Focus on being proactive in all that you do, rather than reactive. As long as you strive for moral correctness, you will receive what you need from the nonphysical even at times it does not feel like it. One step at a time, with your Oversoul and God-Mind leading the way.

- Does the word fertility automatically bring a positive connotation to your mind?
- Do you have to remember that positive always has an opposite side of the coin?
- Are you mindful to not allow your negative ideas and programming to be fertile?
- When you have new ideas, are you disappointed when they do not come to fruition?
- Do you always know that *Rejection is God's protection*?
- Is this easy to say with the logical part of your brain, but emotionally challenging to accept?
- Do new ideas need to be planted at a specific time and location to be successful?

- Are new ideas sometimes blocked from germinating because they need more strengthening before they can be successful?
- Are new ideas sometimes blocked from growing because there is something better waiting that you cannot yet see?
- Have you combined the *Name Frequencies* with the Hyperspace Archetypes that you know?

Name Frequency #19

Conscious Source Connection

Lamed Vav Vav
Read Hebrew Letters Right to Left
Name Frequency Pronunciation
Lah Wah Wah

You are always connected to your Oversoul and God-Mind, even when it may not feel like it. Often, you do not want to hear the answers that are being sent your way, so you create internal blocks as a form of Self-protection. Then, you think you are not getting an answer which means you can blame your Oversoul and God-Mind vs. putting the blame where it belongs, which is upon Self.

Some people say that you cannot lie to your Self, but I have found out that you can. Believing in something because you want to believe in it is a form of lying. You want to believe what you want to believe is correct, so you do everything that you can to justify what you want to believe. Some people go to extremes. When you want doors to open but they don't, then doors closing are your answers. Instead of accepting this as your answer, you say that God doesn't hear you nor are your prayers being answered. Doors closing can be the answer to your prayers.

Denial of the reality of life is something that I see continually with people. I see people moaning and crying when they do not get what they want. It is challenging for people to give thanks for receiving what they need when what they need is not what they want. Sometimes, I am right there with them having my emotional hissy fit even when logically I understand Spiritual Law. This doesn't always mean I like it. I allow my Self to have my hissy fit moment, then do my best to get over it. Sometimes this is easier said than done, even for me with all I know.

There are so many *Name Frequencies* already discussed that you can use to help pull your Self out of a negative mood. No one puts you in a negative mood but you, usually because you do not get what you want, how you want when you want, if at all. Rather than say your prayers are not being heard, be honest about what is happening and why. Know that you are heard, you are being protected in spite of your Self and you have exactly what you need. You can ask for an explanation from your Oversoul and God-Mind. You may or may not be given an explanation. Sometimes the answer is no answer. Programming always tells you that you are not heard; programming always tries to strengthen your own internal illusion that you are separate from Source. You can succumb to the programming and stay in Self-pity, or you can move through the programming into the reality that forces you to become Self-responsible and act like a mature adult.

Maturation is only for the strong. The more you assume Self-responsibility the more you know that your prayers are heard, you have answers, you accept even what you do not like, and the blocks that you create to keep conscious communication fall away. This *Name*

Frequency helps dissolve these blocks so you come from a place of inner knowing that you are connected, heard, cared for, and protected in all ways.

- How often do you feel that your prayers go unheard?
- Is it easy to say that you are not being heard; much more challenging to say that you are not hearing the answer?
- How easy is it to create inner blocks that your inner communication process?
- Is there a natural inclination to not hear what you do not want to hear?
- Are inner blocks that you create a personal safety valve?
- Can the truth upset people to the point where they become mentally, emotionally and/or physically ill?
- Is part of programming's function to make you feel separated from Source?
- Can you ever be separate from Source?
- Have you studied the Oversoul Matrix in the **Hyperspace Plus** book?
- Is it challenging to accept no answer as an answer?
- Is it challenging when doors close one after the other?
- When doors close, does your focus narrow?
- Do closing doors force you to stay on a specific path, whether you like it or not?
- Are hissy fits childish or part of the process?
- Are there times in your life when you realized that you were lying to your Self?
- When you are truly stressed and upset, how easy is it to feel that you are not being heard?

- How easy is it to create blocks that prevent communication from your Oversoul and God-Mind from reaching your conscious mind?
- Sometimes, are you afraid of what you might hear?'
- If you have been through trauma, have you felt like Source abandoned you?
- Is it possible that conscious answers from Source might further traumatize you?
- What other reasons do you create blocks from Self to Source?
- Is it easier to say that Source doesn't hear you than admit you don't allow Self to hear Source?

Name Frequency #20

Releasing Addictions

Fey Hey Lamed
Read Hebrew Letters Right to Left
Name Frequency Pronunciation
Feh Heh Lah

In our ***Alternative Medical Apocrypha*** book, there is an extensive chapter titled *Addictions*. Be sure to review this chapter to broaden your knowledge of addictions because addictions are much more than most people realize. Most people are addicted to something that they usually turn to when the Animal Mind is stressed. Addictions usually have to do with Animal Mind instant gratification of some kind. When you feel overwhelmed, you want comfort, and the sooner the better. When I feel stressed and overwhelmed I tend to start picking at food throughout the day. Sometimes I don't even realize I'm upset until I realize that I'm picking at food because nothing tastes good. Physical food does not taste good because the mental/emotional food

I'm dealing with does not taste good. I have to stop and think about what is really bothering me.

You can be addicted to things like feeling guilty, Self-punishment, and even anger. You can be addicted to a person who emotionally and mentally is not healthy for you. You can be addicted to your programming so that you constantly fall back into the triggers that keep you looping. Anytime anything has control over you, you have an issue. If a chocolate candy bar can control you then think how easily a nefarious person could control you.

You can be addicted to things that others might consider positive, but in excess is not. For example, you might diligently exercise to the point where you actually destroy your body. You might have such a strict diet that your body is starved for nutrients and nutrition causing ill health and disease. You might be a loving kind person who is so addicted to giving to others that you do not take care of your Self. The list goes on and on. Addictions can change. At one point in my life, I was addicted to sugar. I stopped eating sugar but I replaced it with overconsumption of fruit. I was still a sugar addict but I didn't realize it at the time. There are so many things that you can be addicted to without even realizing it. Addictions often feel normal because it becomes a part of your life. Use this *Name Frequency* to help identify your addictions and release them to your Oversoul and God-Mind for good.

- What do you do in times of stress that give you instant gratification/relief?
- Has what you turned to in times of stress changed?
- Do you sometimes not even realize that you are back in old habits until something internal kicks in that finally wakes you up to what you are doing?
- Have you had addictions that others might consider positive, but were not?

- Do you know what triggers triggered your reaction?
- Do you know where/when/how your addictions began?
- Are there people you need to forgive and release so you can release your addictions?
- Have you been so addicted to something that it felt normal?
- What negative addictions have you had/do you have?
- When you are upset, stressed and/or overwhelmed, do you immediately realize what is going on?
- Or, do you have specific behaviors that seem to automatically kick in?
- Do you sometimes realize after-the-fact that you are/were engaging in addictive behavior?
- Have you read the chapter in **Alternative Medical Apocrypha** titled *Addictions*?
- If so, what did you discover about your Self?
- Do you need to do forgiveness and release work on your Self because of your behavior?
- Are there people to whom you owe apologies, either in person or on the Oversoul level, as a result of your addictive behavior?
- Are you addicted to your programming?
- Can you use this *Name Frequency* in conjunction with your other Hyperspace/Oversoul work to release your addictions?

Name Frequency #21

Root Causes

Nun Lamed Khaf
Read Hebrew Letters Right to Left
Name Frequency Pronunciation
Nuh Lah Khah

Anyone who has done any kind of work in the soil knows that what you see on top of the soil can be highly deceiving. For example, a dandelion plant may not look that big, but if you try to dig it up you will find that the roots are extremely deep and quite resistant to removal. I have also dealt with plants that only show growth every few feet, yet under the soil, they are all connected. Some plants are extremely tall yet have shallow root systems that easily come out of the ground. If you cut off branches on a tree, but do not get the trunk, the branches are going to grow back. If you do not get the roots under the ground, the roots may start sending up new seedlings, or the roots may stay buried in the soil, not allowing the ground to be easily cultivated. So too with your mind-pattern. This is why sometimes you think that you are done with an issue only to have it pop up somewhere else quite unexpectedly. Getting to the root of any physical, emotional, mental and/or spiritual issue can be quite challenging.

You may want the ills of society to go away but they cannot go away until the mind-patterns of the people release them. The more you do your own internal work, the more you set the frequency for others to do the same. Sometimes on social media, I see people who want to pray for the eradication of cancer or other diseases. Prayer is always a plus, but you cannot take away the lessons of another. Perhaps if cancer did not exist something worse would creep up to take its place. Until the people are willing to let it go, cancer is here to stay. People often pray with the best of intentions, but without some of society's tragedies, people are still too reactive vs. proactive. As much as you want the world to be a better place according to your standards and wishes, you have to understand the bigger picture. The best way to learn about the world is to learn about you. Use this *Name Frequency* to bring forth Root Causes of your issues that you may not even realize are interconnected. Each person must start with his/her issues so the world can reflect this back.

- Is this Earth an excellent place to learn?
- Are the lessons here challenging?
- If every person does his/her work and the Earth changes into something different, what happens to the Souls who need this planet for their classroom?
- If you bring forth the root causes of your own issues and you release them, will your mind-patterns then attract your Soul to a different plane or planet?
- Is it possible that humanity goes through cycles with the same group incarnating here repeatedly until the group lessons are learned?

- And then the group graduates as a whole and goes on to another plane/planet?
- And then a new incoming group of Souls arrives that repeat the process?
- Have you worked with the soil and been amazed at the extensive root systems of some plants?
- Have you worked with plants that looked huge and sturdy, only to discover that their root systems were not so big at all?
- Have you found mind-patterns that looked overwhelming and then you were surprised at how easily you were able to uproot them?
- Have you found mind-patterns that just keep popping up no matter how many places and times you remove them?
- Have you found mind-patterns that were interconnected, but so well hidden that it took a herculean effort to figure them out?
- Can you use this *Name Frequency* for others and humanity as a whole?
- How important is it to be proactive vs. reactive?
- Do you need the reactive lessons first to turn you proactive?
- Can you be proactive-out-of-balance?

Name Frequency #22

Filtering Negativity

Yud Yud Yud
Read Hebrew Letters Right to Left
Name Frequency Pronunciation
Yuh Yuh Yuh

This *Name Frequency* is a tricky one. I have read various explanations and most indicate that you can stop the *wrong* people from coming into your life. My issue with this is that what may outwardly appear *wrong* may be exactly *right* for the lesson the Soul needs to grow. So, yes, you can use this to stop people from coming into your life. But if you do not take your medicine now, the medicine may be stronger and even far less palatable later. Use this *Name Frequency* to filter negative energy to keep Self as proactive as possible. This means to ask that you get your lessons in the least uncomfortable, most gentle way possible. So instead of a train wreck to which you have to immediately react, proactively search out your inner negativity that would attract such incidences. When your mind-pattern is wide open without any filtration your energy basically has a sign on it that says "come on in".

Using this *Name Frequency* helps to filter out the extraneous lessons while allowing those you absolutely need to come to you. You may even be able to mitigate parts of your lesson as long as you remain proactive. However, your Soul has specific needs and goals that your conscious personality may try to stop. As uncomfortable as you might get, it can always be worse. Through it all, search your mind-pattern to see why you are attracting the negative so you can pull it out, release it, and mitigate the lesson as much as possible while extracting the most Soul Growth. This takes practice, time and talent. This *Name Frequency* can be your ally as long as you work with it and not against it. You might even want to try adding the color Violet to your energy field while focusing on this *Name Frequency* to see what might come up for you.

- Do you always need to consciously get something while working with these *Name Frequencies*?
- As you experiment with them, do you ask your Oversoul and God-Mind to continue to direct what does or does not happen?
- If you use the *Name Frequencies* and various thoughts or images come to mind, do you work with what you get?
- Do you chastise Self when working with these *Name Frequencies*?
- Does chastising Self block information from coming forward?
- Is Self-chastisement a form of protecting Self from receiving information for which you do not feel ready?
- Does new information always mean change/growth?
- Can this be frightening because you may want one answer but you need something else?

- Logically, are you willing to take your medicine now but emotionally you are challenged to do this?
- Do you keep in mind that no matter how bad something seems, it can always be worse?
- When life appears to take a turn for the worse, do you keep in mind that life is taking a turn for what you may not consciously want, but this doesn't make it "worse"?
- When one path in life ends that you enjoyed, how challenged are you to be proactive rather than reactive?
- Would you like to be able to keep all the "wrong" people out of your life?
- Now that you know what you know, how challenged would you be to try to decide who are the "wrong" people and who are the "right" people?
- What happens when you use Violet with this *Name Frequency*?

Name Frequency #23

מלה

Dark to Light

Mem Lamed Hey
Read Hebrew Letters Right to Left
Name Frequency Pronunciation
Meh Lah Heh

When you study what others have written about each *Name Frequency*, you can meditate on the specific frequency and ask what the *Name Frequency* really means. I was reading one book written many years ago in which the author states that for every breath of information he shares, there is one mile of information that he does not share. This reminds me of the Oral ***Torah*** and the Written ***Torah***. When you speak to a person you can say much more than you can when you are writing something down.

When I wrote ***Decoding Your Life*** I was 25 years old. It is Universal Law that came to me every night after my meditation. Sometimes I was woken up in the night with the information in my head that

I wrote down so I could work on it upon arising. When I finished **Decoding Your Life**, I thought my work was done. All people had to do was read the book and they could fix their lives. But I found out it didn't work that way. People still wanted to talk to me, ask questions and they still needed help and guidance. I was quite surprised that they could not use the book without a person to help them along. Now, with my years of experience, I understand why. I also know that if I were to write it today it would be different. I wrote it when I wrote it the way it was supposed to be written. It still holds true to this day and is a marvelous tool for those willing to use it. When I taught the webinar classes, it took us 3 years to get through the book! I'm sure you would not take that much time to read it on your own even if you refer to it every now and then. The webinars contain an immense amount of information that you will not find in the book.

Now, extrapolate the above paragraph to the **Torah**. This means the task of studying the **Torah** could take up many lifetimes. In fact, in one book I recently read the author states that he spent 9 months translating the **Torah** and writing the book. I cannot imagine translating something of that magnitude in only 9 months. If he would have said 9 years, I would have easily believed him. This is why it is important that whatever you choose to read or study, that you continually ask your Oversoul and God-Mind to explain it to you in the way you, personally, need the information. Truth is ever present; it is your mind-pattern that determines what comes to you. I use the written word as a guide, but I always take everything up to my Oversoul and God-Mind for clarification. Just because it is written in a book does not make it true. The more you work with frequency, the more you get your own information.

The reason I am telling you all of this is because I was reading another ancient book about **Kabbalah** and one of the things it said is that *Light Shines in Darkness*. This is the motto of the Waldensian people, who have Hebrew genetics. This was particularly interesting to me. So this is what I am labeling this *Name Frequency*. All the work that you are doing makes a greater impact on humanity than you realize. Think of all the people around the globe concentrating on this *Name Frequency*. Candle flames in the dark, encompassing the world. Think of all of us gathered in one place. There is strength when we are physically together, but there is strength when we spread out with our lit candles united in the inner worlds. Physical and nonphysical worlds are impacted tremendously by your inner level work.

- Do you sometimes feel like the lone candle flame in the darkness?
- Is it challenging to realize that doing your mental work makes a difference?
- Do those who need darkness gravitate to darkness?
- Do you think this is why the majority of the violence is concentrated on the West Coast?
- Is it possible that this is a ploy to lure the dark energies there?
- Could the looting and destruction be the sounding call to those living there to get out of these areas?
- Is it better to have the darkness gravitate to a few areas rather than be spread over the Earth?
- If the darkness concentrates on specific areas, does your Light have more impact?
- Are we in a Spiritual War?
- Is this End Times?
- Is your time better spent in prayer and meditation than marching in the streets?
- Is there a difference between Oral instruction and written instruction?

- Do you need to read every book from cover to cover or can you use the book as a guideline for your personal prayers and meditations?
- Does your *Light Shine in Darkness*?
- Does this feel like an overwhelming responsibility sometimes?

Name Frequency #24

Releasing Jealousy

Chet Hey Vav
Read Hebrew Letters Right to Left
Name Frequency Pronunciation
Cheh Heh Wah

Jealousy is a huge issue for most people because it is a function of low Self-worth. When you do not have inner knowing that you are okay as is, then you want what other people have, whether it is their physical looks, mental abilities or opportunities. It is much easier to wish good things for people when they are at a distance. When people are up close and personal, this is when people get jealous. The challenge in this world is that there are such disparities in all things that it is challenging to understand why.

Jealous people can become angry people because they think they will never have what you have. This makes them resentful and angry which covers up fear which covers up the feelings of never having, getting or being what you have and are. For the same reason, jealous people can become extremely depressed because they feel life is passing them by. On one hand, they may be happy for you but sad for themselves.

Like all frequencies, jealousy is a spectrum. This means as you work your way through this frequency, you may find jealousy popping up at odd times. Most people are more jealous of their next door neighbor than they are of people who make millions and billions of dollars every year. This is because they can relate to the next door neighbor but they cannot relate to the millionaires and billionaires. Jealousy causes many clashes, but as you know, you have to work on Self first. Jealousy is a Lime Green color. Lime green was the favorite color of one of my aunts. She was a wonderful person with lots of personal issues due to low Self-worth. She always wished everyone else well, but she felt undeserving of the positive things of life. She eventually created some kind of mass in her pancreas which the doctors interestingly described as "the shape of a lime". They did not know what it was and the location made it inoperable.

Like so many negative frequencies, jealousy can be extremely toxic. However, jealousy can be a motivator, too. If someone else has it and you want it, jealousy can motivate you to try a little harder so you can have what others have. I once had to stand on the beach while my friends all snorkeled in Hawaii because I was afraid of putting my face in the water. I was so jealous that I forced my Self to face my fear so I could join them. It wasn't easy but jealousy was my motivator and I did it. Every negative emotion has a positive side. Once you understand both sides of the coin you are well-positioned to release old mind-patterns and build new ones in their place. Stand in the *Eternal Now* as you use this *Name Frequency* to release your jealousy and whatever negative mind-pattern is underneath it.

- Do you recognize when you are jealous?

- Can you logically determine why you are jealous?
- Can you remember the first time you ever felt jealousy?
- Have you used jealousy as a motivator to change for the positive?
- Do you like or dislike the color Lime Green?
- As you increase Self-worth have you found Self less jealous of others?
- Do you sometimes feel happy for others but sad for Self when others have what you want?
- Do you do your best to remember that you have what you need vs. what you want?
- Do you feel resentment when you do not get what you want?
- What other negative emotions are buried underneath your jealousies?
- Does this *Name Frequency* help to bring up long-forgotten memories?
- As jealousy leaves, what can you use to fill in the empty space it leaves?
- Do you use specific affirmations to help with your inner healing as well as to increase your Self-worth?
- Does labeling your specific jealousies make it easier to face them?
- Is jealousy an emotion that is easy to ignore?

Name Frequency #25

Giving & Receiving Truth

Nun Tav Hey
Read Hebrew Letters Right to Left
Name Frequency Pronunciation
Nuh Tah Heh

Be careful what you ask for because you just might get it when you use this *Name Frequency*. As much as you say you want to hear the Truth, sometimes the Truth is something other than what you are prepared to hear. This means that the Truth Frequency can shock your energy field so much that you can become physically ill. This, then, is your opportunity to clear out the old so the new can come forward. Or, this can be your opportunity to pass on, and the new still comes to you, but in the nonphysical. Even positive Truth can shock your system to the point of physical illness. If you have such low Self-worth that your energy field is filled with low level frequencies, positive Truth is so contrary to what you know that a giant shakeup can occur to such an extent that you become physically ill as the negative frequencies have the opportunities to leave.

Too much of a good thing can make you ill. Carrots, for example, are a wonderful vegetable. But, they are high in Vitamin A which is not water soluble and can build up in your system to a toxic level. This is why Truth is a huge wake-up call. Truth literally shakes you to the core of your Being. When I was the director of an art gallery and thought I was doing a wonderful job. One day a board member phoned to tell me that I was pushy, harsh and difficult to get along with. I broke down crying hysterically and locked my Self in the storage closet because I was so besides my Self in disbelief. I was literally "beside my Self" meaning this news jerked me partially out of my physical body. I guess she did not expect her Truth to impact me, since she saw me as such a hard person. When she realized how upset I was she came rushing down to the gallery to try to get me to come out of the storage closet. I refused!

Hearing the Truth is challenging for many people on many levels. Be mindful when you tell someone else the Truth because you can literally push someone over the edge, even activating Suicide Programming. Even when people ask for the Truth this does not mean that he/she is prepared for the answer. This is why you must always do your best to go to the Oversoul level to ask to know Truth in the way that is most correct and beneficial. You must also ask for guidance in speaking the Truth in a way that is most correct and beneficial. Truth is a valiant ideal, but the reality is that Truth is a full spectrum frequency that must be handled with care.

When you use this *Name Frequency* you can use the Pale Orange Frequency for Truth in addition to the Maroon Frequency for the Courage to hear or speak the Truth, depending upon your circumstances. If you are asking your Oversoul and God-Mind to show you Truth with explanation, you still must proceed with caution.

- Have you ever been devastated when Truth was spoken to you?
- Have you ever unwittingly devastated someone when you spoke the Truth to them?
- Are you challenged to speak the Truth?
- Are you challenged to receive the Truth even from your Oversoul and God-Mind?
- Do you know that the phrase "beside my Self" literally means that you are partially thrown out of your body?
- Have you felt this way from hearing the Truth?
- Or observed others who definitely reacted this way to knowing Truth?
- Has too much of a good thing ever made you ill?
- Are you always mindful to be careful about what you ask for?
- Have you gotten what you asked for and then wished that you hadn't?
- Do you feel it is important to proceed with caution when giving and receiving Truth?

Name Frequency #26

Order from Unrecognized Patterns

Hey Aleph Aleph
Read Hebrew Letters Right to Left
Name Frequency Pronunciation
Heh Ah Ah

Most people call unrecognized patterns chaos. I have always said that chaos is order not yet understood. Use this *Name Frequency* to help you find that hidden order in any area of your life. Keeping your life in chaos is a fabulous distraction from actually accomplishing what you came here to accomplish.

It is very easy to see that the world is in a state of chaos. Yet, when you move through the outward appearance you can understand why. Everything that is happening can be explained via mind-pattern. The fires on the West Coast of the US have to do with burning inner emotions that have not been dealt with so now the nonphysical is manifesting in the physical. Rioting and looting are the inner angers that have not been dealt with. Pedophilia has to do with all the adults who were abused as children and never dealt with their leftover emotions. Coronavirus has to do with your internal viruses that have been left to grow and spread. None of this could be projected in the outer world if it did not live somewhere within the consciousness of humanity. And whoever is directing this chaos recognizes these patterns, thus is exacerbating them.

These are bitter pills to swallow, but it is forcing people to Self-empower one way or the other. The dark forces already feel empowered, because too many people have turned a blind eye to their own inner negative emotions. Now, people are being forced to choose sides. People are being forced to leave their homes, jobs and businesses. Families and friends are being divided by politics. What seems horrible in the short term may be what saves these people in the long term. Reactive learning is the most challenging. All the recognized order in your life is being purposefully and systemically destroyed.

This *Name Frequency* will help put you in a proactive position. This does not mean easy, but it does mean easier. Keep up your protection work as well, because during chaos is when it is easiest to let your guard down. You do not know where to look or where to turn. You may feel way up one day and way down the next. Maintaining a balance of some kind is imperative. The chaos on the planet has gone on for months with no end in sight. You may have a tendency to allow your home environment to become chaotic as a result. Do your best to sort through the physical chaos to help sort the nonphysical chaos. You may not have control over the outer world per se, but you do have control over your inner world which ultimately controls your personal outer world. In this case, one hand definitely feeds the other. As you unravel your own internal previously unrecognized order, it becomes increasingly easy to recognize order within chaos. One step at a time.

- How easy is it to let your home, or places within your home, turn into chaos?
- How much time does it take to straighten it out?
- Why is it challenging to find the time to straighten out home chaos?
- When you look at chaos for so long, do you quit seeing it as abnormal?
- Do you use chaos as a distraction?
- How do you feel when your physical chaos is in order?
- Is it especially important to get all areas of Self in order to help the outer world settle down?
- Or, is it possible that only your corner of the outer world will settle down but others with different mind-patterns still need to go through the chaos?
- Can you have compassion for those people who are in a reactive position?
- Does everyone need reactive learning?
- Are you doing your best to stay proactive?
- Is it challenging to have so many days, weeks, and months of chaos?
- Has there always been underlying chaos that people have been denying?
- Is it better sometimes to have a giant upheaval that no one can ignore forcing an immediate response vs. a slower pace of change?
- Do most people need a metaphorical hit over the head to change directions?
- Do you think that there is some kind of higher hand directing all outer chaos in an order this person/Being/Force recognizes?
- Ultimately is All directed by the One Same Source?

Name Frequency #27

Tithing

Yud Resh Tav
Read Hebrew Letters Right to Left
Name Frequency Pronunciation
Yuh Reh Tah

Tithing is actually based on the *10 Sefirot*, which are explained in more detail in Stewart's **Template of God-Mind** book. You have 10 fingers and 10 toes for a reason. This is also the reason that tithing is always set at 10%. Some people give more; some give less but the standard tithe is always 10%. Tithing sets the frequency for whatever you have to flow easily to you, through you, and back to you again. Some people tithe only to get something back. Because this is a Spiritual Law you will get something back. But this keeps you tied to the Animal Mind. When you are greedy you set Self up for unpleasant falls. Greed is usually the result of low Self-Value and trying to fill nonphysical emotional holes with something physical. I have watched many, many people operate this way. These people limit their income stream by doing so. Greed opens the doorway for more negative forces to enter. People lie, cheat, even kill to obtain the money, possessions, and life insurance policies of others.

Tithing opens doors. Even the global elite tithe, setting up various charitable organizations and events. Whether you believe in the cause is inconsequential. They follow Spiritual Law by tithing and this definitely increases their financial income streams. Others tithe because they like to help with receiving something back as a secondary cause for giving. This is what elevates you to the Spiritual Mind.

I tithe by giving to my children and grandchildren. I tip as appropriate. I send many, many books into the prison system without charge, praying that this information will help the incarcerated correct whatever needs correction. I tithe by giving my no longer necessary possessions to those in need. There are many people who I help from time to time. Even **Expansions** is my tithe. There is no way that I can ever be monetarily compensated for all that I do and the hours I spend. Use this *Name Frequency* to help give for the correct reasons, in the correct way, to the correct causes/people, in the correct timing.

- Do you consciously tithe?
- Do you hoard what you have or are you generous in what you give?
- Would you be generous in a disaster?
- Do you see others stepping up to help each other in disasters?
- Are these opportunities to tithe?
- Is giving money the only way to tithe?
- Is tithing a Spiritual Law that anyone can follow and still get results?
- Do you have to be a good person to follow Spiritual Law?
- Can a bad person follow Spiritual Law and still have positive results?

- What is the difference between a good person and a bad person following Spiritual Law?
- Have you ever hoarded only to lose what you hoarded?
- Why do people hoard?
- In what ways do you tithe?

Name Frequency #28

Soul Mates

Shin Aleph Hey
Read Hebrew Letters Right to Left
Name Frequency Pronunciation
Shih Ah Heh

Soul Mate. Technically everyone in Existence is your Soul Mate because we all come from One Source. If you think of a tree, we all originate from the trunk. But as you follow the trunk up into the branches, you can see that the branches split off in many different directions. The closer the branch on the tree, the more alike they are. This is why you can feel close to other people, whether it is a chance meeting on the street, a neighbor, colleague, or friend. These people might be very close to you on this giant tree that comprises humanity. However, just because they are close does not always make them compatible. They have different experiences that bring them to this point in their lives than you do. You can resonate immediately with someone but then not like their politics or personal morality.

This was my issue with so many people. I always held my Self to such high standards I eventually realized that no one could really meet my standards. Then I realized that my own standards were so impossibly high that I really was not meeting my own standards either. I learned that everyone is a unique package. You have to decide what you will and will not accept. Sometimes you accept much more than you realize for a variety of reasons. You need Compassion for Self to have Compassion for others. It is challenging to have Compassion for the parts of Self or others that you do not like. This is why I tell you that it is important to understand people so you can explain their actions. Explaining their actions does not excuse the actions. But it gives you a starting place so that you can logically understand what happened even if emotionally you are still processing everything.

Sometimes a branch on a tree is split into one or more parts. When this happens, the result is a multiple birth such as twins, triplets or even more. These multiples are known as *identical* even though no two people can be identical. Fraternal multiple births mean that each Soul is from a different branch of the tree, but they are coming in together at the same time for the lessons each needs If you are looking for your *other half* this means you both come from the same branch. You may or may not be the opposite sex in this lifeline. You may not both be in your physical body at the same time in this lifeline. Regardless, you each will have different Soul experiences so when you come together you may be more opposite than alike, but opposite in such a way that the totality of your experiences creates the whole branch. No one ever completes you, just like one cell has a unique identity. But together, like cells create bigger and better identities. One heart cell is not as powerful as all the cells of the heart put together. Yet, each cell is important with an intelligence of its own. In the same way, when a branch is split each piece has unique characteristics but when all the pieces come together it is definitely stronger and more cohesive.

Underlying all of this is Color, Tone and Archetype. The closer the branches are on the tree, the more matching Color, Tone and Archetype. Again, people often think *positive* but the reality is also *negative*. This is why you feel so drawn to someone but then eventually the negative side of that person comes out. This is also why you have to proactively deal with your own negative side so you can explain and understand it. The more you know your Self, the more you know others.

Asking for one or more Soul Mates is fraught with as many pitfalls as every other request. This can be a positive, negative or both. Always be mindful when you ask for something, that your prayers include getting what is most correct and beneficial for you at all times.

- Is it challenging to think that Soul Mates can be negatives?
- Is the idea of a positive Soul Mate an easy fallacy to fall into?
- Can this be a distraction that causes you to reject others when they display negative qualities?
- Is it challenging to remember that ultimately every person in Existence is a Soul Mate of all others?
- Have you ever met someone who you felt was a Soul Mate based upon the typical definition?
- Does Soul Mate always mean romantic love?
- Is it possible to mistake love for a person as romantic love?
- What is the difference between love and romantic love?
- Do you need personal space no matter how close you are to someone?
- When you come to bumps in the road with Soul Mates, do you dump them or move through the issues?
- How can you tell how close on the tree your branch is to the branch of someone else?

- Can someone seem highly familiar, you like them but for some reason, you are in different places in your life stream so you do not stay in touch?
- Do you feel let down when people you feel in sync with leave your life?
- Can you truly be in sync if they leave?
- Does this mean no matching Color, Tone or Archetypes?
- Or can it mean a very deep level of matching Color, Tone or Archetype rather than the matching archetypes that are needed for daily activities?
- How about matching archetypes that are needed for daily activities but no matching Color, Tone or Archetype on the deeper levels?
- How is all of this possible if you are connected to the same tree?
- Do you like the idea that someone completes you?
- Is this based on the idea that ultimately everyone in existence completes/defines what is the God-Mind?
- Does God-Mind have Compassion for you?

Name Frequency #29

Releasing Hatred

Resh Yud Yud
Read Hebrew Letters Right to Left
Name Frequency Pronunciation
Reh Yuh Yuh

Hate is such a challenging emotion to deal with because it seems that you should hate negative emotions, actions and people. You know that whatever you give out comes back to you. This means giving hate out means getting hate back. I have really had to work with this emotion because throughout my life there have been so many people who have done so much evil to me and my family. The interesting thing I realized is that these kinds of people thrive on hate and other negative emotions. So if I give out hate, it only makes them stronger while holding the emotion makes me weaker. What you have to do with these emotions is pass them out through the top of your head, up into your Oversoul. All the hating that you feel and every negative thing that you want to do to the other person, you do to them on the Oversoul level. This removes the Color, Tone and Archetype from you.

Then, you have to do forgiveness work on your Self for allowing these people and incidences into your life as well as forgiveness work on those people. If you do not, you will only attract more. And, the root of it all is someplace inside of you that hates a part of Self. Maybe you hate that you are always late. Maybe you hate the way you look or some part of your body. Maybe you hate that you aren't smarter. Maybe you hate not to be more talented. The list of small hates is enough to add up to a huge, perhaps hidden, hate frequency within.

Even hating the evil in existence is a hate that serves no purpose because ultimately it is a reflection of Self somewhere, some way. When you no longer hate any aspect of Self, then the hate in the world has no matching Color, Tone and Archetype to attract it. And finally, remember that everything in Existence is a part of God-Mind, including evil. So when you hate, you hate a part of God-Mind.

- When you really think about it, what do you hate in the world?
- What do you hate in other people?
- Who do you hate and why?
- What do you hate about your Self?
- Do you hate your Oversoul and God-Mind?
- Can hate exist in this world if there is no hate inside of each person?
- Does it matter if you only hate a little bit?
- Is a little bit of hate enough to draw hateful experiences to you?
- Does hate going out mean hate coming back?

- How challenging is it to not hate anyone who has harmed you or loved ones?
- Does hate hide within the hearts of most humans?
- Is there such a thing as justified hate?

Name Frequency #30

Building Bridges

Aleph Vav Mem
Read Hebrew Letters Right to Left
Name Frequency Pronunciation
Ah Wah Meh

When I was researching this frequency, at least two authors wrote that this *Name Frequency* can be said in English and sounds like the chant of Eastern religions that say OM/AUM. As you know, the Hebrews spread all over the world, with some tribes going to the East. Stewart has written about this in his ***Template of God-Mind*** and ***Revelations*** books. Knowing this, it makes sense that this is a chant/mantra that people would use to build a bridge to God. The *10 Sefirot* are also about building bridges to God.

You can use this *Name Frequency* to build inner bridges to the various parts of Self that need healing of some kind. This could be mental, emotional, and even physical. There may be people in your life who pulled out of your life who you want back in. Ask on the Oversoul level if it is appropriate for a bridge to be built from you to them. Or, there may be people who you released from your life. You can ask your Oversoul if you need to build a bridge here or if it is okay that you have moved on. The more inner bridges you get in order, the more the world has the opportunity to come into order. You can even build inner bridges to help with internal communication, from one part of Self to another.

Be aware that like all things, bridges can be built that are not correct or beneficial. Think of the pedophiles, con artists and thieves. You must be ever vigilant with your protection work as well as be mindful to only do what is correct and beneficial to the best of your ability.

- Do you have bridges to other people that have been broken that you would like repaired?
- Do you have bridges to other people that have been broken but you are not sure if you want them repaired?
- Have you ever been the victim of someone who spent a lot of time building a bridge to you that was for nefarious purposes?
- Is this the same as psychic cords written about in **Decoding Your Life**?
- What parts of your inner Self do you need to build a bridge to and from?
- What if you try to build a bridge and the other person rejects it?
- Is it possible that an inner part of Self rejects a bridge that you try to build?
- Does this *Name Frequency* sound like OM/AUM??
- Why is it important to use the oldest version of Hebrew possible vs. modern Hebrew?

Name Frequency #31

Completion

Lamed Khaf Bet
Read Hebrew Letters Right to Left
Name Frequency Pronunciation
Lah Khah Veh

Completing whatever you start is generally thought of as a positive. Once you start something it seems that you should finish it. I have always struggled with completion. I get almost done and then whatever I'm working on just sits there. I have to force my Self to do the last little bit. Programmed people are often programmed this way so that nothing they do ever comes to fruition, Because of this, they are often unsuccessful, feel worthless, and thus, depressed. Then, the cycle starts over again. For this reason, I usually work on several projects at once. I also generally read several books at once. Working linearly in almost any area of my life is challenging. I use this to my advantage because this aids my understanding of multidimensionality. Usually, I complete many things at the same time because I begin many things at the same time. Often, I think about what I need to complete long before completion takes place. Sometimes, I think about completion before I even begin, that is how well I know my Self. I do not want to start something and then have a mess sitting there waiting for me while I complete it.

Even though my kitchen has been completed for a few months, it is not organized the way I want. I have a couple of pantries that need to be cleaned out, which I started doing, things that still need to be put in their proper places. I have started cleaning my office several times without completing the process. I shop quite a bit online. It is rare that I fill my shopping cart and then pay for it immediately. Usually, I have to think about my purchase for a day or two. Conversely, you may be good at completing the negative things you start. When you work with this *Name Frequency* of Completion, be mindful of your thoughts. Be careful what you ask for, because you may get it.

- Are you good at negative Completion?
- What kinds of negatives have you completed?
- Can this *Name Frequency* reverse negative Completion?
- When you use a recipe to make a cake, does it matter who you are?
- Are these *Name Frequencies* equivalent to a recipe that you follow?
- Could a person with evil intent use this *Name Frequency* to bring something evil to Completion?
- Do you understand the responsibility any person with any knowledge has?
- What kinds of projects have you started that need completion?
- What do uncompleted physical projects represent in your mind-pattern?
- What mental work have you started that needs Completion?

- Do you work linearly through your projects until they are completed?
- Do you work on many projects at one time?
- Do you complete many projects at one time?
- Do you have an issue with completing projects?
- If you complete projects, does it take you a long time once you start something?
- Are you mindful of what you ask for because you may get it?
- When you ask for Completion, does it matter how it is completed?
- Do you want only positive completions in ways that are most correct and beneficial?
- Do you filter your wants, hopes, and desires via the Oversoul level so that you have continual guidance from the highest parts of your Soul possible?

Name Frequency #32

Memory

Vav Shin Resh
Read Hebrew Letters Right to Left
Name Frequency Pronunciation
Wah Shih Reh

Memory is definitely a multi-layered challenge. Some memories never fade and some you cannot retrieve no matter how much you try. Many years ago, when life was not so complicated, I used to work on building my memory as well as my eyesight. One of the exercises I did was looking at something and then closing my eyes while recalling every single little detail. For example, I would look at the top of my dresser and then recall each and every item. Or my desk, shelving, nightstand, inside a drawer or cabinet. This exercise is a bit more challenging than it may sound.

Negative memories seem the easiest to recall. I used to recount many of them as examples in my classes and blogs. Through the years, as I have dealt with them I do not like to speak about them anymore. I realize that I spoke about them as part of my releasing process. In fact, sometimes I have to think really diligently to pull the negative memories up in their entirety. When this happens to you, it means that you have released the memory or you have suppressed it.

Your experiences come into you from your Oversoul via your solar plexus/Animal Mind. It is an energy that you take in and live. Then when the experience is complete you clean up that strand of energy by giving your experiences back to your Oversoul. When that strand of energy is cleaned up, your Oversoul recasts it to you with another experience. This means both positive and negative experiences. This also means that to get more positive experiences you have to give those back to your Oversoul as well. Good can always get better. Some people even forget the positive experiences because they are so overwhelmed with the negative. This happened to me growing up with my Mother. I allowed the negative experiences to overshadow the positive. It took me decades to reconcile my memories and feelings. Some people think you should forget the negative memories and move on with your life. The issue with this is that if you do not reconcile your memories you will get more of the same experiences and they can be much worse. Without understanding, this is what happens to most people.

If you do not release the positive memories you do not have room for more positive experiences. Each physical body plus energy field can only hold "x" number of experiences. If you fill the space with old memories, your space becomes stagnant, the nonphysical grows heavy, settles into the physical body and voila, you have health issues. This is another reason why it is important to do the *Green Psychic Flush* exercise so that your energy lines are always in motion. This exercise breaks up any energy blockages so your mind, body and emotions can more freely flow.

Use this *Name Frequency* to help pull up any memory that still has unlearned lessons, both positive and negative. You can also do the *Green Spiral Staircase* from the **Hyperspace Helper** book in conjunction with this *Name Frequency*. You must learn from your past because that is what today is built upon. Your Hyperspace/Oversoul work improves your memory because as you empty it out, buried memories can rise to the surface, just like plucking one tissue after another out of a tissue box. This *Name Frequency* also helps improve your memory for the same reason.

- Do you think your memory needs improvement?
- Is a bad memory a way of dealing with life by not dealing with life?
- Do people with dementia and Alzheimer's Disease take the easy way out by not dealing with their lives?
- Has Hyperspace/Oversoul work brought up memories that you had long-forgotten?
- Is it important to deal with negative memories?
- Is it easier in the short-term to ignore negative memories?
- Can buried, suppressed negative memories come back to harm you at a future date?
- Do you remember to release your positive memories or do you conveniently forget to do this?
- Do you like to recount your negative memories to others?
- Do you like to recount your positive memories to others?
- Is recounting your memories a way of reliving them?
- Do you know people who continually tell the same stories?
- Do you think people who do this do so for you or for themselves?
- Do you do the *Green Psychic Flush* to keep your energy flowing?
- Do you do the *Green Spiral Staircase* to access buried memories?

- Do your negative memories sometimes overshadow your positive memories?
- Are negative memories the easiest to recall?
- Have you ever done any memory building exercises that proved helpful?
- Why is memory so tricky?

Name Frequency #33

Confronting Darkness

Yud Chet Vav
Read Hebrew Letters Right to Left
Name Frequency Pronunciation
Yuh Cheh Wah

Every person has dark places hidden within. Sometimes it can be quite challenging to look at your own dark places. It is always easier to look at other people and point the finger of blame at them. The challenge, when bad things happen to good people, is to identify what was within those good people to attract such a dark and negative experience. Your responsibility is always to proactively shine light into your own internal darkness. If you do not, sooner or later something will happen to force you to reactively confront these hidden places. Even when you are proactively looking, you can be challenged to dig out your own darkest corners. This is why you attract experiences that force you to reactively acknowledge what was hidden within. Many people do not want to look in their dark places because they do not have the tools to handle what they have successfully secluded from themselves. Even when you have the tools, you can be extremely challenged to really look. Sometimes you know what is there, but you do your best to suppress and deny it so that you do not have to face Self. I know many people like this.

No matter how many tools you have, feeling overwhelmed happens. However, there is a difference between feeling overwhelmed and actually being overwhelmed. Being overwhelmed means that you cannot handle it. Feeling overwhelmed means that you feel like you cannot handle it, but you can and you eventually do. This most likely means that you have to force your Self to change emotional expectations. But once you do, you feel free on all levels. Hiding from Self is both the easiest and most challenging thing that you can do.

Use this *Name Frequency* to help you see into the darkest recesses of Self. Flood your Being with Maroon for Courage so you can do what you need to do. You may have positive aspects about your Self that you have hidden away. For example, before I left my first husband I had hidden away much of my inner strength and Self-worth. I felt powerless without the skills to function in life on a daily basis. I hid much of my light from my Self. It was only after I left and time passed that I realized how bad my situation was and how much inner strength, fortitude and courage was within, waiting to be used.

- Why is hiding from Self easy?
- Why is hiding from Self challenging?
- Have you felt overwhelmed, only to realize that you could handle the situation?
- Have you ever been overwhelmed to the point where you imploded rather than handled the situation?
- When you finally face whatever you find within, do you feel a sense of freedom?

- Do you worry that others will find out about your dark secrets?
- Do you have more tools than most people to deal with the dark areas of your life?
- Even when you are proactively searching for your inner darkness, are there certain areas or topics that you avoid?
- Does darkness always contain negative?
- Can darkness contain your positive attributes?
- Do you have concerns about outshining others and thus not fitting in?
- When you outshine others, does this make you an automatic target?
- Do you continue to proactively strengthen your protection as your light grows brighter?
- Is facing Self challenging?
- Why do people not understand that facing the positive aspects of Self can be as challenging or more than facing the negative aspects?
- Have you questioned why bad things happen to good people or why good things happen to bad people?
- As you shine the light on your inner Self, does this help to explain the darkness hidden in others?

Name Frequency #34

Balancing Ego

Lamed Hey Chet
Read Hebrew Letters Right to Left
Name Frequency Pronunciation
Lah Heh Cheh

As I wrote about in **Decoding Your Life**, the ego is an essential part of who and what you are. However, without Self-Esteem, Self-Worth, and Self-Value, you allow the outer world to tell you who you are. This means that you want others to see and hear you so that they can tell you how wonderful you are. You need this outer validation because you do not have the internal validation. Everyone likes praise and compliments. However, when you do what you do to receive praise and compliments this means your Ego is out of balance. Sometimes people go to extremes to set their lives up so they get positive attention so they can feel good about themselves. I had an acquaintance who used to bring phenomenal appetizers to dinners I hosted. She never told me she was bringing them, she would just arrive with appetizers that were more fantastic than the dinner I prepared. Even I loved her food, but it was an obvious ploy to draw attention away from my dinner and onto her. She always got the kudos she desired, but of course, I had to deal with my own inner resentments.

There are a lot of people like this. Perhaps their actions are even unconscious pleas for attention. This usually starts in childhood when a person does not feel like he/she fits in. The bid for attention continues until the person is totally oblivious that he/she is seeking attention because of low Self-Value. When you have inner Value, any attention you get from the outer world is not the intended goal. You do what you do because it is the correct thing to do. I know people who do things for others because they want a big thank you. People who do the most volunteer work are often these kinds of people. They need confirmation from the outer world that they have Value. They need their empty emotional holes filled up so they seek attention and kudos from the outer world.

People with an inflated opinion of themselves have low Self-Value, even though their words say the opposite. I used to know someone who always talked about his material possessions and money. To others, he always came across as bragging. Those who did not have what he had did not like him for this reason. I think he was proud of his accomplishments and did not know his audience. He was like a little boy who wanted all his friends to tell him he had done well. That was not happening.

Ego is a tricky thing because you need it, but you need it in balance. Finding that balance is different for each person. The most important thing is to realize when you have inner validation that you are doing a good job and when you need outer validation. Sometimes outer validation is necessary, for example, if you are learning a new skill. Maybe you are taking music lessons and you need the instructor to guide you. Yet, ultimately, all knowing of who and what you are must come from within. Use this *Name Frequency* to help you find this balance.

- Do most people like praise and compliments?
- Have you received insincere praise and compliments?
- How does sincere vs. insincere compliments make you feel?
- Do you know when you are looking for praise and compliments?
- Have you observed others who definitely are looking for praise and compliments?
- Do you know people who do anything they can to get attention, even at the expense of others?
- Is it challenging to have compassion for these kinds of people?
- Does a lion have to tell you that he/she is a lion?
- If a person is good at something does this need to be stated?
- Do you need others to tell you that you are okay?
- If so, can you trace this back to a time when others told you in some way that you were not okay?
- Are you working on your Self-Value?
- Can you observe Ego coming into balance?
- Have you heard people say that you should not have any Ego?
- If you do not have any Ego would you be without Value?

Name Frequency #35

Sexual Energy

Khaf Vav Kuf
Read Hebrew Letters Right to Left
Name Frequency Pronunciation
Khah Wah Kuh

Sexual Energy is your most primal creative force in this reality. Sexual energy is stronger than your need to eat or find shelter. Yes, people will give up food to engage in sexual activity. And yes, addiction to pornography and sex addiction is real. Stewart and I wrote about this in **Alternative Medical Apocrypha** in the chapter titled *Addictions*.

Instead of being viewed as sacred energy that needs protection, Sexual Energy is exploited by nefarious global handlers to tie people into their Animal Mind. I wrote about this extensively in my **Heights of Relationships** book. When I was growing up, what you see everywhere today was hidden behind a brown paper wrapper at the supermarket.

Of course, covering it up made everyone more curious about what was behind that wrapper. You cannot not see the sexual exploitation because it is everywhere. Once you have seen it, it is something that you cannot un-see. I especially feel for our youth who must deal with it every day. To maintain personal integrity and morality with this bombardment of sexual energy is an assault on the senses. Without awareness of your Chakra system and protection techniques, the lower Chakras fall wide open. This makes children easy prey for those who would take advantage of them. They think attention to their physical body means someone loves them when nothing is further from the truth.

Pedophilia is about people who felt unloved as children and/or were sexually assaulted as children who act out what was done to them. Please refer to **Heights of Relationships** for more information. The fact that this predilection is exploding globally tells you that something is very wrong with our societies. Our job is to protect our young, the future of humanity. Overloading their sexual senses is not protecting them. In the same way, you must protect and honor your own sexuality. Knowing that it is a sacred path that replicates the Original Act of Creation is reason enough to think deeply about your actions. Be sure you read **True Reality of Sexuality** to further understand this concept. Programming can also activate sexual predilections, but programming still has to be hooked into something within. And, just like an alcoholic, only you can stop doing whatever it is that is not elevating and uplifting.

This *Name Frequency* helps you get your sexual energy in order and in its proper perspective. Your sexual energy does not define you; it is a part of the whole. Use this *Name Frequency*, along with asking your Oversoul, to allow your sexual energy to flow in the way that is most correct, beneficial, uplifting, and elevating for you. In addition, be sure your Chakra Bands are in order and in the correct colors. Use the *Green Psychic Flush* to keep everything flowing, including your sexual/

creative energy. In addition, you can even use the *Brown Merger/Self-Integration Archetype* in the lower Chakra Bands to help hold your energy field together. Be responsible in thoughts, words and actions.

- Are you mindful to keep your Chakra Bands in the correct colors and all flowing in the same direction?
- Do you use the *Green Psychic Flush* to keep your psychic energy flowing freely through your physical body?
- Do you use the *Brown Merger/Self-Integration Archetype* at various places within your energy field depending upon what you need?
- Do you observe people who allow their sexuality to define them?
- Is it challenging to always be responsible for your actions?
- Do you feel for youth who are continually bombarded with sexuality at a time when they are most vulnerable?
- As a society, should we be doing more to protect our youth?
- Do you understand how deep societal mind-control runs?
- Are all addictions about your loss of control?
- Does your loss of control of any aspect of your life open you to nefarious activities?
- How challenging is it to stop addictions of any kind?

Name Frequency #36

Fearlessness

Mem Nun Dalet
Read Hebrew Letters Right to Left
Name Frequency Pronunciation
Meh Nuh Dah

Hopefully, you are already diligently working on removing Fear, as I wrote about in detail in ***Decoding Your Life***. Fear is at a maximum now between the Covid plannedemic and the riots and looting. You can see what fear does to people. In my opinion, it can bring out the worst and it can bring out the best. The worst is when people go deeper into fear. The best is when people confront their fears, making a conscious choice to not let fear control them. The chapter I wrote in ***Decoding Your Life*** on Fear was a result of my own conscious decision to get over my fears. I felt that fear had controlled me most of my life so I did what I knew at the time to face every fear that I possibly could. My final fear was leaving my first marriage. When I was ready, circumstances appeared which forced me to make a choice. Stewart was not going to wait forever for me to make up my mind. It was a now or never situation, especially if I was going to have children because I already was 39 years old. I faced my fears, made the leap of faith, and here we are today.

I know a lot about fear but because of this, I know a lot about courage. I focused on building my courage while deflating my fear energy. Fear has a proper place, but fear out of balance can bring out your most negative attributes. I did not want to live my life in fear, so my only other option was to face it, walk through it and come out on the other side. A healthy dose of fear can make you stop and think before doing anything foolish. Too much fear can also cause you to be paralyzed. Speaking in public used to paralyze me. My mind would go blank, my knees turned to jelly, I couldn't catch my breath and I felt like I was going to pass out. Once you stop breathing, your brain does not have enough oxygen so you are not going to think, much less act or physically move when it's time to run.

Use this *Name Frequency* to help eliminate excess fear as well as establish courage in its place. Always remember that when you remove something you must add something or the old will be right back in again. Maroon is the color of courage, so you can use Maroon in a variety of ways. You can wear Maroon colored clothing, use Maroon in your environment, even sleep on Maroon bedsheets or under a Maroon comforter. You can use Maroon towels. Flood your entire Being with Maroon, allowing the frequency to permeate each and every cell. Be creative as you use this *Name Frequency* in conjunction with your Hyperspace/Oversoul work.

- Are you already diligently working on removing fear?
- Do you consider your Self a fearful person?
- Can you make a list of your big fears?
- How about little fears?

- Do you keep in mind that enough grains of sand can fill a glass?
- Have you ever been paralyzed by fear?
- Were you a fearful child?
- Were you raised in fear?
- Have you made a conscious choice to not live in fear?
- Have you observed fear bringing out the worst in people?
- Has this happened to you?
- Have you observed fear bringing out the best in people?
- Is it important that fear be in balance?
- Is it important to keep some fear?
- What is the biggest fear that you have faced?
- Do you have any current fears that you are avoiding?
- Do you use the Maroon Frequency to help instill courage?
- When you release fear, do you remember to ask your Oversoul to fill up the empty spaces?

Name Frequency #37

Big Picture

Aleph Nun Yud
Read Hebrew Letters Right to Left
Name Frequency Pronunciation
Ah Nuh Yuh

I have a friend who talks about "playing the record to the end". In other words, whenever you think about what you want to do, you have to think beyond the current moment so you can make an informed decision. For example, some people make a conscious choice to drive while legally intoxicated. If you play that record to the end, your chances of having an extremely negative outcome are quite high. Even if it is your first time driving while intoxicated, potential consequences could drastically affect the rest of your life. When you decide to change jobs/careers, the initial phase may be very exciting. But once you settle in, *wherever you go, there you are*. So when you play the record to the end you have to decide if this truly is the most correct and beneficial move. Some people get pets because in the moment there is an emotional connection. But the reality is that pet guardianship has a lot of ups and downs, with many years of commitment and dedication. You have to play this record to the end so you do not have a pet that you do not want or cannot care for in a few years.

In the same way, the more years you have, the more you can see why you did what you did. The big picture of your life begins to come together. In your first few decades, you may feel like your experiences are not related. But, there comes a time when you look back on your various experiences to see how you needed those various experiences to put you exactly where you are now. Even if you do not like your current moment, it is exactly what you need or your Oversoul would have put you somewhere else. When most people look at the big picture of anything, they tend to focus on only the positive that can happen. Then, when the negative happens they think they made an incorrect decision. Others focus on what could go wrong to such an extent that often they never leave their status quo. Use this *Name Frequency* to help you look at the big picture as an objective observer who considers both positive and negative in your linear past, current status and potential future.

- Even when you consider both positive and negative, are there still usually unexpected circumstances?
- Do you have the tools to handle unexpected circumstances?
- Are unexpected circumstances Self-tests?
- Have you focused on the positive of a situation so much that you were surprised when negatives popped up?
- Or focused so much on the negatives that you did not embrace something from which you might have highly benefited?

- Have you noticed that as your life evolves that you are beginning to put the pieces together of prior seemingly unrelated events?
- Do you consider that the positives and negatives together create a rich and varied life?
- Do you need Clear Vision to be able to look at the big picture?
- Have you ever put together a jigsaw puzzle and compared that to seeing the big picture of your life?
- Right now, in this moment, are you comfortable with your big picture?

Name Frequency #38

Growing by Flowing

Chet Ayin Mem
Read Hebrew Letters Right to Left
Name Frequency Pronunciation
Cheh Aye Meh

Many years ago I had a friend who owned a jewelry store. The store often struggled financially. My friend told me that when business slowed down she knew she had to spend some money so more could flow in. This is superb advice. When your finances are low, the tendency is to hoard what you have rather than *let go and let God*. I believe in giving and I believe in receiving. Giving has always been easy for me. Receiving has been more challenging although I am much better than I was. I can even create, but then not allow my Self to accept what I could be receiving. Flowing means giving, accepting and receiving.

I read the story of a woman who sent her daughter to borrow some salt from a very poor neighbor. When the girl returned she asked her mother why because they already had salt. The mother explained that this way the neighbor would feel more comfortable if she needed to borrow something from her. The mother thus set the stage for the neighbor to be able to accept and receive.

Many people give to charities. I prefer to find a specific person or family in need because then my donations go directly to those in need. Stewart and I send our books to prisoners without charge when they request them. I have helped people with their research when it comes to book publishing and other areas in which I am especially knowledgeable. We give where we see a need and when the giving is sanctioned by Source. Sometimes it takes very little. Even a smile and/or a kind word can make a difference. Whatever you can give opens the door for you to receive. The key is that you are able to accept what is coming your way. God-Mind is never stagnant so this is why it is important that you follow your inner calling to give, accept, receive.

You can even give to your Self. For example, I no longer wait for special occasions to justify paying for special food. When I am in the mood for something, I spend the money on me. I AM worth it. If I need some quiet time, I give that to my Self and go sit in my room for a while. I keep the flow going as much as I can. Not everyone can accept what you want to give them. You must know your audience. Use this *Name Frequency* to promote the cycle of giving, accepting, receiving for Self, others, animals, places and ultimately All of Existence.

Of course, you can also keep the negative growing by flowing. You may be great at accepting the negative in life rather than the positive. Be mindful to not give negative, not accept or receive the negative!

- Are you good at accepting or receiving the negative?
- Are you good at giving negative?
- Do you keep your life flowing?

- Does your life feel stagnant?
- How does hoarding stop growing?
- Why do you so often need to do the opposite of what you feel like doing?
- Is life designed to pull you down or pull you up?
- Or is life what you make it?
- Do you give to your Self?
- When you give to your Self do you feel guilty?
- How do you give to others?
- Does giving to animals and places help to keep life flowing?
- Is volunteering giving?
- Do you easily accept from others?
- Do you easily accept from Source?
- Do you know your audience?
- Have you ever tried to give to someone who could not accept?
- How do you grow by flowing?

Name Frequency #39

Transformation

Resh Hey Ayin
Read Hebrew Letters Right to Left
Name Frequency Pronunciation
Reh Heh Aye

You can take your blocks and turn them into stepping stones. Too often, people only see blocks as blocks. That is the end of their progress. The challenge is to know when a block is redirecting you and when it is put there to see if you have the strength and inner fortitude to surpass. I am the type of person who does not take no for an answer. I keep going until I find a way to use the perceived block to my advantage. However, there are times when no matter what I do, what I try, where I go, the block is a block is a block. It is my redirection into something better whether I like it or not. Sometimes it is there for my total protection. The most important thing is to ask your Oversoul what to do when you come to a block. This additional tool also helps you to determine whether you are being tested to move forward or tested to label the block as redirection.

According to **Kabbalah**, this is the *Name Frequency* that Moses used to feed the starving Israelites in the desert with Manna from heaven. As you may recall from the **Bible** story, the Manna transformed into the taste of any food the person desired. In the same way, you can ask your Oversoul to transform your life experiences into what is most correct and beneficial for you. As you already know, sometimes what you want is not what you need. However, the more you grow the more what you want/need comes into alignment so that they are the same thing. You always want to be cautious to not transform your negative into more negative. This is why it is important to recognize a block to test your tenacity from a block that is put there to redirect you. The closer you are to balance, the more challenging it is to discern the difference between the two.

Interestingly enough, people with much stress who are surpassing become stronger and more radiant. I am always amazed when I see someone after a period of time and they are simply glowing! When I tell them how great they look, they inevitably say that they have been under tons of stress. Stress is a huge pressure that will either tear you down or turn you into a beautifully polished piece of jewelry. My clients often tell stories of their lives that sound horrible yet I can see the inner strength in that person. Without that inner strength, that person would not be here. This reminds me of one of my favorite sayings, "That which does not kill you makes you strong." Use this *Name Frequency* to use whatever is going on in your life for positive inner transformation.

- Is it challenging to know which blocks are put in place for your protection and which ones are part of your obstacle course?

- Have you been in the position where if you did not surpass you knew you would no longer be here?
- Have you ever felt like giving up, yet some inner spark kept you going?
- Did you ever feel like you were just about ready to go under, then the stress let up?
- Or, the stress intensifies to push you beyond current boundaries into a new, improved state of transformation?
- Has stress transformed you into your worst at times?
- Has stress transformed you into your best at times?
- Do you acknowledge your inner strength and fortitude that keeps you going when others would have given up long ago?
- Are your needs/wants aligning more now than they used to?
- Have you seen people under a great deal of stress who still look better than ever?
- How do you feel about your Self when you realize what you just went through and survived?

Name Frequency #40

Speaking Correctly

Yud Yud Zayin
Read Hebrew Letters Right to Left
Name Frequency Pronunciation
Yuh Yuh Zye

Speaking the correct words 100% of the time is challenging for everyone. To do this, you would need to maintain left and right brain balance 24/7. You may be in the process, but life challenges can easily throw you off-center and out of balance in a variety of ways. Once this happens, your tongue follows whatever mind-pattern is evoked and you are off and running, usually not in the correct direction.

Too often people think that they should only say kind words. Yet, kind is subjective. What may sound kind to you coming from your mouth may not be kind according to the recipient. I once had a client who went by a really horrible nickname. When I asked her if I could call her by her given name, she said yes. In the following phone conversation, I used her given name and she became enraged, yelled, slammed the phone in my ear and I never heard from her again. I have shared information with people who then thought I was showing off how much I knew rather than being helpful. My list goes on and on. When this happens, and given the opportunity, I do apologize for any misunderstandings.

Sometimes, the correct words to be spoken are harsh. If someone is coming at you aggressively, you may be directed by your Oversoul to throw out some harsh words to stop the attack. Sometimes, people only respect you if you are as nasty as they are, otherwise, they think you are a patsy that they can walk all over. Their nastiness is like a test because they judge nasty as someone with a backbone vs. someone who can easily be walked upon. Every situation is quite unique and calls for different words. Regardless of what words you use, it is always important that you release them up to your Oversoul as you speak for distribution on the Oversoul level. Let the involved Oversouls figure it out. This lessens your efforts as long as you do your best to follow the words your Oversoul directs you to speak.

When you are not sure, say what you need to say. You will know by the response if what you said was correct or not. So much of what you do is trial and error. Trial and error is your unique guide so you eventually know without a doubt because of your own experiential learning. Your training must prepare you for all situations, so you are given a variety of experiences to create flexibility and become impervious to external pressure. This makes you quick-witted and able to respond to anyone, anywhere, anytime without flinching in the least. Use this *Name Frequency* to help guide you in this inner process.

- Are you able to correctly respond to anyone, anywhere, anytime?
- Do you ask your Oversoul for the correct words to speak?

- Do you remember to release your spoken words up to your Oversoul as they flow out your mouth?
- Do you sometimes think you are saying the correct words only to have others tell you that you are not?
- Have you upset someone by using what you thought were kind words?
- Is kind subjective?
- Have you had to apologize for being misunderstood?
- Have you needed to be aggressive with your words because of circumstances?
- Are there some people who can only understand negative communications?
- Is gossip negative communication?
- Is speaking ill/poorly of someone negative communication?
- Can your words contribute to someone becoming ill or poor?
- Is it challenging to always choose the correct words for each unique situation?

Name Frequency #41

Self-Value

Hey Hey Hey
Read Hebrew Letters Right to Left
Name Frequency Pronunciation
Heh Heh Heh

Self-Esteem, Self-Worth, Self-Value. All these frequencies are about how you feel about you. It is so easy to try to feel good from outside input, but that input is fleeting. Soon, you feel empty again and you look for more outside input. Filling empty holes from the outside never lasts. You must do the inner level work so that you feel good about your Self from the inside.

I love the chapter in ***Decoding Your Life*** that teaches you how to release Self-judgment and Self-criticism. These are the 2 frequencies that can pull you down faster than anything else. I give you simple affirmations in that book that I used for many years to help me help my Self.

I release the need to criticize and judge My Self.
I AM okay as is.

If anyone says anything negative about you, it is your choice to accept or reject. When you are doubtful of your own Self, you accept the negative to feed what is already within. When you know who and what you are, you reject whatever anyone says about you that is not true. This is your test which you will repeat until you determine that Self-Esteem, Self-Worth, and Self-Value all must come from within. No one can give it to you; no one can take it away.

Everyone is a work in progress. Know that considering who you are, where you came from and the experiences that you have had, that you are okay as is. Life is a process that teaches you as you go. Everyone is a package of both positive and negative; everyone is being tested; no one passes all his/her tests on the first try. Most people take dozens, hundreds, even thousands of the same increasingly challenging tests before they pass. You can spend your time criticizing and judging Self or you can make a conscious choice to Value who and what you are in this present moment. You cannot compare your Self to other people. You can observe them and understand that they, too, have challenges that you do not see. Each person is a unique flower in the garden of life. One is not better or worse than another. Just as each flower is beautiful in its own way, so are you. Use this *Name Frequency* to enhance your Self-Value on all levels of your Being.

- Why is it usually easier to denigrate than praise Self?
- Have you been around people who love to praise themselves, yet you see they have extremely low Self-Value?
- How do most people react to these kinds of people?
- Can you have compassion for these kinds of people or do they try your patience?
- Does a lion have to tell you that he/she is a lion?

- Are you challenged to Value Self in the present moment?
- Do you think that you will Value Self after you have done this or that?
- Why is it challenging to Value a work in progress?
- Do you think that you will not meet the expectations of others?
- Do you have unrealistic Self-expectations?
- If so, where did these come from?
- Have others said negative things to you that you accepted because of your inner low Self-Worth?
- Does your doubting mind-pattern pull these kinds of people to you?
- Do you have to be beaten down enough until you finally say you have had enough?
- Can these types of experiences push you further down or help you find your inner gumption to get up and get going?
- How easy is it to use other people's words and actions as an excuse to not do anything?
- Have you learned to not judge or criticize Self?
- Have you tried to fill empty emotional holes from the outside?
- How did that work for you?
- Was your fulfillment long-lasting or fleeting?
- How challenging is it to feel good about Self from within?

Name Frequency #42

Revealing the Hidden

Mem Yud Khaf
Read Hebrew Letters Right to Left
Name Frequency Pronunciation
Meh Yuh Khah

When I first used this *Name Frequency*, the visual of an iceberg immediately popped into my mind. When you see an iceberg, in general only 10% is above the surface while 90% is below. It is interesting that in my study of the *Sefirot*, I am learning that from the *10 Sefirot* emanates many other things in groups of 10, such as 10 fingers and 10 toes. When you think about this, you realize that what animates those 10 fingers and 10 toes is also hidden. You see the outer, but you do not physically see the bones, nerves, blood vessels, muscles, and other internals that exist behind these, nor do you see the psychic energy, life force, and flow of consciousness. When you think about it, you do not see most of the world because most of it is hidden.

Much is hidden from you because if you could see it all you would be on sensory overload. You are challenged to deal with your life on a daily basis with what you do see. The more knowledge you have, the more responsibility. As you demonstrate that you can deal with your life as it is now, then more and more is revealed to you. Yes, that which is hidden is interesting, but so is your daily life. Except for some reason, when something is hidden it is much more interesting than that which is in plain sight. Just like something sitting on a table is not as interesting as when it is wrapped in gift paper with a fancy bow on top. What is hidden in that box piques your interest much more than the same item sitting in plain sight on the table.

Your life is like the item sitting on the table. No mystery, no intrigue, no desire to explore. But when it is wrapped up and hidden, then you are more intrigued to make the inner quest to the Center of You. You cannot reveal too much too soon, because that can change your life too much too fast. So you are allowed to tiptoe around and have a peek. This way you can adjust your inner sight and thus your outer life. Use this *Name Frequency* to unwrap your inner Self, but ask your Oversoul and God-Mind to do it in a way that is most correct and beneficial for you. Too much truth too fast can put you on overload.

- Have you had a truth revealed to you too fast that put you on overload?
- Does your current life feel dull and boring compared to the mysteries of life that you seek?
- Is your current life part of the mysteries of life, except because it is not hidden it does not feel interesting or intriguing?
- Is it challenging to keep your focus on your current life while you explore your inner mysteries?
- Is it important to keep a balance of your inner and outer work?

- Do you think that 90% of how the world works is hidden from you?
- Would you be on sensory overload if you saw 100% of the way the world works?
- Does more knowledge mean more responsibility?
- Do you have to prove to Self that you can handle your current life before more is revealed to you?
- Is only seeing 10% of the way the world works a protection for you?

Name Frequency #43

Mind Over Matter

Vav Vav Lamed
Read Hebrew Letters Right to Left
Name Frequency Pronunciation
Wah Wah Lah

The strength of your mind is astounding which is why the global handlers spend so much time trying to negatively influence you every way they can. The amount of money spent on advertising is phenomenal, practically beyond comprehension. The reason for this is not to get you to buy their product, but to gain control over your mind. The fight by others to control your mind is intense. As one of the songs on my ***Peace in the World*** album says, your mind is the strongest tool you have. Every day you read stories of people who overcome various crises. They were told that they would never walk, have children, secure meaningful employment, get out of poverty and more.

When the going gets tough, the tough get going.

Life tempts you to give up and quit. It is your mind that says, "No way." That inner spark that was discussed at the beginning of exploring these *Name Frequencies* is alive and well. You are pushed to extinguish your spark, but no one can do this except you. You can buy into this scenario or you can use it as a pushing off point to rise beyond the naysayers into someone bigger and better than even you can imagine. In the same way, your Animal Mind wants to run your life, putting food, shelter, and sex above everything else. Your Spiritual Mind must take control to elevate and uplift the physical body. Fasting is an excellent way to gain control of the Animal Mind if the Animal Mind is in control of you.

You always have your mind. No one can take that from you, but they can make you believe that you are weak, worthless, gutless, and lower than a snake's belly. You are continually challenged to accept or reject this type of thinking. The lower your Self-worth, the easier you are to control. No one can take anything from you, but you can willingly give away or shut down the Brilliance of Your Being. Use this *Name Frequency* to maintain and strengthen your Mind Over Matter. But like everything you do, always be certain that what you are doing is most correct and beneficial for all involved.

- Do you have personal experience with Mind Over Matter?
- Have you ever been told that you could not do something, but you did it anyway?
- Just because you can do something, does this mean that action is the most correct and beneficial?
- Are you able to identify programming of the masses that dumbs them down as well as weakens, subverts, and redirects their wills?
- Have you had to fight against mass programming?

- Must you continually be aware to not accept negative mass programming?
- How do you deal with others who have fallen into the programming trap of temptation?
- Do you have control over your Animal Mind or does your Animal Mind have control over you?
- Why is your mind so valuable that everyone wants to own it?

Name Frequency #44

Eliminating Judgment

Yud Lamed Hey
Read Hebrew Letters Right to Left
Name Frequency Pronunciation
Yuh Lah Heh

Whatever you give out comes back to you. This is one of the most basic Spiritual Laws. When you judge others, that same judgment comes back to you. There are so many ways that you judge people, places, and things every single day. You may be judging clothing, attitude, driving, big business, politicians, the economy. No matter what it is, judgment means you are labeling it good or bad. Sometimes what you label bad is most correct and beneficial for the situation. For example, negative gets people to move. Without negativity, people may get complacent and lazy. Sometimes what you label good is not the most correct and beneficial for the situation. Maybe you give someone money to help with bills. Since the person's bills are paid, he/she decides it is okay to not go to work for a few days.

Not liking something does not make it bad. I do not like eggs, but there are many people who do. I do not label eggs bad because I don't like them. Liking something does not make it good. Someone may like to party, drink alcohol excessively, or smoke cigarettes, but this does not make these items good for you. When you learn to observe, as I wrote about in **Decoding Your Life**, you understand with wisdom and without judgment. This is not easy. Some people may label you cold and unfeeling. But the reality is that you care so deeply that you allow All That Exists to be what it is without judging it. You understand with wisdom why it is what it is and what place it has within Existence. Instead of labeling God's World good or bad, you accept what is along with its purpose and mission in life.

When you feel judgment rising, release it up to the Oversoul level and ask for an explanation of whatever you are thinking about. Everything exists for a reason. Becoming an objective observer instead of a judge means that you stop judging your Self which allows you to observe who and what you really are. The change in perspective and thus attitude is amazing. In addition, the outer world must reflect this back, meaning that others will release the need to judge you. Use this *Name Frequency* to stop the Judgment and help install a mind-pattern of objective observation.

- How challenging is it to observe without judgment?
- Are you programmed to believe that everything is good or bad?
- Is it challenging to not think of everything as good and bad?
- If a thief successfully robs a store, is that a good day for him/her?
- If a thief gets caught, is that a bad day for him/her?

- If you miss your plane, is that a bad day for you?
- If your missed plane crashes, is that a good day for you?
- Was it most correct and beneficial for you to miss your plane?
- Do other people judge you?
- Do you judge them?
- Who allows you to be you without judgment?
- Why is it important to be an observer vs. a judge?

Name Frequency #45

Prosperity & Wealth

Samech Aleph Lamed
Read Hebrew Letters Right to Left
Name Frequency Pronunciation
Sah Ah Lah

Money is the first word that comes to the minds of most people when they think of the word Prosperity. As you already know, you can have lots of money and not be prosperous. You can lose money or things, but with a mind-pattern of Prosperity, you always have what you need. When you are grateful for what you have, then you are well-positioned to align your needs/wants with the wishes of your Oversoul and God-Mind.

Prosperity comes in many forms, but the place to start is always within. You may be prosperous in friendships, prosperous in knowledge/wisdom, prosperous in positive attitudes, prosperous in your vegetable/flower gardens, prosperous in your artwork. Prosperity is always in your mind-pattern first and then the outer world can reflect that back to you.

You can limit what comes to you and how it comes to you by only thinking about money. Expand your awareness to include True Prosperity so that whatever you need easily finds you. As your inner alignment with your Oversoul and God-Mind comes together, what you need and what you want has a better possibility of merging into one. This means that your needs are met and your wants are met. I have a friend who owns a condominium in Hawaii. I used to go every year with her. I had a wonderful vacation with very little cost and she had a traveling companion. Some people are paid to go on vacations to help with children or elderly people. I have another friend who is a potter. I wanted a dinnerware set, mixing and baking bowls, soap dishes, goblets, vases, and a myriad of her other handmade items. I worked for her in exchange for all these things, including many gifts that I gave to others. No money changed hands, but both of our needs/wants were fulfilled.

Without a Prosperity mind-pattern, no matter how much comes, you cannot hold onto it or enjoy it. Perhaps you get extra money and then your house needs a major repair so there goes your money. Or, you have a health issue so your money goes to health expenses. Maybe your car breaks down so the extra money must also cover car repair. When you have a Prosperity mind-pattern what you need automatically comes to you. As your Prosperity mind-pattern strengthens, what you need aligns with your wants that are most correct and beneficial for you. Life can vastly improve without the exchange of any money or perhaps you get paid to do what you already love. Friendships blossom, careers take off, gardens produce in abundance. Use this *Name Frequency* to strengthen and expand your Prosperity mind-pattern.

- Do you only focus on money to meet your wants/needs?
- Is a Prosperity mind-pattern more valuable than money?

- Do most people only think of money when they think of Prosperity?
- During the Plannedemic, were all of your needs met?
- Was toilet paper more valuable than a barrel of oil?
- Could money buy all the toilet paper you wanted?
- Have you had unexpected money come, yet it was spent quickly?
- Has your mind-pattern attracted what you need/want without any exchange of money?
- Are you careful to ask your Oversoul to only bring to you what is most correct and beneficial?
- As you more correctly define Prosperity, is your Prosperity mind-pattern strengthening, deepening, expanding, and aligning with your Oversoul and God-Mind?

Name Frequency #46

Absolute Certainty

Ayin Resh Yud
Read Hebrew Letters Right to Left
Name Frequency Pronunciation
Aye Reh Yuh

This *Name Frequency* helps you push up through doubt and confusion. Doubt and confusion make you stop and question what you are doing, why you are doing it, and if it is most correct and beneficial. Sometimes, if you go straight from one area of your life to another without questioning, you can cause something that is not most correct and beneficial to happen. For example, you may have a relationship that you want to work, so you use this *Name Frequency*. If you use this *Name frequency* to force the relationship, you may be cutting off another relationship that may be more correct and beneficial for you. And, if you have to force a relationship you may get it to find out why it should not have happened at all.

On the other hand, this *Name Frequency* can enhance your positive emotions and attributes. For example, you can use it to know without any doubt or confusion that:

I AM okay as is.

I AM consciously connected to my Source 24/7.

I surpass my programming.

This *Name Frequency* allows you to know with absolute certainty that whatever happens is most correct and beneficial. You must be extremely cautious how you use this *Name Frequency* so that you do not push through something that ultimately is what you want but not what you need. As you know, there are many *Name Frequencies* like this. You must always do your inner level work so that whatever you do it is under the guidance of your Oversoul and God-Mind.

You are learning that your Hyperspace/Oversoul tools and techniques are neutral. This is how the global handlers get away with what they are doing. They learn to manipulate the laws that remove themselves and put you in the position of being responsible for making a negative choice. They set the path and you walk it. The temptation is great to get what you want now to satisfy the Animal Mind vs. taking the time to wait a little longer to satisfy the Higher Spiritual Mind.

For example, the transgender agenda. No one is coming around, knocking on your door and taking your children for experimentation. Parents are willingly giving their children to the medical community for this purpose. Social media is another fantastic example. No one is forcing you to enter your personal information into a huge gigantic database. You willingly do this. The global handlers can set up their agendas and then slap this *Name Frequency* on it so that they know with absolute certainty that you will walk the paths that they set for you. Without Soul-level discernment, you are going to walk that path. Use this *Name Frequency* with caution and only under the direction and guidance of your Oversoul and God-Mind.

- Is it tempting to go for short term, immediate satisfaction?
- Do you see others do this all the time who appear to get away with it?
- Do you get frustrated that your own path takes so long?
- Because your Soul is ageless, in the overall scheme of things, is your current lifeline just a blip?
- Is it always important to be mindful of what you ask for, because you may get it?
- Is it challenging to remember that the global handlers know how to manipulate Spiritual Law in their favor?
- Do doubt and confusion slow you down so you ask the correct questions and wait for the correct answers?
- Have you ever asked for something, gotten it, and then wished that you had not?
- Why must you always be so careful to ask for what is most correct and beneficial?
- Can you easily determine how to use this *Name Frequency*?

Name Frequency #47

World Peace & Global Transformation

Ayin Shin Lamed
Read Hebrew Letters Right to Left
Name Frequency Pronunciation
Aye Shih Lah

After I turn off my computer every night, I check my phone to scroll through social media. I can count on people to be posting the latest news because as you know, that changes moment by moment. I happened to click on a video that showed inane, senseless violence. I was so stunned at what I saw, tears began forming in my eyes at the depravity of the actions. I felt a deep sadness for those who were attacked as well as for those who did the attacking as I quickly clicked out of the video. Of course, there are no accidents, so as I contemplated what I had just witnessed it came to me to see if there is a *Name frequency* for World Peace. I opened up one of my books at random, found my Self on the Table of Contents, and right in front of my eyes I read "World Peace". That seemed pretty amazing so I opened another book to see if the *Name Frequency* had a different Name, which it did. This other book is called the same *Name Frequency* **Global Transformation**.

As you already know, the outer world reflects somewhere your own inner state. Somewhere on the deepest levels, you need peace and transformation. The more your internal peace and transformation gain strength, the stronger it emanates into the world so that those who are ready can find their own inner peace and transformation. If you feel a victim in any way, then you are adding to the collective victim mentality mind-pattern. If you attack anyone, including your Self, then you are adding to the oppressor mentality mind-pattern.

The work that you are doing now is extremely important because you are helping to hold the higher level fabric of humanity together. This means that you must release the lower level fabric of humanity within that holds you down. If you desire global transformation then you must have inner transformation. Yes, the work you do is extremely important. Enough grains of sand fill a glass. Enough people doing this work populates a neighborhood, a city block, a county, a state, a country, and yes, the world. Collective Humanity is Healing so all the dirt is coming up. Healing is not easy and does not always happen in what most people would call a positive way. Increasing the speed of your own inner peace and transformation enhances the speed for the rest of the world.

- Are you an oppressor of Self?
- Do you attack your Self or support your Self?
- Do you beat your Self up?
- When you do this, do you add to the negative collective mind-pattern of Humanity?
- Do you clean up after your negative Self-attacks, give all to your Oversoul and apologize for your behavior?

- Is it easy to point the finger and blame someone or something else?
- If something exists in the outer world that you do not like, where is the best place to start the healing process?
- Do you sometimes feel powerless when it comes to changing the world?
- Do you remember that empowerment begins with you?
- Are you one grain of sand in a glass?
- Are you willing to do your part and add your grain of sand to the glass?
- Is Humanity Healing different than you would like to see humanity healing?
- Can healing encompass some very rough stuff?
- Do the victims need the oppressors to teach them whatever it is they need to know?
- What kinds of mind-patterns do the victims have to attract horrific physical lessons?
- Does someone have to play the part of the oppressor?
- Do you have compassion for all?
- Do you have compassion for all parts of Self?

Name Frequency #48

Unity

Mem Yud Hey
Read Hebrew Letters Right to Left
Name Frequency Pronunciation
Meh Yuh Heh

When you only think of your Self as one grain of sand that can do little if nothing at all, you do a disservice to all the other grains of sand that are trying to come together to unite into an even greater power. When I farmed in Eastern Washington State the soil was comprised of sand. I saw the power of sand during sandstorms as well as other anomalous events. This leads me to share this poem by John Godfrey Saxe 1816-1887 to remind you of the power of a group mind working together.

THE BLIND MEN AND THE ELEPHANT.
A HINDOO FABLE.

I.

IT was six men of Indostan
To learning much inclined,
Who went to see the Elephant
(Though all of them were blind),
That each by observation
Might satisfy his mind.

II.

The First approached the Elephant,
And happening to fall
Against his broad and sturdy side,
At once began to bawl:
"God bless me!—but the Elephant
Is very like a wall!"

III.

The Second, feeling of the tusk,
Cried: "Ho!—what have we here
So very round and smooth and sharp?
To me 't is mighty clear
This wonder of an Elephant
Is very like a spear!"

IV.

The Third approached the animal,
And happening to take
The squirming trunk within his hands,
Thus boldly up and spake:
"I see," quoth he, "the Elephant
Is very like a snake!"

V.

The Fourth reached out his eager hand,
And felt about the knee.
  "What most this wondrous beast is like
  Is mighty plain," quoth he;
  "'T is clear enough the Elephant
  Is very like a tree!"

VI.

The Fifth, who chanced to touch the ear,
Said: "E'en the blindest man
Can tell what this resembles most;
Deny the fact who can,
This marvel of an Elephant
Is very like a fan!"

VII.

The Sixth no sooner had begun
About the beast to grope,
Then, seizing on the swinging tail
That fell within his scope,
"I see," quoth he, "the Elephant
Is very like a rope!"

VIII.

And so these men of Indostan
Disputed loud and long,
Each in his own opinion
Exceeding stiff and strong,
Though each was partly in the right,
And all were in the wrong!

MORAL.

So, oft in theologic wars
The disputants, I ween,
Rail on in utter ignorance
Of what each other mean,
And prate about an Elephant
Not one of them has seen!

https://en.wikisource.org/wiki/The_poems_of_John_Godfrey_Saxe/The_Blind_Men_and_the_Elephant

Every day, people argue about an elephant in the room. Having a different viewpoint does not make another person incorrect. It is always important to listen to many different viewpoints to see the entire picture. In the same way, you may be sorting out a variety of inner viewpoints as you try to come to conclusions about various aspects of your life. This infighting sets the stage for inner dissension rather than inner unification. Stop your infighting by unifying Self. In turn, this must be reflected in the outer world.

When you really think about your infighting, there is much more going on than you realize. I told you about my hairstylist who wanted to cut my hair on the Thursday I was traveling. I was really upset that she felt safe to cut my hair Thursday afternoon but not safe to cut my hair only a few hours later at my regularly scheduled 9am time the next morning. I practically begged her to do my hair, she talked to me like I was a little child, telling me that she knew I was disappointed but it was important that everyone was safe. I am a huge believer in loyalty. I had been her client for close to 10 years, always accommodating her schedule. The one time I really needed her, she brushed me off like a pesky fly on her shoulder.

All during the lockdown, I was so upset with her. I did not know what to expect when the lockdown was lifted. I did not want to do the incorrect action for the incorrect reason. My two appointments with her were not pleasant and she did not apologize. I decided to change salons. Now, in the overall scheme of things, getting one's hair done is way down on the list. But the disloyalty I felt bothered me more than my hair. Thus, infighting with my Self for months. A few grains of sand in my cup.

My new stylist is the owner of his salon. I like him a lot. My new infighting was whether to tip him or not, as protocol says not to tip the owner. I have tipped salon owners before and no one ever told me not to. I would feel funny not tipping. More infighting. More grains of sand in my cup. My day of the appointment came and I still was fighting with my Self on what to do. All through the appointment, I was fighting with my Self. Finally, when it came time to pay, I told him that I was terribly embarrassed to ask, but I wasn't sure about protocol for tipping owners. He said that there was a saying that owners worked 2x as hard as anyone else at half the pay, so extra was always appreciated. I was so relieved. I was relieved to know that I could/should tip him. I was so relieved to be done with the old salon. I was relieved to have answers and actions that I could live with. Inner unification at last!

I have been upset that my son has to take the nasal Covid-19 test. I had been infighting about whether to say anything to the university or keep my mouth shut. More grains of sand in my cup. Finally, I decided to write to them. They answered and told me he could take a saliva test. I felt so relieved. But then he doesn't have a primary doctor so I called the local Covid hotline to find out that they do not do saliva tests but there is a new nasal test that barely goes inside the nose, that he does himself that was only one week old. And yes, they would schedule him. Hallelujah! I have been praying that something would happen before he had to take the invasive test. Unity within.

- How easy is it to infight and put grains of sand in your cup that divide rather than unify?

- How many times a day do you fight with your Self?
- How does your infighting divide and cause inner conflict?
- Are the answers to larger issues easier to see than smaller issues?
- Or is each issue unique?
- Is there always infighting when you have to make a decision?
- If you go to a restaurant and have to choose food from a tantalizing menu do you infight over what to have/not have?
- Do you find unity within only to have something else come up that causes the infighting to come up again?
- If you put enough grains of sand in your infighting cup can you bury your Self?
- Is infighting necessary and a natural process as you come to balance?
- Is there another way?
- If everyone is infighting, does this add to the fighting/divisiveness in the world?
- Is infighting in society a natural process or is there another way?
- Can we unify through our differences as well as our similarities?
- Does each piece of the pie have to be the same?
- Do all the pies have to be the same?
- Is there strength in diversified unification?
- Does internal strength come from uniting your own diversified parts resulting in all of you is going in the correct direction for the correct reason with the correct timing?

Name Frequency #49

Happiness

Vav Hey Vav
Read Hebrew Letters Right to Left
Name Frequency Pronunciation
Wah Heh Wah

Many people think of Happiness as a kind of a Spiritual High that keeps ascending and never stops. My life experiences show me that life is a mixture of positive and negative depending upon what you need at the time. From my experience, Happiness is more a fleeting emotion that pops in and out of my life. I prefer a more consistent and steady flow of emotion so I focus on satisfaction, contentment and gratitude. My dogs, for example, can make me happy. But that can dissipate when they dig, whine or refuse to eat. When I feel depressed looking at my dogs can boost my attitude. When I feel better, then I can get on with my day.

Good news from my children makes me feel happy, but again, I get on with my day and onto other emotions. This also makes me think of good times with friends and family. When I am with them I am Happy, but other emotions come along especially if we venture into deeper subjects. Then I am more satisfied, content, and grateful for my friends. However, if they live at a distance there is that nagging feeling in the background that knows I will be sad when we part.

You already know Happiness that comes from material possessions is always fleeting. You may initially feel Happy, but eventually, you come back down again. I was Happy when we purchased our home. Now, I enjoy it but there is always maintenance. I am grateful that I have a home. Getting a home in Italy to be near my family would make me Happy, or a home on Long Island to be near our family there would make me Happy. But these would have to be second homes or I would not be that Happy. Being nearer to anyone you care about brings up more inner issues.

- With all of this in mind, how would you use this *Name Frequency*?
- What makes you Happy now?
- What do you think would make you Happy?
- From experience, does Happiness stay?
- Is Happiness always a fleeting emotion?
- Would you want to be perpetually Happy?
- Does perpetual Happiness preclude other emotions?
- If you were always Happy, would you miss the diversity of negative emotions?
- What other positive emotions could co-exist with Happiness?
- Would there be other positive emotions that you would miss out on?
- Do you have a personal definition of Happiness?

Name Frequency #50

Limitlessness

Dalet Nun Yud
Read Hebrew Letters Right to Left
Name Frequency Pronunciation
Dah Nuh Yuh

There are reasons why you place limitations on your life. Some are in place as protection by your Oversoul. Others are your own Self-limitations because you do not know that you are worthy of partaking in the vastness and richness of All That Is. I come from a very limited mind-pattern as discussed in my ***Heights of Wealth*** book. My grandparents were farmers and railroad people. My parents were working class. My dad sometimes had 4 jobs at one time to keep our family going financially. I learned not to expect much and to work hard to pay for my own extras as a child.

When I met Stewart, he came from an entirely different background. Whatever his family had, they spent. I was amazed when

I went to family dinners. His mother usually had several different cold appetizers followed by several different hot appetizers, followed by several different kinds of main courses, many side dishes, fresh fruit, and always many different desserts. This did not happen in my household. Before my first barbecue for them, his mother asked me about my menu. I told her hamburgers and hotdogs. She was aghast that was all I was having. She told me that I should consider those people who did not want hamburgers and hotdogs. She said I had to have chicken, steak, fish, and sausage too. I was aghast that she would expect me to prepare so much food, but of course, I did to keep her happy.

I also found out that you could not have too many cartons of ice cream open at the same time. Even if my parents had several cartons of ice cream in the freezer, we started one carton and finished it before we opened another. Same with different kinds of jam. One jar at a time. No matter what his family did, to me they seemed extravagant. His parents were very generous. His mother always said that whatever she had, her friends and family had. That was very true. Stewart is also very generous. I am grateful for his attitude. I was raised much more conservatively, so between Stewart and me, we have a good balance.

One of Stewart's favorite sayings is "More is more" and he maintains his no-limit attitude in all that he does. I have definitely come a long way, and I definitely defer to my Oversoul to provide or protect, or both. The mind-pattern has to be there to support more, or whatever positive you get is soon gone. However, only expecting less does not give you an appreciation for the vastness and richness of All That Exists. First, you must determine if your limitations are Self-imposed or Oversoul-imposed. This Name Frequency helps you remove Self-imposed limitations under the guidance of your Oversoul.

- Do you think of your Oversoul limiting you for your own Self-protection?

- Is it easy to realize how you Self-limit?
- Were you raised with limitations of what you could or could not have?
- How do you Self-limit in your daily life?
- Can you encompass a "More is more" attitude?
- Are you a generous person?
- Are you conservatively generous or liberally generous?
- Are you generous to your Self or only to others?
- Or to Self and not others?

Name Frequency #51

Repentance

Hey Chet Shin
Read Hebrew Letters Right to Left
Name Frequency Pronunciation
Heh Cheh Shih

Repentance is a helpful frequency when you want to make amends with your past. Everyone has things that happened that at the time might have seemed the correct thing to do, but looking back now with more knowledge you realize were not. One incident for me happened decades ago. I was carrying a handmade pottery bowl set for a friend of a friend. The set slipped from my hands and broke into dozens of pieces. I felt terrible and apologized but for some reason, I did not offer to pay for a replacement. I still don't know why I didn't. Even after all these years, this incident stays with me. I have apologized to her many, many times on the Oversoul level. On the Oversoul level, I have apologized to my mother for not being the daughter she wanted, to my ex-husband for marrying him to get away from my mother, and the list goes on. When I drive on busy streets I do my best to let cars into my lane when I can. There have been occasions when time was of the essence so I could not. On the Oversoul level, I have apologized to these people, too.

Whatever you did or did not do needs to be cleaned up as best as you can on the Oversoul level. This *Name Frequency* helps you do this as well as bring up incidences that you may have long-forgotten. I remember when I was around the age of 5 trying to get a neighbor boy to drink soap bubbles. When I tried to demonstrate to him how easy it was by pretending to drink some, the bubbles went into my mouth! I knew at that time that I deserved that and I quit trying to convince him to drink them. Yes, I have apologized to him as well as to my Self and Oversoul for my behavior. You have all kinds of memories and emotions locked away that need to come out for resolution. Repenting for your behavior, apologizing to the person, giving it all to your Oversoul, and filling the space with healing Color, Tones and Archetypes is a process that this *Name Frequency* can help you with.

- Have you spent time repenting for past behavior?
- What is your earliest memory of doing something that was or could have been harmful to another person?
- How many memories do you carry for which you still need to repent?
- Or, have you tried to release these memories yet you still feel bad and guilty for what you did?
- Have you given these situations to your Oversoul?
- Have you asked your Oversoul to fill the space with healing Color, Tones, and Archetypes so that you could finally release your bad feelings?
- Do you use these incidences to emotionally beat your Self?

- As a result of these incidences do you feel you deserve to be beat by life?
- Do you accept life beating you?
- Are you good at receiving the negative?
- Can you use this *Name Frequency* to help pull this out of you so you can move on?

Name Frequency #52

Passion

Aleph Mem Mem
Read Hebrew Letters Right to Left
Name Frequency Pronunciation
Ah Meh Meh

When you are depressed or troubled, it is easy to lose your passion for life. Negative thinking is like quicksand. The more you struggle the faster it pulls you in. I have definitely had periods in my life where I felt like I was going through the motions of my daily tasks. Periods of time like this make you feel like they will never end. Each day feels like a torturous eternity that drags on forever. This is when you have a choice. You either fall deeper into the pit or you do what you need to do to pull your Self out.

These have been a rough few months for most people. When your structure is suddenly pulled out from underneath you, you are left flailing for some sense of normalcy. Everyone needs a routine of some kind to keep going. Your structure is a template for your life. Yes, everyone needs a respite for a few days here or there. But I know when the respite is over I am always ready to get back into my daily routine/structure. Once you are in the structure it is much easier to find your passion. Even if you do not have time for what you love, at least you know what you love to do. When the time is most correct and beneficial, that comes together for you.

Sometimes people think that as you gain more years you lose your passion for life. From my observations, older people have *been there, done that* and do not want to go there or do that again. Instead of acknowledging they did it and they don't want to do it anymore, they often say that they are too old. I did a lot of things decades ago that I do not want to do anymore. There is a time in your life for everything. I found out that when you don't do what you want to do at the time you want to do it, you often lose the passion. Then when you can do it, you do not want to do the same things because you have changed. This means that your needs, wants and priorities change. Societal programming says that you are old so you should just give up and die, so people do.

Whenever life changes unexpectedly, your foundation/structure changes. Even when the change is positive, until you get a new foundation/structure, you can experience a wide range of varying emotions that may leave you laughing one moment and despondent the next. Negative changes may leave you depressed as well as feeling like your years of living are slipping away. Age is meaningless when you recognize that the Soul is ageless. Allow your physical body to reflect the agelessness of your Soul.

Use this *Name Frequency* to help recapture your Passion for living. Using this *Name Frequency* may mean that certain life situations and even people drop out of your life while new doors of opportunity open. You may feel like you are going through the motions, but this is the place to start. Logically you know what you need even if you do not yet feel it emotionally. You need a place to begin, so here you are. Begin!

- Have you ever lost your Passion for living?
- Or have you lost your Passion for various aspects of your life?
- Are you waiting for a new Passion to reveal itself?
- Do you feel despondent or depressed over your age?
- Do you use age as an excuse to not do something, whether you want to do it or not?
- Did you use to have more Passion for living?
- Have you had periods in your life when you were despondent or depressed?
- If so, how did you get out of it?
- If you already have a Passion for living, can using this *Name Frequency* to make good even better?

Name Frequency #53

Unconditional Sharing

Nun Nun Aleph
Read Hebrew Letters Right to Left
Name Frequency Pronunciation
Nuh Nuh Ah

Unconditional Sharing is giving because it is the most correct and beneficial thing to do. Many people give because of what they will get back, including feeling good because they gave. I have been around many people who see what they want then they determine how to get it without ever asking if this is in their highest interest. I have been around people who give to get back. They want something so they think about what they have to give to you so you will give to them. I know one woman who managed to get her entire house remodeled by doing this. I know people who volunteer so they can be publicly acknowledged for what they gave. Even people who give to churches and schools often want some kind of acknowledgment about what they give and the size of the gift.

Sometimes you think you are sharing unconditionally, but you may not be. Once I gave a raise to a woman who had worked for me for one year. She took the raise and then one week later told me she had another job. I'm sure she knew this when she took the raise. I gave her the raise to thank her for her loyalty and excellent work. I felt betrayed that she did not tell me that she had another job when I gave her the raise. Yet, I did not give her the raise to ensure she would stay. I gave it as a thank you, therefore I realized I needed to deal with my reactions to her choices.

There can be great inner joy in sharing with others. But like everything else, there is the responsibility of sharing the correct thing in the correct timing in the correct way for the correct reasons. Unconditional sharing encompasses all of this plus only the acknowledgment of your Oversoul. If you expect more than this, then you are not sharing unconditionally. Even when I write my books, I think about when someday I will not be around but people will still have access to the information. Yet, having my name on the books holds part of my Soul-personality energy here. Unconditionally sharing the information is more important than people knowing my name. Part of me wishes I did not have to put my name on the books at all. Unconditional sharing is much more complex and simple than it seems at first glance. Use this *Name Frequency* so what you do is for the Glory of the Creator and not for the sole Glory of Self.

- Is Unconditional Sharing challenging?
- Do most people give to get something back?
- Do you share because it makes you feel good or because it is the correct thing to do?
- Is win/win sharing unconditional?
- When you share, do you want acknowledgment?
- If you give a gift, do you want a thank you?
- Does sharing with others bring you inner joy?

- Does your inner joy come from seeing or knowing the reaction of the recipient?
- Do you feel the same inner joy if you do not see or know the reaction of the recipient?
- Have you thought that you shared unconditionally only to realize from your own reactions that you did not?
- Are you careful to share the correct thing in the correct timing in the correct way for the correct reasons?
- Is the acknowledgment of your Oversoul more important than the acknowledgment of the outer world?

Name Frequency #54

Correct Death

Nun Yud Tav
Read Hebrew Letters Right to Left
Name Frequency Pronunciation
Nuh Yuh Tah

Death represents an ending of something which means something new is beginning. When you do not like the ending or even the new beginning, you label death bad. When my last aunt passed away it was the ending of her life on Earth, the ending of my physical time with her, but the beginning of her life in another plane of existence which meant a new way for me to communicate with her. I did not like her choice to leave, but it was not my place to try to stop her. I did not like the new beginnings for me although I knew she was ecstatic to be reunited with other family and friends who had passed over before her.

Death goes beyond the physical passing of someone. Anytime anything ends, it is a death. It can be the death of a friendship, the death of a business, the death of a dream. Endings always mean new beginnings even if at the moment you do not like either. When you do everything that you can to stop something from ending but it ends anyway, then this is a redirection from your Oversoul. Usually, the life force leaves long before you actually realize something is dying. Like a relationship, for example. You may be surprised when someone ends their relationship with you, yet most likely there were signs long before it happened.

When I had a group of friends leave me years ago, I was devastated. I did everything I could to try to save the relationships except compromise my morals and ethics. I finally had to admit it was over, but it did not lessen the hurt. Then, in the subsequent months that followed, I had other friends tell me that this group of friends had been talking behind my back for some time. The friendship had been dead for some time, only I didn't know it. Even though emotionally it took many years for me to heal, logically I could see that it was for the best. I did not like the ending and I did not like the new beginning without them.

I know people who have gone through the loss of their businesses. Death was not fun, yet once the business was gone new avenues opened which eventually brought them more personal fulfillment. Yes, there is correct death whether you like it or not.

You can pray to stop the death of anyone or anything, but you must always ask for the involved Oversouls and God-Mind to make the final decisions. As you already know, if you interfere with the lessons or paths of others, you will have a steep price to pay. Even when you do not want the death of any kind to happen, you must always acquiesce to the Higher Powers regardless of your pain and sorrow. As challenging as it was for me to let my aunt go, I know she was ecstatically happy. I am happy for her, sad for me. Life is full of these kinds of experiences. One door closes, another opens. This does not mean easy even if the door opening shows you the most correct and beneficial new beginning. Use this *Name Frequency* so only that which needs to die, dies as well as to direct you to your new beginning with clarity, wisdom and understanding.

- Is the Death of anything ever easy?
- Does Death always denote change?
- Does Death ever truly happen suddenly?
- When you see that Death is inevitable, how often have you fervently increased your prayers to stop it?
- Or, if you see a person or animal suffering, have you prayed for a correct Death?
- Even when you know that a relationship or a business is waning, is it challenging to ask that Death come quickly to end it?
- Have you prayed to save someone or something that you knew most likely would not make it?
- Is it challenging to trust that when one door closes another opens?
- How many times have you had new beginnings that you did not like?
- Is it easier to understand the logic behind Death than deal with your emotional upheaval?
- Have you been through Deaths that brought peace and relief?
- Do you have any circumstances now to which you could apply this *Name Frequency*?

Name Frequency #55

Actualize Ideas

Mem Bet Hey
Read Hebrew Letters Right to Left
Name Frequency Pronunciation
Meh Veh Heh

I am a person of action. When I make up my mind to do something, I do it. That is the way I like to think of my Self. I have learned that I really do not like to speak about my plans until they come to fruition. When you speak too soon, you dissipate the psychic energy necessary to actualize your ideas. This is where the saying, *all talk, no action* comes from. Or, you can spend so much time and energy dreaming about what you want to do someday, that someday never comes.

But, I also have a side that procrastinates. I have a lot of things that I need to do, but these are further down on my list of priorities. I like to wait until the need to do turns into a want to do. When I need to do something, I do not have the passion, so the task takes a lot longer. When I want to do something it is much easier, faster, and with better results. Turning what you need to do into what you want to do is a matter of aligning your needs and wants. This *Name Frequency* can help you do this.

Some people never start because if they never start they never fail. Of course, there really is no such thing as failure, only redirection. Sometimes the redirection produces a better result than if your original plan had succeeded. When I was learning to cook softshell crabs, I accidentally grabbed a bag of unmarked powdered sugar that was sitting next to my potato starch. I thought it had fallen out of the potato starch box. I seasoned it with salt, pepper, and other savory spices. While I was frying it, I thought it smelled sweet, so I tasted it. I was mortified, but it was obviously too late to change anything. So, I told Stewart that our crabs would have an "Asian flare". They were actually very good, although a bit too sweet for our tastes but now when I make the mix I add a tablespoon of sugar into it. This also helps them to brown and crisp better. If I hadn't made that gaffe I would not have been redirected to do this to my recipe. I have learned to not be afraid of failure because the important thing is to start and keep going, no matter how slow and/or awkward. Use this *Name Frequency* to Actualize Your Ideas.

- When you want to do something, are you challenged to get started?
- Are you afraid of failure or success?
- Why are people afraid of success?
- Have your failures ever turned out better than your original ideas?
- Is failure redirection?
- Do you procrastinate?

- Do you speak too much about your ideas, thus removing the energy to propel them forward?
- Is it easy to get lost in dreaming about your ideas without putting your thoughts into action?
- Why is action so important?
- Are tasks easier when what you need to do aligns with what you want to do?
- Do you pledge to start and keep going no matter how slow and/or awkward?
- If so, do you follow through with this pledge?

Name Frequency #56

Releasing Anger

Fey Vav Yud
Read Hebrew Letters Right to Left
Name Frequency Pronunciation
Feh Wah Yuh

I have been talking to you about releasing anger since Day 1. ***Decoding Your Life*** has tons of information to help you. As you know, anything on the negative side of the Red Frequency can easily control you before you can control it. This includes hate, resentment, bitterness, irritation, annoyance. Most people are filled with these emotions but have lived with them for so long they may not even recognize that they exist within. This is why it is so important to observe all that you think, say and do.

You can easily use the outer world as a reflection of what is within you. Everywhere you look, you see people expressing these negative qualities to some degree. Even justified or righteous anger is still anger.

Holding onto it in any way destroys your cellular structure. Lashing out at anyone or anything ensures that this is what is going to happen to you. What you give out comes back, always. All the negatives of the Red Frequency feed the adversary, making him/her/it stronger and stronger. If you feed it from your own negatives, you are helping to grow the very thing that you want to be destroyed.

The worst thing that you can do to your adversary is to give him/her Unconditional Love and Acceptance via the Oversoul level in the form of Pale Pink. Pouring Pale Pink onto your adversary is like pouring boiling oil onto a normal person. It is up to the involved Oversouls whether your adversary accepts or rejects it. In addition, because this is what you are giving, this is what will return to you. You always must ask your Oversoul and God-Mind what is most correct and beneficial for each situation. If by chance you are told to give out a negative Red Frequency it must be from a place of neutrality where you use the Frequency and it does not use you. To do this, you must come from a strong internal place, anchored deeply within your Oversoul and God-Mind. In the meantime, do your best to continue your release work. Using this *Name Frequency* is another layer that helps you remove all the excess negative Red Frequency that is no longer appropriate in your life.

- How long have you been removing excess Red Frequency?
- Are you surprised at how much is within?
- Which of the negative Red Frequency emotions are the most challenging to release?
- Are you challenged to not give negative energy to your adversaries?
- Are you mindful that what you give out comes back to you?
- Are you challenged to not allow your negative emotions to control you?

- Are you challenged to release your anger that you consider righteous and justified?
- Are righteous and justified anger judgments rather than observations?
- Do all adversaries exist for a reason?
- Do all adversaries come from the same Source as you and All That Exists?
- When you do not understand something is it easy to judge it?
- Must you always ask your Oversoul and God-Mind before you open your mouth or move your body?
- Are outer world circumstances bringing up your deep buried negative Red Frequencies that you perhaps thought you had vanquished?
- Do you need the negative Red Frequencies in your toolbox for when it is appropriate to use them?
- Have you used the negative Red Frequencies as tools without them using you?

Name Frequency #57

Soul Connection

Nun Mem Mem
Read Hebrew Letters Right to Left
Name Frequency Pronunciation
Nuh Meh Meh

Soul Connection is one of the foundational pieces of Hyperspace/Oversoul work. You can never not be connected to your Source. Illusion exists to make you think and feel separate. Conventional religions continually tell you that God is out there rather than in here. The reality is that God is everywhere.

There is not a spot where God is not.

I learned this in my church when I was little. I can remember being extremely challenged to realize that God was in a rock. I was a product of public school educational indoctrination where you are taught the difference between an animate and inanimate thing. I could easily identify with animate things having a Soul and God being there, but a rock was a bit beyond my child's mind comprehension. It is challenging for most people to realize that they are already connected and only need to be conscious of this. The Oversoul Matrix as presented in **Hyperspace Plus** book is an excellent visual to give you an idea of the depth and vastness of your inner connection to Source. Use this *Name Frequency* to continue opening your conscious connection to Source 24/7. Know that good can always get better.

- Are you aware of the depth and vastness of your Soul/Source connection?
- Is it challenging to think that there is not a spot where God is not?
- Do you have issues visualizing God in a rock or other objects you were taught were inanimate?
- Does programming teach you Separation of Soul and Source?
- Do education and conventional religion indoctrinate you with Separation of Soul and Source?
- How do you know that you are One with your Source at all times?

Name Frequency #58

Letting Go

Yud Yud Lamed
Read Hebrew Letters Right to Left
Name Frequency Pronunciation
Yuh Yuh Lah

Letting go is another foundational Hyperspace/Oversoul tool that hopefully you have been practicing since Day 1. This sounds like it should be easy, but it is not as easy as you would think. Most people are consciously eager to release their negative experiences, yet it is these negative experiences upon which people often build their lives and identity. I know from experience that releasing the negative is not as easy as it sounds. And, there are layers upon layers within layers of the same negative experiences that need to be sorted through, understood and lessons learned so that you can move on. Some negative experiences take many years of sorting to gain all the rich knowledge embedded therein.

Sometimes, you are so used to specific types of negative experiences that you do not even realize that they are negative. For example, you may use Self-deprecating language without realizing it. You may say:

I hate it when...

I don't have enough time...

I am so stupid...

I should have known better...

You most likely have and use many such negative terms when you refer to Self and your life experiences. This is just the beginning point of what needs to go. The minute you uncover one layer, another one pops up. You cannot take out all the negativity or you would be left without any foundation at all. In the same way, people do not want to release their positive experiences because fear tells them there might not be more to fill the space. Good can always get better, but for some reason, the majority of people seem to forget this. And even when you logically know this, emotionally you may still live in fear that nothing will ever fill the space.

Your emotions are always much more complex than you realize. You must do the inner level work to really understand and appreciate the process of letting go. This *Name Frequency* helps to pull up both the positive and negative so you can grow on into some bigger, better, and more magnificent on all levels of your Being. Do your best to also release impatience, because this is a process that allows you to create a new way of Being in a way that you can most comfortably handle in the midst of your discomfort. Letting go means change. Only you can determine your own process. Trust the pace set by your Oversoul and God-Mind. Do your best to stay motivated to keep going.

- How many years have you worked on letting go?
- Is it a much longer and more intense process than you first realized?

- Have you uncovered more depth within your experiences than you expected?
- Have you grown to appreciate your negative experiences more than you thought you ever would?
- Do you use Self-deprecating words?
- Are your thoughts filled with negative inner talk about you and your life?
- Have you built your life around your past identity?
- Do you view your past identity subjectively or objectively?
- Do you easily let go of positive experiences?
- Are you challenged to accept that good can get better?
- Do you trust the process of Source?
- Are you ready to claim the Magnificence of Your Being?
- Does Your Magnificence incorporate both positive and negative aspects of your Soul-Personality?

Name Frequency #59

Feeling Safe

Hey Resh Chet
Read Hebrew Letters Right to Left
Name Frequency Pronunciation
Heh Reh Cheh

Feeling safe comes from Trusting Source to take care of you at all times. This is truly challenging for most people because you are consistently pushed to Trust Source. No matter what happens, how others treat you, where you are, how much money you do or do not have, it is imperative that you anchor into Self, Oversoul and God-Mind. Most people have the trust beaten out of them either metaphorically or physically. Trusting the process is overwhelming because it is too easy to focus on the unknowns in negative ways. Knowing that whatever happens is most correct and beneficial and for your Highest Good is a strange concept that few can grasp. Animal

Mind consistently fears not having needs met for physical survival. Fear of not surviving is always present and a top priority.

When you understand the Oversoul Matrix as presented in ***Hyperspace Plus*** you realize that you are connected to your Oversoul multidimensionally. Life on Earth is an illusion built upon the 13x13x13 holographic matrix of this reality. As long as you are here, the illusion feels very, very real. This is the way it is supposed to be. But ultimately, there is never a time when you are not connected. You are always protected and watched over. Only your doubt makes you feel otherwise.

- Is it challenging to always feel safe?
- Is it easier to trust in outer methods of protection than inner ones?
- Is there a place and time for utilizing outer methods of protection?
- Is it easier to place your faith in what you can see vs. what you cannot see?
- Can you see your inner connections to Source?
- Does doubt serve a positive purpose?

Name Frequency #60

Freedom

Mem Tzadi Resh
Read Hebrew Letters Right to Left
Name Frequency Pronunciation
Meh Tzah Reh

Freedom means moving forward. Too often, when you break out of where you were, you expect the next level to give you more freedom. Well, you are correct, you do have more freedom but you also have more Self-responsibility. I have heard so many people talk about childhood and how it was a simpler time, therefore they wish they were this age or that age instead of their current age. As you know, every age and stage in life has its challenges. No matter where you were or how wonderful it was, there were challenges. When people get stressed they want to go back to what they know.

I have also questioned many of my life decisions at various times. When I was most uncomfortable was when I most wanted to go back to the old ways even though I knew the old ways were not that great. And, once you leave the old ways you really cannot return because you are now a different person. It is challenging when you are not in the new, you are out of the old and you are somewhere in between. I wrote about this in **Decoding Your Life**. Many people feel like this right now. I know one of my pleasures in life that gave me a bit of change was going out to eat once or twice a month. When you work from home you never get away from your work. There are many days when I wish I could go out to dinner, which is my old way. The new way says if you do go out, you have to wear a mask, everyone around you has to wear a mask, the servers have to wear a mask and I do not want to do this. One of the rules at one of my favorite restaurants says you have to keep your mask on at the table until your food arrives. Not fun or relaxing! I am waiting for this idiocy to settle down. The old way isn't working and the new way isn't working for me, so I am in between.

Anytime the honeymoon period wears off of any new venture, you begin to question if you did the correct thing. In the beginning, you may be so enamored that you only see the positive. But as time goes on, the negatives are going to pop up. The adjustment period can be extremely uncomfortable. This is when you want to go back, even when it is not possible. These are all emotionally challenging places to be. Freedom is wonderful, but there is always a price. The price for freedom is Self-responsibility. Sometimes I have wished I had someone to make decisions for me and take care of all my responsibilities. But if this did happen, I would be on the other side of the fence wishing I could take care of my Self and my own responsibilities. Use this *Name Frequency* to help you adjust from one level of Being to another. Like all things, there are 2 sides to every coin.

- Do you sometimes wish that you had someone to make your decisions and take the responsibilities off of you?
- Do you think ultimately you would resent someone like this?

- Do you want to be in charge of you or do you want someone else to be in charge of you?
- Is there always an adjustment period when you move from one level of Being to another?
- Have you made a forward moving change, only to question what you did?
- Did you have a honeymoon period first, where everything was wonderful?
- How long did it take for the reality of your decisions to come to you?
- Whenever the new ways stress you, is there the desire to revert to the old ways?
- Have you ever thought, "What have I done"?
- Have you ever tried to go back?
- If so, how did this work for you?
- Have you ever wished to return to a different age and stage in your life?
- Is this a realistic thought?
- Does Freedom always bring more Self-responsibility?

Name Frequency #61

Emotions

Vav Mem Bet
Read Hebrew Letters Right to Left
Name Frequency Pronunciation
Wah Meh Veh

Because in physical reality emotions are symbolically represented by water, you can use this *Name Frequency* to help correct the water/emotions within Self as well as the water/emotions of the World. Water is necessary for all life forms. Frozen water, ice, is classified as a mineral. Water comprises over 65% of the human body. When I was farming, water rights for irrigation purposes was a huge issue. In the Columbia Basin in Washington State, every piece of farmland had the right to a certain amount of cubic feet of water. Irrigation ditches traversed the Columbia Basin paralleled by dirt roads. Every day, I put my water order in a glass jar next to the outlet for my farm. The ditch rider, as he was called, picked up the card and opened the locked water gate to disperse the water allocation. If that water was used up for the season, you had to buy extra water that someone else had not used, if it was available. Maintaining the irrigation district was a major operation. Even then, farmers said that one day water rights would be a global issue, which it definitely has become. Since that time, water rights have definitely grown in complexity.

Although I have only consumed steam-distilled water for decades, most people did not think of purchasing any kind of bottled water at that time. Now, purchasing bottled water is the norm for many people. However, even bottled water has a variety of additives so you have to be careful what you buy. Clean drinking water has always been an issue and continues to grow. Some people walk long distances for drinking water. Once I saw an extremely interesting video on social media where two young boys in an African country actually went to a dirty river, got water, and then set up their own filtration system using sticks and stones. The result after only a few minutes was clear, clean drinking water.

The best water I have ever had was in the Cottian Alps where my family lives in Italy. When I drink that water I truly feel like every layer of my body is being purged of negative emotions. This makes sense because water represents emotions. The purer the water intake, the more your body can purge of its toxins. My cousin's father even said that their water makes you urinate more. My cousins do not want to drink water from the ground, only from the mountains. They even haul their drinking water from their high mountain home to their lower mountain home. That is how important their water is to them.

The water in your body is imprinted with your thoughts, words and actions. This is why sometimes when you listen to music the song plays repeatedly in your head. The sound waves are replicating through your body. With this in mind, think of the global noises that are imprinted upon all bodies of water and the impact of this imprinting throughout the world. The outpouring of humanity's emotions have imprinted the water in ways that are not always positive.

Kabbalah says that water can heal, rejuvenate and is the secret to immortality. Use this *Name Frequency* to help correct the water/emotions within Self as well as the water/emotions of the World.

- Is it odd to think that water has a specific taste?
- In general, can you describe the taste of water?
- Where did you taste the best water?
- Where did you taste the worst water?
- Are fluoride, chlorine, and other water additives necessary?
- Did you know that ice is considered a mineral?
- Have you had songs repeat in your head?
- Or been to a live concert where you can feel the music in your body?
- Have you felt the music in your body long after you left the concert?
- What is the mind-pattern of people who attract dirty drinking water?
- Could the solution to dirty drinking water be as easy as a few sticks and stones placed in the correct way?
- What is the mind-pattern for people who have limited access to drinking water?
- Why are water rights such an issue?
- Why are people attracted to bodies of water such as streams, rivers, ponds, lakes, oceans?
- Why are some people frightened of bodies of water?
- Why do people feel compelled to look at or swim in water?
- Why do some people feel like they will drown if they go into the water?

Name Frequency #62

Living Example

Yud Hey Hey
Read Hebrew Letters Right to Left
Name Frequency Pronunciation
Yuh Heh Heh

You are a living example. What you are a living example of is up to you. I have met many people who make me grateful that I am not like them. These kinds of people inspire me to change my ways because I do not want to be like them. I do my best not to judge them, but to observe and be grateful because *there but for the Grace of God, go I.*

I used to love to help everyone any chance I could. I felt my mission was to share what I knew so that we could all grow together. I wanted to be a positive example that inspired others. But I found out that most people lose interest after your first few sentences. They do not want to be told what to do. So, I learned to keep quiet until someone started asking questions. Then I was thrilled to tell all I knew. Again, this overwhelmed people so I had to take another step back. I learned to really listen to what the person was asking and then not give too much information in answer to their questions. Now, I am not that eager to tell what I know. I try to say the most salient points as succinctly as possible. Of course, I do know that I am a living example. However, this is still subject to interpretation by the people with whom you interact. Regardless of how you are, others will put their own perceptions onto and into you. Ultimately most people want to be their own teachers.

Even if you barrage someone with questions, your goal is still to experience for your Self, not live through someone else's experiences. Those who want to live through you are afraid of either failure or success. Emotions are complex. No matter how much you want to help others, the best way to do this is by helping your Self. Be a living example of upliftment and elevation in every way you know how. Use this *Name Frequency* to positively enhance Your Living Example.

- Do you think of your Self as a Living Example?
- Of what are you a living example?'
- Do you teach because you exist?
- Do you teach others how they want to learn?
- Do you teach others how you want them to learn?
- Are you excited to share what you know?
- Do you feel dejected or rejected when others do not really care about what you share?
- Does every person want Self-experience?
- Are some people afraid of success and failure?
- Do you demonstrate what you know by Being?
- Have you been inspired to change your negative ways because of an example by another person?

- Has what you wanted to share and how you share changed through the years?

Name Frequency #63

Appreciation

Ayin Nun Vav
Read Hebrew Letters Right to Left
Name Frequency Pronunciation
Aye Nuh Wah

An attitude of gratitude is paramount to progressing in any area of your life. Yet, I know when you are thinking about where you want to be vs. where you are, it can be challenging to be appreciative of current circumstances. Sometimes when I get depressed, I start making mental lists of everything for which I am grateful. I am truly amazed at how much I have to be grateful for that is so easy to take for granted. I have a home, food, water, employment, family, pets, health and my list expands from here. This helps to put my life in perspective as well as keep me focused in the *Eternal Now*.

There is a very clever parable that I want to share with you:

There was once a man with a large family and a very small house. He decided to ask the village wise man what to do. The wise man said:

Move your cow into the house.

The man was surprised, but because he believed in the wise man, he moved the cow into the house. Now, the house was more crowded, so the man went back to the wise man to report this. The wise man said:

Move your horse into the house.

The man was incredulous at this piece of advice, but he went back home and moved the horse in, which did not improve the situation. So, he went back to ask the wise man what to do. The wise man said:

Move your chickens into the house.

Even though the man was puzzled, he went back home and moved his flock of chickens into the house. The man was becoming desperate so once again he went back to the wise man to ask him what to do. The wise man said:

Move all of your animals out of the house.

The man rushed home, moved all of the animals out, and could not believe how much room was in the house. Now, he was appreciative of the size of his home.

Most people most of the time do not realize what they have. Therefore, they focus on what they do not have rather than be appreciative and grateful for current circumstances. Here is another example of being grateful for what you have:

A man with an old car wishes for a new car.

A man with a bicycle wishes for any car.

A man who is walking wishes he had a bicycle.

A man in a wheelchair wishes he could walk.

This *Name Frequency* helps you focus on what you have in this moment. Once you appreciate this moment and everything within it, then you are prepared for the next moment.

- Do you ever feel distraught about what you do not have?
- Do you worry that you will be stuck in the present moment forever?
- When you live in the *Eternal Now*, is each moment forever?
- Do you remember that you are unique?
- Is it easy to try to compare your life to others?
- Can you name 10 things for which you are grateful, and then another 10 and another 10, and keep going?
- Does this easy exercise make you feel even a little better?
- Is it easy to take some things for granted until they are gone?
- Is it true that sometimes you do not know what you have until it is gone?
- Does being appreciative help hold and increase the positive in your life?

Name Frequency #64

Appropriate Influences

Mem Chet Yud
Read Hebrew Letters Right to Left
Name Frequency Pronunciation
Meh Cheh Yuh

Objectively Observing Self is a challenge for most people because Objective Observing means moving through your perceptions and illusions into what actually is. The further removed someone or something is from you the more objective you can be. For example, it is much easier to be objective about a stranger down the road who you do not know well than someone living in your own household. This is why I have an entire chapter on Objective Observing in *Decoding Your Life*.

The more you know about the *72 Name of God* Frequencies, the more you understand why the basics are so important. You must know the basics to get the most correct and beneficial results from these

Name Frequencies. Like anything else, you can force results, but forcing results means you are playing God and there are negative consequences for such actions. Never neglect your foundational basics because these are the Spiritual Laws upon which other Spiritual Laws are built. Just like in the study of Mathematics. If you do not get your foundational math, you are going to be lost the further you go until one day, you just give up. Do your best to not get your Self in this position.

When you Objectively Observe Self you find that some areas are not as bad as you thought they were and some areas are not as great as you thought they were. You might love your voice, for example, but your voice may be full of anger. You can become so accustomed to hearing it that you cannot hear any anger in your voice. Others may definitely hear this and think of you as an angry person even if you do not. You might dislike your eyes, thinking that they are too wide-set or too narrow-set, but others may think you have beautiful eyes. These are simple examples, but, you interact with hundreds and perhaps even thousands of people every year who are going to perceive you according to their illusions vs. who/what you really are. They do not have a clue how to Objectively Observe.

When people know your negative qualities, they can use them against you. Even your Positive qualities can be seen as weaknesses. I have had many con artists cause a lot of problems because they take advantage of my kindness. I have had to learn to strengthen my boundaries. Sometimes you need more tough boundaries than kind boundaries. There are so many fine nuances to use this *Name Frequency* of Appropriate Influence. There are some people that need to see you as tough; others need to see you as gentle and kind. Because you do not know what influences their behavior or their goals and agendas, it is important that you ask your Oversoul and God-Mind to Appropriately Influence them in the way that is most correct and beneficial for all.

- Is it challenging to present your Self in a way that is correct and beneficial for all persons involved?
- Is it always best to be who you are?
- Do you practice Objective Observing of others and Self?
- Can you Objectively Observe others easier than Self?
- Do you know your positives and negatives?
- If you are still learning about Self, can you expect others to know you as you are?
- Can others sometimes see what is within you that you cannot yet see or have the courage to acknowledge, both positive and negative?
- Do you ask your Oversoul and God-Mind to Appropriately Influence others to see you in the way that is most correct and beneficial?
- Do you try to hide your negative qualities?
- Is negative bad?
- Is being tough bad?
- Is kindness good?
- Is being kind always good?
- How challenging is it to know others with whom you interact?
- Do you communicate via the Oversoul level with others?
- Even with all you know, can Oversoul communication be a challenge to interpret?
- Regardless of everything you know and do, when you are supposed to experience something, is it going to happen whether you want it to happen or not?

Name Frequency #65

Acute Observation

Dalet Mem Bet
Read Hebrew Letters Right to Left
Name Frequency Pronunciation
Dah Meh Veh

I once told someone that he had made an astute observation. He then asked if this was good or bad. Acute is another word for astute, both meaning a very perceptive observation, so yes, both words are positives. Observing without judgment is mandatory. The more details you objectively observe, the more perceptive your conclusions. For example, you can objectively observe that a person sitting alone on a park bench. In addition, if you observe that the person is wearing a heavy coat, hat and gloves you know that it is cold out. You may observe that the person is drinking a hot liquid from a cup. If you observe a brand name on the cup, you may be able to identify what the person is drinking. If the person has a dog on a leash sitting by him/her, you know that the person likes dogs. By the breed of dog and its appearance, you can tell more about the person's personality. The more details you objectively observe, the more you know about the person sitting on the bench. This does not imply any judgment.

When I was growing up, I was taught in my church that "God is Love" and to see the God in everyone. I was very puzzled as I reached adulthood why, even when I saw what I knew to be the God in everyone, everyone did not respond likewise. This led to my eventual conclusion that God is everything, which means negative as well as positive. Once I understood this, I had coping skills. When I was the Director of a small art gallery, a customer asked me what church I attended. When I replied that I did not go to church, he said, "Aren't you afraid you're going to die?" This answer shocked me. His implication was that without going to church, I was going to hell. I do not remember my response, I only remember that I was incredulous that someone would only go to church because he/she thought this was the way to escape hell.

I do not fear God. I do not fear my Self. I do not do what is morally correct because I am afraid of negative consequences. I have learned through the years that some people do fear God, they fear Self, they do what is morally correct because they fear negative consequences. This *Name Frequency* can help you with all of these conundrums by helping you Acutely Observe Self and others.

- Do you fear God?
- Do you fear Self?
- Do you do what is morally correct because you fear negative consequences?
- Is Objective Observation a skill?
- Is Acute Observation another skill level of Objective Observation?
- Can others use Acute Observation of you to your detriment?

- Can you see the positive aspects of God in everyone?
- Can you always treat someone as if the positive aspects of God are shining through them?
- Do you sometimes "cast your pearls before swine"?
- Why is it important to always practice Acute Observation under the direction of your Oversoul and God-Mind?

Name Frequency #66

Self-Responsibility

Mem Nun Kuf
Read Hebrew Letters Right to Left
Name Frequency Pronunciation
Meh Nuh Kuh

No matter what is going on in the world, no one can ever do anything to you unless there is something within that attracts the experience. This can be an extremely challenging concept because most people hold the mind-pattern of victim mentality. You have to put something out somewhere, some way for something to come back to you. This means both positive and negative experiences.

This was a challenging lesson for me. I used to think that if I treated someone kindly and with respect, the same thing would come back. Through the years I realized that not everyone can accept kindness and respect. And there are those people who perceive these qualities as weaknesses, so they take advantage of you. Instead of reacting surprised and overwhelmed when negative experiences come my way, I do my best to sort out what I did to attract such an experience. Negative experiences always push me to stretch further and deeper so I can understand. These can be really tough lessons but ones that you do not forget.

Blaming others is not taking responsibility for your part. Many legal battles happen because one side is so busy accusing the other that no one takes any accountability. This means that the only ones who really win are the attorneys whose fees mount the more each side fights with the other. Sometimes you may want to end an interpersonal quarrel but the other side does not. You must then determine how you are holding on. When you let go, the situation goes away because then there are no matching Color, Tone, or Archetypes. Again, more challenges. This can be especially frustrating when you are applying all your Hyperspace/Oversoul tools and nothing seems to be what you need. Use this *Name Frequency* to help clarify what is within the situation that reflects you and you need to learn, take responsibility, and move on without self-pity or thoughts of revenge.

- Have you wanted to emotionally move on but you could not let go?
- Or, it seems someone else could not let go?
- Can it be challenging to determine where you are holding on when you think you have let go?
- Have you ever been involved in a legal battle that you wished had never started?
- Can attorneys feed negative situations so much that determining an equitable answer is nearly impossible?
- When things are not going your way is it challenging to look inside?
- Is it easier to see what the other person did than what you did?

- Do negative experiences push you to stretch further?
- When you give out kindness and generosity do you expect these to be well received?
- Can others see these as weaknesses, thus try to take advantage of you?
- Sometimes do you blame others even when you know better?
- Are you sometimes challenged to find your victim-mentality mind-pattern that contributed to negative experiences?
- Do you do your best to be Self-responsible 24/7?

Name Frequency #67

Eternal Now

Aleph Yud Ayin
Read Hebrew Letters Right to Left
Name Frequency Pronunciation
Ah Yuh Aye

Time is elusive for most people. When you are having a fantastic time, hours turn into minutes and seconds; time flies. When you are having a miserable time, minutes and seconds turn into hours; time slows down. When you want something to happen, sometimes it seems the more time you invest the further away your goal becomes. Focusing on the linear future takes your focus off the present moment. It is always your present moment that is the key to optimizing your life.

This is another extremely challenging concept because it is too easy to focus on the goal instead of the process. The goal is something that has not happened in linear time. The process is right now. What happens right now determines if your goal even stays the same or changes. The process can change you, thus your goal changes. I have long given up my expectations of others, what life is or isn't as well as what I should or should not get from life. Rarely has anything ever turned out as I expected in the way I expected. I am most satisfied when I keep my focus in the *Eternal Now*, doing what I know to do in the moment and allowing my life plan to reveal itself.

In the meantime, I do everything that I can to the best of my ability, extracting as much learning and meaning from every second of my life. I also do my best to give every second equal importance I know that what I do in this second determines the next second. I proactively make each second the best second of my life. Use this *Name Frequency* to bring your focus into the *Eternal Now* and to give more meaning to each second of your personal process.

- How challenging is it to live life without grandiose expectations?
- If you take away grandiose expectations, do you deflate disappointment?
- How challenging is it to give every second of your life meaning?
- Do you live every second to the best of your ability?
- Have you ever reached your goals in the way and timing you expected?
- Does the process change you?
- Have you changed your goals because of the process?
- Or reached your goal and because you changed, the goal was not that satisfying?
- Do you expect too much from others, only to be disappointed in them?
- Do you expect too much from your Self?

- Do you live in the linear future instead of the *Eternal Now*?
- Do you have Soul-satisfaction and meaning in your process?

Name Frequency #68

Contacting the Departed

Chet Bet Vav
Read Hebrew Letters Right to Left
Name Frequency Pronunciation
Cheh Veh Wah

There are many methodologies for contacting those people who have passed on. *The Healers' Handbook* has several such methods listed. This *Name Frequency* can be used in conjunction with those methods, or on its own. What is most important is that you stay in heavy protection firmly anchored in your Source at all times. There are always departed souls vying for attention from those who can hear or see them. Often, these are tortured souls who have unfinished business on the Earth plane and are therefore reluctant or unable to move on. Many such souls will seek your help, but this may not be to your benefit.

In addition, there are such tortured souls as well as astral entities and demonic forces that pretend to be your loved ones. This is another reason why it is especially important to stay in heavy protection if you use any of these methodologies. You know to flush them in Pale Orange to bring out the truth, as well as Violet, Silver and Gold. Anyone or thing of a lower frequency level cannot handle these higher frequency colors.

You can use this *Name Frequency* when you pray for those who have passed on as well as if you want to contact them. When you ask via the Oversoul level if the time is correct to connect with them, be careful with the answer that you receive. While time is different in other dimensions, your loved ones may be busy or they may have another incarnation. You can, however, always contact them via the Oversoul level. You may have to wait for an answer, but this technique will always ensure your safety, which is paramount. Use this *Name Frequency* for additional protection and to send messages to those who have passed on.

- Just because you can do something, does this make it correct to do it?
- Must you always be wise with your inner level work?
- Is it easy to be tempted to go into dangerous territory?
- Without proper instruction can it be challenging to know what is dangerous territory?
- Does wanting to connect with the departed sound innocent?
- Are there people in body who take advantage of the innocence of others?
- Do those people change when they no longer have a body?
- Did you know that some Black Lives Matter founders invoke the souls of the departed to work through the living to get what they feel is justice?

- Have you had communications with departed loved ones?
- How did you know that these souls were who they said they were?
- Who initiated contact, you or them?
- Have you had departed loved ones contact you in the dream state while you were sleeping?
- Is it always challenging when loved ones pass on?
- What, if anything, provides you with comfort?
- Is it easy for charlatans to take advantage of grief-stricken family and friends of the departed?
- Do you keep your protection in place 24/7?

Name Frequency #69

Spiritual Direction

Resh Aleph Hey
Read Hebrew Letters Right to Left
Name Frequency Pronunciation
Reh Ah Heh

Losing your Spiritual Direction is common. There are so many distractions along the way, you may question the existence of God or perhaps stop believing in God altogether. This may seem like a huge negative but it is the negative that makes you question so you can refine and redefine where you are and what your Source is. When I questioned why seeing the good in others did not actualize the good in them, I was given another layer of information telling me that God contains all things, which means negative as well as positive. This was an eye opener for me, which definitely broadened my Spiritual knowledge and understanding. When things did not seem to be going the way I wanted, I questioned my Spiritual work to determine if there was something else that I wanted to do. Regardless of how much I pondered, I always came back to yes, this is my purpose. There is no one else doing what I am doing in the way I am doing it.

Sometimes people fall into deep temptation like discussed in the *Addictions* chapter of our **Alternative Medical Apocrypha** book. This does not make you a bad person, but it does show you your weaknesses. When people get far enough down, they often turn to their Source to guide them out. When you do get out, you have another set of vast knowledge that you can build on as well as help others who may have the same or similar weaknesses. Nothing is ever wasted within the Mind of God. Use this *Name Frequency* to help guide you deeper into Source, so that you set your foot on the correct path for you. When you feel lost, this frequency shows you the way.

- Have you ever lost your Spiritual Direction?
- Have you questioned long held beliefs?
- Have you questioned the existence of God?
- Have negative experiences put you on a deeper, more positive path?
- Have you fallen into deep temptation which you feel led you away from God?
- If so, what or who pulled you out?
- Can your most negative experiences be the impetus for your most positive experiences to begin?
- Do you know that nothing is ever wasted within the Mind of God?

Name Frequency #70

Finding Direction & Movement

Yud Bet Mem
Read Hebrew Letters Right to Left
Name Frequency Pronunciation
Yuh Veh Meh

As you are already learning in your Hyperspace/Oversoul work, chaos is only order not yet understood. There is always something in your mind-pattern that is chaotic to attract chaos in the outer world. Often, chaos is a positive sign that something is moving. Movement is always a positive even if it is uncomfortable. God-Mind is never stagnant so as long as you are moving somehow, someway you are working on some part of Self.

When you clean out any area of your home, the room, closet or cabinet can look quite chaotic as everything is moving around, coming out, being discarded, upgraded and replaced. When we redid our kitchen it was total chaos that lasted for months longer than we anticipated. But as the kitchen proactively fell apart, we discovered many areas that were connected that also needed to be upgraded and replaced such as plumbing, wiring, venting and more. The more work we did, the more revealed itself. We were grateful that we had an excellent contractor who was willing and able to correct the errors. It was a slow process and frustrating at times, but worth the effort. Much of what was completed will never be seen by anyone, but how we feel inside is priceless. Just like after you clean and organize a cabinet or a closet. No one really ever sees it but you, yet you feel so great even when the doors to the cabinet and closets are closed. You feel the difference between order and chaos.

We recently had some shelving put in our furnace room as well as a janitor's sink. This allowed us to get everything that was piled up on the floor onto shelving so we could get to what we need. Of course in the process, we tossed many things that we do not use and yes, the corners of this room were filthy! We even uncovered a dead mouse! No one but us ever goes into that room but knowing that it is in order makes me feel wonderful. I did not know the corners were so filthy or that there was a dead mouse there. Now that I know, emotionally I feel so grateful to have this room cleaned up. Your home represents you. When your home is in chaos, you are in chaos. Many people keep the inside of their cars in chaos. Your car represents your path in life. If your car is in chaos then your path in life is in chaos. You need to find the order in your emotional, mental, Spiritual and physical chaos to create a smoother flow of existence for the totality of your Being. This *Name Frequency* will help aid in the process.

- Is it challenging to always remember that chaos is only order not yet understood?
- Do you have chaos in your car?
- In your cabinets, closets and drawers?
- Can you have chaos without dirt and filth?

- Do you have mental, emotional, Spiritual and physical chaos?
- Are you a slave to chaos?
- How are you proactively eliminating chaos from your life?
- Does chaos overwhelm you?
- Can you bring order to chaos one tiny, tiny step at a time?
- What happens to chaos if you never begin to organize it?
- Will it dissipate on its own?
- Will you be forced to reactively deal with it?
- Are health issues that are left too long the result of chaos?
- Are financial issues the result of chaos?
- Are relationship issues the result of chaos?
- What can you do right now, today to begin to establish order out of chaos?

Name Frequency #71

Simultaneity

Hey Yud Yud
Read Hebrew Letters Right to Left
Name Frequency Pronunciation
Heh Yuh Yuh

There is a reason why you are here and not there, wherever there may be in your mind. Because you are a multidimensional Being, technically you already exist wherever your mind goes. But, because you are here, this is where your focus needs to be. In other words, there is one aspect of your Soul-Personality focused in this reality, giving you the illusion of a life stream here. Your Hyperspace/Oversoul work teaches you to focus here, so that as you do your mental work, you move your consciousness wherever it needs to be. Yet, you have a point of return. Without that point of return, you would literally be crazy.

Mind-altering substances unbutton you from your physical body so that you have no point of reference. Some people never recover. Their bodies are here but their minds are locked somewhere in the space/time continuum without a way for them to return. You can also become unbuttoned from your physical body via a severe accident, trauma, illness, and programming as well as demonic/astral attachment and/or possession. Flushing the physical body with White Light can unbutton you from your Chakra Band System, which is why when people are close to physical death they often have White energy fields.

The *Eternal Now* holds all of your existences simultaneously, but this does not mean that it is mentally healthy to access them all at once. There is a reason your Soul chose to focus on this life stream in this moment, exactly as it is. Some people want to know their linear future so they become obsessed with tomorrow instead of today. Yes, you can look at your tomorrow but this may put more stress on what you do today. As you develop your appreciation for the *Eternal Now*, then you may be more prepared for the linear future. On some level, you already know. It is a kindness to not know the negatives in advance as well as the positives. Even the positives may scare the part of you with low Self-Worth/Value. This means that you could sabotage the positives and prevent them from ever actualizing. Being aware of simultaneity helps you expand your knowledge of what is a Soul. Use this *Name Frequency* for Self-education, but be careful of what you ask for; always use protection, do your basic preliminaries and ask your Oversoul and God-Mind for guidance.

- How important is it to understand Simultaneity?
- Have you had experiences that opened your eyes to Simultaneity?
- Does the concept of Simultaneity continue to expand your knowledge of what is a Soul?

- Do other life streams in other existences influence you both positively and negatively?
- Why do people want to know their linear future?
- Is it a kindness to not know the future?
- How do you keep your Self buttoned into your physical body?
- Is it challenging to think of your life stream as an illusion?

Name Frequency #72

Spiritual Cleansing

Mem Vav Mem
Read Hebrew Letters Right to Left
Name Frequency Pronunciation
Meh Wah Meh

This *Name Frequency* goes right along with the **Healing Past Spirituality Affirmations**. You are such a conglomeration of so many influences that you can be challenged to sort your current Spiritual Belief System. It is important to merge the best and release the rest. When you do not know exactly what to do, you can use the visualization of *Merging with Aspects of Alternative Selves* from **Healing Archetypes and Symbols** page 46, to pull into this physical reality traits and characteristics from your alternative realities as well as to bring current goals to fruition by merging with your Self in the *Eternal Now*. As you are working with these concepts, it is important that you continue your release work to let go of old ways that prevented you from spiritually growing as well as clean up your thoughts, words, and actions that were counterproductive and even harmful to your Self and/or others. Include your forgiveness work, asking any person, place or thing that you knowingly or unknowingly harmed to forgive you via the Oversoul level. Use this *Name Frequency* to clean up and heal your past as well as the present. This sets you up for a clean and clear linear future.

- Do you know what the best parts of you are in this lifeline?
- Can you ask for the best parts of you in other lifelines to merge into this one?
- Sometimes is it challenging to sort out the old spiritual belief systems from where you are now?
- Can it be challenging to know what your spiritual goals are?
- Can you unknowingly harm others?
- Can others unknowingly harm you?
- Are you consistent with your forgiveness and release work?
- Have you asked your Oversoul to merge the best and release the rest?
- Are you ready to accept a clean and clear linear future?

AFFIRMATIONS—FREQUENCY

You already process frequency on every level of your Being. With awareness you can learn to focus in on specific frequencies or tune out specific frequencies, just like tuning into a specific channel/frequency on a radio. Working with your Oversoul becomes easier and clearer as you deepen your ability to know by knowing.

I AM consciously aware of more than I realize.
I slow down my conscious awareness.

I AM always anchored in my Oversoul and God-Mind.
I AM always connected to Source.

I feel the difference between my Soul and my body.
I feel my Oversoul and Source pulsing through my Soul.

I feel the frequencies in my energy field.
I feel what is me and what is not me.

I breathe my Self into my Center.
With my mind, I create a Violet bubble around All That I AM.

With my mind, I create a mirror on the outside of my Violet bubble.
I breathe my Self into my Center and exhale up to my Oversoul all that I no longer need.

Within my Violet bubble, I differentiate what is me and what is not me.
I know what I feel like.

I release all that is not me up to my Oversoul to give to the Oversoul of the owner of these frequencies.
I AM clean and clear within my Violet bubble.

I know my own colors, tones and archetypes within my Violet bubble.
I follow my own colors, tones and archetypes deeper into Me.

I immediately identify anything that slips into my Violet bubble that is not me.
I immediately fortify my inner and outer security.

Via the Oversoul level, I consciously explore frequency.
Via the Oversoul level, I AM connected to All That Is.

My Oversoul directs my Frequency exploration.
My Oversoul opens and closes doors as is appropriate.

I accept the decisions of my Oversoul.
When doors close, I search for the open doors.

I AM already in a constant state of knowing by knowing.
I know which doors to enter.

I use my knowledge wisely.
I know that I AM always Source-connected.

I release my need to be disappointed.
I accept the knowing of my Source.

I trust the plan.
I release the need to know the entire plan.

I know that one step takes me to my next step.
I trust that I know what I need each step of the way.

I follow the frequencies of the open doors.
I AM always guided by the frequency of my Soul Parent.

Every issue is already resolved on the Soul Level.
There is a reason why I know what I know on the human level.

My focus in the Eternal Now keeps me calm.
I trust in the process of my Soul-Parent.

I always know the frequency that my Soul-Parent casts for me.
I know when I am on frequency and when I am off frequency.

My Soul-Parent explains to me on a need-to-know basis.
I trust the decisions of my Soul Parent.

I release the need to try to control the decisions of my Soul-Parent.
I accept all decisions of my Soul-Parent whether I like them or not.

I do my best to follow the wishes of my Soul-Parent.
I easily identify the frequencies of what is most correct and beneficial.

I release the urge to do what I want to do without Soul-Parent permission.
I always ask Soul-Parent permission before I open my mouth or move my body.

I know by knowing in less than a blink of an eye.
I AM safe and protected when I trust the plan of my Soul-Parent.

I recognize that Soul-Parent always sees the bigger picture.

I AM grateful to be focused on my portion of the bigger picture.

All That Exists Is Frequency.

I always know what I need to know.

My ability to know by knowing deepens.

My conscious Source connections grows exponentially.

Kabbalah

You now know that the *72 **Names of God*** each are specific frequencies. These come from the 3 ***Bible*** verses in the ***Torah*** about the *Reed Sea* in *Exodus*. Technically, the entire ***Torah*** is considered the *Name of God*. Yes, all 304,805 letters of the ***Torah***. This is why you cannot say the *Name of God*; you cannot say 304,805 letters all at the same time! This is also why some people use the 4 letter *Name of God*. This 4-letter *Name of God* represents the 304,805 letters of the ***Torah*** all strung together without spaces. This 4-Letter *Name of God* is generally just called "The Name".

Hebrew Letters Right to Left Yud Hey Vav Hey

English Letters Y H V H

Name Frequency Pronunciation Yahweh or Hahvahyah

This 4-letter *Name of God* is also known as the Tetragrammaton. Each of the 4 letters are meaningful because each is related to the verb "to be". YHVH ultimately means that God was, is and will be.

In a synagogue the ***Torah*** is kept in a special cabinet called an Ark. Inside the Ark is the ***Torah*** with a special covering. It is considered an honor to be allowed to remove the ***Torah*** from the Ark, which is then usually carried through the congregation while songs are sung. The congregants may not directly touch the ***Torah*** but may use a scarf or prayer shawl to touch the ***Torah***. Then the scarf/shawl is taken to your lips to receive the blessing of the ***Torah***.

Next, the covering from the ***Torah*** is removed and laid on a special platform in the front of the synagogue, where it is unrolled by touching the wooden dowels upon which it is rolled. The ***Torah*** is never touched. When reading, a special pointer stick is used by the reader to keep his/her place. The ***Torah*** is meant to be sung rather than read. If a ***Torah*** becomes damaged in any way, it is no longer considered viable as the complete *Name of God*, so it must be buried with proper prayers. You may have seen God written as "G-d" to represent the *Name of God*. Anything with God's Name written out in any way is considered a Holy Object and therefore must be properly disposed of according to Jewish Law, which is by burial.

- Did you realize that the ***Torah*** is considered the complete *Name of God*?
- Do you think Holy Objects should be treated differently than other objects?
- If everything comes from One Source, ultimately is everything Holy?
- What do you think is the reason behind specific rituals at specific times on specific days?

- Do rituals help to align energies/frequencies?
- What makes the Hebrew letters important archetypes?

The Original ***Bible***, the ***Torah***, also known as the *5 Books of Moses* is a code for life, not a religion, and was given/revealed/transmitted to Moses approximately 3600 years ago. The oral ***Zohar/Book of Splendor*** was revealed to a Rabbi approximately 2000 years ago and is said to be the Soul of the ***Bible/Torah***.

The Original ***Bible/Torah*** was written in what is now called Biblical Hebrew. Translating from Hebrew to English is difficult. Plus, you will find a difference between Modern Hebrew and Biblical Hebrew. Knowing and understanding the Hebrew AlephBet will aid your study and application of these Archetypes including the Sounds of Creation.

The ***Torah*** was written without vowels or punctuation. The vowels were understood, but because of the disbursement of the Jews, the written pronunciations of the Biblical Hebrew became forgotten and lost. This was a challenging concept for me until I read an article where someone demonstrated the principle in a way that I could understand. For example, you can probably read the following sentence without vowels; the vowels are understood:

Th bk ws lng wth mny pgs bt th stry ws xcllnt.

Translation:

The book was long with many pages but the story was excellent.

However, if you did not know the language the consonants would most likely not be enough to help you understand the words. If someone did this with Italian, I know I would not be able to fill in the vowels. I would definitely need some help! The vowel notations in the section following the Hebrew Letters were added much later to help the Jews read their all but lost and forgotten language.

The Hebrew Letters

Name	Form	Sound	Numerical Value
Aleph	א	silent	1
Beis	בּ	b	2
Veis	ב	v	2
Gimel	ג	g	3
Dalet	ד	d	4
Hay	ה	h	5
Vav	ו	v[1] or oo	6
Zayin	ז	z	7
Khes	ח	kh	8
Tes	ט	t	9
Yud	י	y	10
Kaf	כ	k	20
Lamed	ל	l	30
Mem	מ	m	40
Nun	נ	n	50
Samekh	ס	s	60
Ayin	ע	silent[2]	70
Pay	פּ	p	80
Fay	פ	f	80
Tzadi(k)	צ	tz	90
Kuf	ק	k	100
Raysh	ר	r	200
Shin	שׁ	sh	300
Sin	שׂ	s	300
Tav	תּ	t	400
Sav	ת	s	400

Default Name	Default Form	Final Name	Final Form	Sound
Khaf	כ	Final Khaf	ך	kh
Mem	מ	Final Mem	ם	m
Nun	נ	Final Nun	ן	n
Fay	פ	Final Fay	ף	f
Tzadi(k)	צ	Final Tzadi(k)	ץ	tz

Certain Letters at the End of Words

When appearing at the end of a word, five Hebrew letters change forms. Although they look different, they are still pronounced exactly the same. Here are the final letters:

The Vowels

As noted, the Hebrew letters themselves consist entirely of consonants. Additional symbols (placed below or on top of letters) make vowels, known as nekkudot (dots). These nekkudot make a string of letters into pronounceable and meaningful words. The names of vowels, below, indicate how the nekkudot are pronounced by Ashkenazim as well as by Modern Hebrew speakers, whose accent has been heavily influenced by Sepharadic tradition.

Komatz

Looks like a "T" and can be found under the letter, makes a short "u" sound (as in fun)3

Patach

Looks like a flat horizontal line under the letter and makes an "ah" sound (as in barn)

Note: The Modern Hebrew (Sepharadic) pronunciation for both the komatz and the patach is the sound, "ah."

Tzayray

Two side-by-side dots under the letter, make a long "a" sound (as in day)

Segol

Three dots arranged as an inverted pyramid under the letter makes a short "e" sound (as in bed)

Note: The Modern Hebrew (Sepharadic) pronunciation for both the tzayray and the segol is a short "e."

Sheva

Two dots stacked below the letter, can either have no sound at all (this is called a sheva nach) or it can make a quick "ih" sound, as in tick (in which case it is called a sheva na)

Cholam

Can either make a long "o" sound (as in bone) or among some Ashkenazim it makes an "oy" (as in boy). The cholam can either appear as a dot at the upper left of a letter, or it takes the form of a vav with the dot above it.

Cheereek

A single dot below the letter makes a long "e" sound when followed by a yud. Otherwise, it makes a short "i" sound.

Shoorook

Makes an "oo" sound (like boot) and appears like a vav with a dot to its left

Kubutz

Makes a shorter "oo" sound like in "book" and appears like three dots, arranged like an ascending staircase below the letter

(At times, the komatz, patach and segol may appear with a sheva on their right side. In this case, they are pronounced more briefly but are known as chataf komatz, chataf patach, and chataf segol.)

Gematria (Numerical Value)

In Hebrew, every letter has a numerical value. The first 10 letters (aleph to yud) each correspond to a number, one through ten. The next nine letters (khaf to kuf) represent 20 through 100, and the final three letters (raysh, shin and tav) are from 200 to 400. Similar to Roman numerals, letters are added together to equal a given number, and the letters retain their essential worth no matter where they are placed in a sequence, so tav, khaf, and aleph, for example, equal 421. With this system, any word or phrase can be given a specific numerical value, known as gematria. Often, great secrets of the **Torah** are steeped in gematria. In fact, one of the most popular commentaries on the **Torah**, written by Rabbi Jacob ben Asher, known as the *Baal Haturim*, uncovers layers of hidden meaning in the text by way of gematria (and other close analysis of the texts).

Ever wonder why the number 18 in Judaism represents life? The word "life" in Hebrew is pronounced, "Chai," which is comprised of two letters, "khet" and "yud." "Khet" represents the number eight, and the letter "yud," ten. These two letters added together equal 18. "L'Chaim!" To life!

The Code to Creation

The Hebrew letters are not just a handy tool to transcribe Hebrew speech. Rather, they are the vessels through which Gd created the universe. As told in the opening chapters of Genesis, Gd spoke ten utterances, and the world came into being. These ten statements are the "garments" through which the Divine energy is translated into physical existence. How about the things, such as computers and books, not mentioned specifically in the ten utterances? That is where gematria and other exchange systems come into play. These allow the Hebrew terms, based on the ten utterances, to "become" the Hebrew name of every given item, which is its life-source.

https://www.chabad.org/library/article_cdo/aid/4069287/jewish/The-Hebrew-Alphabet.htm

https://www.chabad.org/library/article_cdo/aid/4426636/jewish/Hebrew-Alphabet-PDF-Chart.htm

- Is it challenging to think of writing English without any vowels?
- Would it be challenging to read any foreign language without any written vowels?
- If every word has a frequency, how important is pronunciation?
- If words create, is a mispronounced word likely to create an aberration?
- Does sound disturb/move the air?
- Do words therefore carve something out of the air?
- Are words spells?
- Do you understand the concept of Gematria?
- Is there a reason why one word is chosen over another word that means the same thing when the numerical value is taken into account?
- Or one letter with the same sound as another is chosen?
- Does the formulation of each letter that you think or speak disturb the air or ether in some way?
- Is ether finer in substance than air?

Oldest Language on Earth

Hebrew is said to be the oldest language on Earth. This means that it is closest to the Original Process of Creation. The oldest book is said to be the ***Sefer Yetzirah***, also called in English the ***Book of Creation*** and sometimes the ***Book of Formation***. The ***Sefer Yetzirah*** is said to be about 4000 years old and originally given to Abraham.

The ***Torah*** came 400 years later. The ***Torah*** was not meant to be a religion. The ***Torah*** was meant to be instructions about life. Another 1600 years passed before the ***Zohar*** made its appearance. ***Zohar*** means "Splendor" so technically it is The ***Book of Splendor***. The ***Zohar*** is a commentary to explain the ***Torah*** and is said to be the Soul of the ***Torah***.

You could spend lifetimes studying everything that has been written about everything. Your goal is to discover the salient points that you can utilize to help you understand your life and your purpose in the *Eternal Now*. The more you understand frequency, the more invested you become in knowing by knowing vs. knowing by reading. I read via the Oversoul level, with my Oversoul directing my learning. I have read extensively all of my life. Too many people think that if it is in writing it must be true. You are instructed to cite the work of others whenever you write any research papers. While I do agree that this is important you must also remember that generally speaking, words are clothed with the energy of the person writing it and literally colored by their personal experience. Objective writing is unusual. However not only do I read via the Oversoul level but I also write via the Oversoul level. This is why every time you go back and reread my books you pick up something different. The books are written energetically specifically to those who are led to pick them up.

You will never read much of what is hidden information. You have to remember that many ancient manuscripts were never published in book form. This means that ancient manuscripts are in private collections, not in the public. Books that are released publicly are done so for a reason, usually to help control the masses who the global handlers want to conform to a specific way of thinking. One of the authors of a ***Kabbalah*** book I recently read stated that for every hairbreadth of information he wrote, one mile remains hidden. Another author wrote that he was ostracized for sharing ***Kabbalah*** with the public. ***Kabbalah*** teaching is traditionally oral teaching. You can understand this if you have studied personally with Stewart and me vs. only reading the books. Even on the blog which is for the general readership, you can receive more specific pointers to the work that you are already doing.

- When you think of the volume of written information available on any subject, can it feel overwhelming?
- Can written information be a distraction?
- Do you read via the Oversoul level?
- Does your Oversoul focus you and point out information specific to you?
- Is reading a guidepost to point you in your inner direction?
- Have you considered the overabundant supply of ancient manuscripts never destined to be put into book form?
- Why is so much information hidden?
- What is the difference between knowing by knowing and knowing by reading?
- When reading do you consider that words are clothed with the energy of the person writing it and literally colored by their personal experience?
- How does understanding frequency help guide you?
- What can the frequency of an older language tell you vs. the frequency of a newer language?
- Did you know that the ***Torah*** was not meant to have a religion built around it?
- Why is this important to understand?

When you think of a subject in which you are an expert, you would be challenged to write it all down in a book or tell someone everything that you know. If someone came wanting your help to learn your subject, you would find few that would be truly dedicated. My dad told me that at one time he wanted to be a philosophy teacher. I told him that unfortunately, most students are interested in a passing grade vs. really learning a subject. My oldest son taught undergraduate physics classes. He said that cheating was rampant and openly discussed. Most took the class because it was a requirement for their major, not because they actually wanted to learn physics. When I was in elementary school, professional storytellers came every now and then who were amazing. These men and women knew how to mesmerize you with their words so that you became one with the story. Traditional stories and songs were not written, they were all orally passed from one generation to the next.

This is why it is so important that you understand frequency. Frequency is behind everything that you say, see and do. To know anything, you must find the frequency and follow the thread back to its origin. I love to read; reading opens up worlds. Reading focuses your attention so the story takes on a life in your mind as you visualize the scenes unfolding. In the same way, when you read through your Oversoul you are focused on specific passages, pages, or chapters. You may be directed to look in a specific book or ignore specific books. I can look at a book and know if it is something for me to read. Sometimes, I think I want to read a book, but no matter how much I push my Self I just cannot do it. Others, I can't put down. Still others I flip through them and get what I need and move on. I do not want to spend my life reading. I love to read, but I also want to experience.

- Is there a balance between reading and experience?
- Is it easy to get caught up in one or the other?
- Do you sometimes feel like there is so much to know that you will never know all of what you want to know?
- Can you tell by looking at a book or holding if it has something of value for you to know?
- Do you visualize what you are reading as you are reading?

- Have you been mesmerized by professional storytellers?
- In what subjects would you consider your Self an expert, or even very knowledgeable?
- Would it be challenging for you to tell all that you know about a specific subject?
- How do you impart knowledge from one person to another?
- Is there a difference between knowledge and information?
- How do you discern within one subject area which is the best path to follow?
- How does understanding frequency help you choose your path?

I often recommend that people read ***Masters of the Far East*** by Baird T. Spalding. Here is the description from Amazon.com:

ELEVEN MEN embarked upon a journey in 1894 with one objective:

...to find the great spiritual teachers of the Far East and witness their uncommon abilities. Since these Masters were scattered over a wide territory that covered a large portion of India, Tibet, China, and Persia, they knew it could take years of searching many secluded villages and hidden mountain communes. Planning each step of the journey became a challenge knowing that countless miles of rugged terrain separated the remote and isolate locations that were imperative to the exploration. Even though they could plot their route on a map and see where they were headed, the destination deep within the souls of eleven scientifically trained men remained uncertain. Baird T. Spalding and the others were practical in nature and the thought of spiritual masters performing miracles seemed impossible. Despite these suspect thoughts, something compelled them to move onward. So they did.

Volume 1: Introduction of the Master Emil. Visit to the "Temple of Silence". Astral Projection. Walking on Water. Visit to the Healing Temple. Emil Talks about America. The Snowmen of the Himalayas. New Light on the Teachings of Jesus. ISBN# 9780875163635

Volume 2: Visit to the Temple of the Great Tau Cross. Visit with the Master Jesus. Jesus discussed the nature of hell; the nature of God. The Mystery of thought vibrations. Jesus feeds the multitude. An account of a healing experience. Jesus and Buddha visit the group. ISBN# 9780875163642

Volume 3: One of the masters speaks of the Christ consciousness. The nature of cosmic energy. The creation of the planets and the worlds. The trip to Lhasa. Visit at the Temple Pora-tat-sanga. Explaining the mystery of levitation. A doubltless convinced of the existence of Jesus. ISBN# 9780875163659

Volume 4: First presented as "The India Tour Lessons." Each chapter has text for study as well as guides to teachers for developing and interpreting the material. Among subjects covered: The White Brotherhood, The One Mind Basis of coming social reorganization Prana. ISBN# 9780875163666

Volume 5: Lectures and articles by Spalding; also a brief biographical sketch. Partial contents: Camera of past events. Is there a God. The divine pattern. The reality. Mastery over death. The law of supply. ISBN# 9780875163673

Volume 6: Thirty-five years after the appearance of Volume 5 of Life & Teaching of the Masters of the Far East, ten dusty cartons were discovered in the DeVorss warehouse, some of which held Spalding manuscripts, paper, letters, photographs, and other materials related to this man whose name has been a legend in metaphysical and truth circles. The New Volume 6 includes: Articles previously omitted from Vol.5, Photographs, The 1935 India Tour and correspondence, Rare letters, Personal recollections of BTS, Spalding's last days, Spalding biography and memorabilia. ISBN# 978087516988

SET 6 volumes: Handsomely boxed in their own sleeves: Since 1924, when these writings first appeared, they have influenced and inspired generations of seekers. Astonished at the interest in his discoveries and experiences, he wrote Volume 2 (1927). Volume 3 (1935) followed along with a 30 city tour. Volume 4 (1948) and Volume 5 (1955) were compiled from his question and answer material and Volume 6 (1996)contains historical reference to his articles for the Mind Magazine 1935-37. ISBN# 9780875165387 https://www.amazon.com/Life-Teaching-Masters-Far-East/dp/0875165389/

These books were originally written as a true story. Then some years ago I read that there are now viewed as fiction. Regardless, even fiction is real in some reality. I think these are fabulous books to get you thinking beyond your current human experience. I have had the experience of being taken out of my body into a cave where there were moving pictures on the walls that showed me true history, similar to watching a movie. If you have not had this experience, it may be challenging for you to understand, but you can understand that when you are destined to know something and the timing is what it is supposed to be, you will get the information that you need, when you need it, how you need it.

When you think, you follow frequency. If you think about a cat, you follow the cat frequency as you explore what you know/do not know. Actual observation of cats teaches you a plethora of information. When you are thinking about cats, your mind might wander into the topic of birds. When you realize that you are now off-topic/off-frequency you have the option to go back to exploring more about cats. This is the same when you explore any topic/frequency. Your mind wanders through the topic exploring as you go. Changing topic changes the frequency.

Books provide a starting point but your own actual observation is what is most meaningful to you. In the same way, when you explore more seemingly abstract information, thinking about it puts you on the frequency. Just like when you do your Hyperspace/Oversoul visualizations, reading about them helps you think about possibilities. When you actually do the exercises you begin to explore various frequencies that are now open to you as a result of your inner level work.

In the same way, when you study **Kabbalah**, you follow the topic/frequency to discern for your Self what is true/not true. You apply what you know about daily topics/frequencies to Hyperspace/Oversoul topics/frequencies to **Kabbalah** topics/frequencies. You give your thoughts and questions to your Oversoul and then follow the frequencies. You know what is most likely truth vs. what is most likely not the truth. For example, if I told you that I have a bright green cat with five legs that talks, you would recognize right away that most likely I am not telling the truth. But if I said I have a cat that weighs 30 pounds and is almost 40 years old, you would more likely believe this tale than the one about a green cat. Still, you would question me until you discern the truth. The further something is from your reality, the more you have to question until you know without a shadow of a doubt what is true/untrue. Staying on-topic is following the frequency.

- When people change topics in a conversation suddenly, does it take you a few minutes to catch up with them?
- Can changing topics suddenly cause confusion?
- When this happens, is your mind/energy/frequency going in one direction and suddenly it has to switch to another direction?
- Does thinking in one direction put you on the frequency of one specific topic?

- If you are talking about cats and a person starts talking about birds, can this be confusing?
- Can you feel the change in energy/frequency when you change from talking about cats to birds?
- If you are mentally exploring a Hyperspace/Oversoul topic do you ask your Self/Oversoul enough questions to keep the topic/frequency expanding?
- Can you recognize truth when you hear it when discussing daily topics?
- What does truth feel like vs. something that is not the truth?
- If you are exploring Hyperspace/Oversoul topics/frequency can you tell when you are on-topic/on-frequency and when you are off-topic/off-frequency?
- How can you expand this into your **Kabbalah** exploration?
- Or when you read books such as the ones by Baird T. Spalding?
- Do you know the frequency of truth vs. not truth always, sometimes, never?
- Do you exercise your mind to stretch the boundaries of what you consciously know?
- Which is most important, reading or experiencing?
- How do you discern what is truth and which path to follow?

Guidance Through the Storm

All of life is frequency. This is why it is so easy to get lost. Every time you think you are where you are supposed to be, something comes along to grab your attention. Without awareness, it is easy for life to pull you from one direction to another until you are aimlessly swinging in the breeze. You must continue to slow your Self down so that you know when you change direction/topic/frequency. If you want to go deeper within, then you need to get on the frequency that takes you deeper within. You need to find an inner roadmap and follow it. This is why I teach you to follow frequency. Your Hyperspace/Oversoul tools each have a frequency. Only you know where you need to go. Only you know which tool to pick up on any given day. Imagine that you are going through a storm, unable to find your way to a place of safety. So, you pick up one of your Hyperspace Archetypes, hold it up in front of you knowing that it will guide you out.

Hebrew letters are another set of archetypes that can guide you out of your inner storm. Just like you focus on your Hyperspace Archetypes, you can focus on the Hebrew letters. You could also do this with any alphabet with which you are unfamiliar. You could use the Greek Alphabet or Japanese Alphabet for example. The reason I am focusing you on the Hebrew AlephBet is because Hebrew is considered the oldest known written language. This means that when you hold Hebrew letters up to guide you out of your inner storm, the letter has the potential to draw you the deepest and farthest down your path. Because of the disbursement of the Tribes of Israel throughout the world, Hebrew genetics are more prevalent than most people realize. Many people have Hebrew genetics who do not consciously know this. Hebrew genetics, even when they are buried deep within, can be activated using the Hebrew AlephBet. This means you are able to access deeper layers of information that already exist within.

- What is the point of drawing out hidden genetic information?
- What kinds of information do your genetics hold?
- Do your various genetics each hold different information?
- Does it make sense to try to access your oldest genetics?
- As you dig through newer genetics to get to the older ones, will the newer genetics also reveal hidden information?
- Can you get lost while trying to follow your genetics?
- Can you use language, both written and oral, as a guide into your genetics?

- Does knowing your genetics take you deeper into your mind-pattern that built the genetics?
- Does getting deeper into your mind-pattern take you deeper into your Creator?
- Does it make sense to access your oldest genetics to access your oldest mind-patterns to access your oldest connections to your Creator?

Hyperspace/Oversoul work is not a religion. You may pick and choose what you want from this body of information. You are always encouraged to get your own information and follow your own path under the guidance of your direct communication with your Creator. I have studied a variety of religions through the years in a variety of ways. I always get something from each one. I read the frequency of what is truth and what is taught for public consumption and control. Hence I belong to no religion.

I belong to the same religion as God.

This answer usually stops most people from asking more personal questions. To me, living your life according to the wishes of your Creator is your Ultimate Spiritual Experience. This varies for each person. For some people, they belong to organized mind-control religion because this is what they need. It is not for me to judge their journey. However, in my opinion, part of the journey for these people is to understand what spirituality is not. Even though I have an interest in the Hebrew language and facets of what the Jews know, I have no desire to take on Judaism as my religion. I have read enough to know that I am not compatible with many of the requirements for their adherents, nor do I want to be. Because of my Hebrew genetics, the Hebrew letters and sounds resonate and activate another level of my Being. Sound creates movement.

Generally, organized religion consists of a group of people who come to a consensus of what everyone should believe and how they should live their lives. I always want to be as free as possible in this reality to follow the dictates of my Creator over the dictates of human-made law. When something piques my interest, I study it to understand why. While I may be interested in the opinion of others, I do not consider anything a fact until I know it for my Self.

- How do you know something for your Self?
- Can something be stated as a fact by many people, yet something within you is still doubtful?
- Do you want to follow a consensus of the opinion of others regarding your spiritual life, simply because a group of people has decided that something is what it is?
- If you are raised within an organized religion and this is all you have ever known, how challenging is it even to know to question your way of life?
- Have you studied various religions?
- Have you found validity within each one?
- Do you want to belong 100% to any religion?
- Does religion take away Spiritual Freedom yet promise this at the same time?
- How challenging is it to wade through the religious ideas of others?
- Can you follow frequency to find your own path through the plethora of choices that are offered?

Anything written down is a 2-dimensional representation of something that is very multidimensional. To begin to fully explore this concept, I suggest that you take any of the Hyperspace Archetypes, put it at your Pineal Gland to explore its multidimensional shape and meaning. Look at it from every direction that you can imagine to begin to understand the Archetype in its entirety. Look at it from above it, beneath it, front, back, facing left, facing right. Allow what you see on paper to come to life. I also suggest you take the first letter of your first name and do the same thing. Explore the meaning of this letter, which is an archetype and represents the frequency upon which you chose to enter into this physical reality. Write your letter on paper. Turn the paper to the left, right, hold it above your head, then look at it from above, Think about what it would like from the front or back. All these are clues to Self.

I have always liked my first name and the sound of the "J". Interestingly, in Italian "Gi" makes this sound. If you straighten the "G" and turn it around, with a little imagination you can see the "J". One day while doing my stretching exercises I became a giant Hebrew Gimmel. This surprised me until a few days later while I was out walking I was shown that in Biblical Hebrew the Gimmel was sometimes written with a dagesh/dot which was then pronounced as a "J" sound. If you turn the "J" upside down and tweak the line across the top of the "J" you can see a Gimmel. You can sort through all of your genetics to find the correct written representation for just that first letter of your first name. All of these letter/archetypes tell you something about your Self. The archetype and the sound have a specific meaning to you.

- What is the Hyperspace meaning of the first letter of your first name?
- If you write it on paper and turn it in various directions, what shapes does it represent?
- If you hold the letter at your Pineal Gland, can you see it expand from a 2-dimensional letter into a multidimensional archetype?
- What does this tell you about your Self?
- What letter of the Hebrew AlephBet makes the sound of your first name?

- What does this Hebrew letter archetype tell you about you when you look at it from various directions?
- Can you put it at your Pineal Gland and turn it in all different directions to understand another layer/level of your inner Being?
- Genetically, what other archetypes are used to write the first letter of your name?
- What sound does the first letter of your first name make?
- Why did you choose that sound?
- Do you like the first letter of your first name as well as the sound it makes?
- Have you explored Hyperspace archetypes in the same way?

Dreams and Symbolism

Pictures in your dreams are simply Hyperspace Archetypes dressed up in clothing that you consciously recognize. Power Archetypes, for example, may be represented by Mountains. DNA may be represented by a Railroad Track or a Ladder. An Oversoul Archetype could be anything from a Road in this shape to a String lying on a table in this shape. A Square is Physical Reality; a Rectangle is an Alternate Reality. Either of these could come through in your dreams as a table where you eat. All kinds of messages come through in this way. In my ***Little Fluffs: Archetypes*** book, you will see several examples of Archetypes hidden all around you in your daily life. There are always layers within layers of meaning in all of these Archetypes. The best way for you to understand the meaning of the picture is to put what you see at your Pineal Gland to see what comes up for you. Then, you follow the picture to see what thoughts, scenes and/or memories come up for you.

In the same way, stories contain many hidden layers of meaning within the archetypes of the letters. As you read, you ask your Oversoul to explain what the story means to you, personally. You want to know what it is teaching you because you know that everything is a reflection of some aspect of Self. Therefore there is a reason that you read what you read beyond entertainment. This is why I often tell you a story about my life. You are really not so interested in my life as much as you are interested in what this makes you think about in your life. The stories I relate about my life are lessons cloaked within a story. In the same way, if I wanted to cloak information I would lay the story out in a code that you would have to think about to break.

Programming is laid out like this. This is why stories such as the Wizard of Oz, Alice in Wonderland, Sleeping Beauty, and Snow White are all stories that keep being reinvented. The programming is coded in the story. Spies use codes and symbols to communicate with each other. The Navajo Code talkers are famous for helping with hidden communications during World War II. Archetypes and symbolism are everywhere. **Decoding Your Life**, the name of my classic book of Spiritual Law, is a fascinating process. The Hebrew AlephBet is another code that helps you do just this.

- Are you the most fascinating person that you know?
- Are you the person who you like to know the most about?
- Is it fascinating to know that by unlocking your own inner codes that symbolism meanings are automatically revealed?
- Because the world is built upon Archetypes, does it make sense that everything in your life has a hidden meaning or code?
- Do you decode your dreams to understand their hidden meaning?
- Do you *Decode Your Life* to understand its hidden meaning?
- Why are there so many layers of meanings to sift through?

- Do you know how to focus on a symbol to determine what it means to you, personally?
- Do you trust what you find?

All life is symbolism. Only focusing on your dreams stops people from focusing on the symbolism of daily life. When you realize that everything has meaning is when you really start to understand Self via Self-teaching, which is what I show you in **Decoding Your Life**. Understanding symbolism does not make you good or bad. Understanding symbolism gives you information. What you do with that information is then up to you. You can use it to create good or bad. This can be a challenging concept for many people.

One of the best examples concerns the *Erev Rav* that I came across in some of my **Kabbalah** studies. Interesting that once again this information had to do with the Exodus of the Jews out of Egypt. As previously mentioned, the Jews were discouraged as they were led out of Egypt, even wanting to return to their life of slavery rather than suffer on their way to freedom even though they had witnessed many miraculous events. While Moses was on Mount Sinai receiving the Ten Commandments, the Biblical story says the doubting Israelites convinced Aaron, the high priest, and brother of Moses, to build a new god out of gold, which he did in the form of a golden calf.

According to the **Zohar** the *Erev Rav* were Jews trained in the practice of Egyptian sorcery by Egyptian priests. Another interpretation of the **Zohar** says that the *Erev Rav* were Egyptians who were studying Judaism. They were presumably forced to accompany the Israelites out of Egypt. However, it is my guess that they were spies and shills whose function was to stir up doubt and dissent. Yunus and Yumbrus were the ones who were behind the creation of the golden calf. The golden calf was made from gold that the two *Erev Rav* effectively drew down through the Sefirot. They tricked high priest Aaron into helping them bring the calf to life. This is something they could not do because of their wicked ways; they needed Aaron for this final act. Yunus and Yumbrus also included sex and drugs as a part of the celebration of this new god. All of this phenomenon was enough to convince the doubting Jews to follow them instead of Moses, who was conveniently away getting The Ten Commandments. When Moses returned, he smashed the idol with the stone tablets of The Ten Commandments.

The *Erev Rav* still exist to this day, hidden but used by those who are interested in world domination. These people do not want you to know what they know because you might become a rival or attempt to eradicate them. The Rabbis working for the good of humanity do not want you to have this information because you might unwittingly use it for evil instead of good. Without proper instruction, you might unintentionally harm your Self or others. There are many good reasons why information is cloaked and hidden from the general populace. One primary reason for hiding information is so that it would only be understood by a few people who are willing to do the work to be able to effectively utilize it in the most correct and beneficial way.

- Is there a good reason why information is cloaked and hidden?
- Is it one thing to ponder hidden information and another to actually know it?
- How much responsibility is there with knowledge?
- Can it be tempting to use what you know for evil instead of good?
- Does evil tempt you by offering short-term rewards?
- Does evil appeal to the Animal Mind over the Spiritual Mind?
- Have you ever done something you thought was positive only to reap negative consequences instead?
- Does understanding symbolism give you information?
- Is it challenging to sometimes know how to proceed with information?

- Is it always important to ask for guidance from your Oversoul and God-Mind on how to proceed?
- Can there be a fine line between good and evil?
- Can you be tempted to do evil while convincing your Self that it is good?
- Is it easy to want short-term over long-term verification?
- Is it challenging to wait for long-term Spiritual rewards while you watch others get short-term Animal Mind rewards?

There is much controversy about giving **Kabbalah** information to non-Jews even though **Kabbalah** and the *Torah* itself are not supposed to be about religion. However, there are many non-Jews, such as my Self, with a lot of Hebrew genetics. There are many Jews who really do not understand their religion or practice all of its tenets. There are also many variants of Judaism with some sects super-strict while some are extremely liberal. Even within Judaism, there is something for everyone. With that said, when I read some of the laws to which they must adhere, I think to my Self, "This is not the way it is supposed to be!" I cannot tell you how I know this, I just know by knowing. What is not supposed to be is human/Animal Mind interpretation of Spiritual Law. Spiritual Law can only be interpreted accurately by Spiritual Mind. When I read I hear frequency. I hear the difference between Animal Mind interpretation and Spiritual Mind interpretation.

When I first started reading the books on **Kabbalah**, I told Stewart that I did not agree with much of what I was reading. His first response was to ask me if I thought I knew more than the Rabbis who studied this for centuries. My reply was yes, I do know what is not accurate. Eventually, as he read on, he agreed with me. He said that there was much that he did not agree with either. In fact, some of what I was reading I said was no more than New Age Judaism. The more I read, the more I disagreed with. This is why I prefer to study on my own. I follow the frequency that leads me through the Animal Mind interpretations and into the Spiritual Mind bits and pieces, plus opens me to what I already know when it is time for me to know.

Sometimes, I am not told anything beyond what is correct or not correct because it is not time for me to know more than that. This is why I do my best to explain my process to you. This is not about getting you to agree with me, it is about sharing a process that you might be able to incorporate into your own studies so that you, too, get your own answers. No one can say anything is true because you read it. You can only say that it is true when you know by knowing. You can explain knowing by knowing all you want to someone, but until they experience this they really do not understand what you are talking about. I often use an orange as an example. You can tell someone what an orange tastes like. They must experience the taste for themselves. Until they actually taste the orange you cannot have an in-depth discussion of what an orange tastes like.

- Have you ever tried to have an in-depth conversation with someone but you could not get a meeting of the minds?
- Can it be a relief when you find someone who knows what you are talking about?
- Is it necessary to always agree with someone?
- Can learning occur via disagreements?
- Is it challenging to listen to someone with whom you disagree?
- Do you automatically shut down when you disagree with someone?
- Is it important to remember that if someone is speaking to you, that person has something valuable to share?
- Can what you learn be something other than what you think you are learning?

- Can the other person be teaching you how to listen via the Oversoul level?
- Can the other person be teaching you how to speak via the Oversoul level?
- How many hidden lessons can be buried in unpleasant conversations?
- Do you know by knowing when something is not correct?
- If so, is it important if you do not know why it is not correct?
- If it is important for you to know why something is not correct, will this eventually be revealed to you?
- Can you tell the difference between Animal Mind interpretations and Spiritual Mind interpretations?
- Can both be correct?
- Why do you think there is controversy about giving **Kabbalah** information to non-Jews?
- Is there controversy about giving **Kabbalah** information to Jews?
- Are there people within any religion who do not understand their religion?
- Can you practice the tenets of any religion without understanding what it means or why some tenets are in place?

My work is filled with personal exercises, processes and questions. You have to do the work to go within to verify for your Self what is truth. I give examples that cloak the moral of the story that I want to express to you. You read the story, you find the moral of the story and then you can apply that moral/knowledge to your own life which in turn reveals more inner truth. Truth is always truth, but your experience of it must come from within. If an elephant is in the middle of the room and you have 4 people looking at it from 4 different directions, each will have a description that is the truth.

They could argue amongst each other for an eternity about who has the correct truth without ever recognizing that each has a piece of the truth. Animal Mind and programming keep people arguing amongst each other. Spiritual Mind tells you to listen with your Spiritual Ears, see with your Spiritual Eyes to discover the entire truth of anything.

Adhering to tenets may not mean that you even understand the tenets. You may pray but not understand the prayers, simply going through the motions. Yet, just like when you say your affirmations, you may not feel them in your heart and soul, but it is all a beginning point of something. Using specific words in specific ways always create. With awareness, you can develop a sensitivity to frequency so you learn from whatever the words are creating. Think of how many ways that you can spell the first name of someone. According to one website, the boy's name Caden, has 52 different spellings and the girl's Aaliyah, has 89 different spellings. Here are examples of the various spellings of the popular boy's name of Michael and its feminized version of Mikayla.

Michael

Mikael, Micheal, Mikhail, Mikel, Mikail, Mikhael, Michel, Mykel, Michal, Mikaeel, Mikal, Mikkel, Miquel, Michale, Mikell, Michail, Mikaele, Mikha'El, Mychal, Maichail, Maikel, Micael, Mícheál, Mickel, Mikaail, Mikaal, Mikayel, Mychael, Mykole, Michaeal, Mickael, Mickeal, Mi'Kael, Mikaël, Mikahel, Mikayl, Mi'Kel, Mikelle, Mikhal, Mikiel, Mikkal, Myckel, Mykael, Mykell, Mykhael, Mykhail, Mykl

Mikayla

Mikayla, Michaela, Mikaela, Micaela, Mckayla, Makaela, Ma'Kayla, Mikhayla, Makaila, Micayla, Mikaylah, Mackayla, Makyla, Michaella, Mikela, Macayla, Makaylah, Mikaella, Makala, Mickaella, Mikala, Makailah, Makalya, Mekayla, Michela, Mickaela, Mikaila, Mikailah, Mikeala, Mikella, Mikeyla, Mykaela, Mykayla, Mackaila, Makaylaa, Ma'Kaylah, Makeila, Makiyla, Makkayla, Ma'Kyla, Makylah, Maykala, Micaella, Micaila,

Micailah, Micaylah, Michayla, Micheala, Mickayla, Mikaelah, Mikahla, Mikalah, Mikaylla, Mikhaela, Mikhaella, Mikhaila

https://www.babycenter.com/0_baby-names-with-the-most-alternate-spellings_20004860.bc

- If the name sounds the same, why do people choose one spelling over another spelling?
- Does knowing the Hyperspace meaning of each letter give you information about the Soul-Personality that chooses its name and the spelling of its name?
- Could your name be spelled differently?
- Do you like the spelling of your name?
- If each spelling sounds the same, why did you choose the spelling you chose?
- Do the letters change the numerical value of your name according to Hebrew Gematria?
- Does the numerical value of your name reveal another layer of who and what you are?
- In general, do people who use Latin alphabets consciously consider the numerical value of names?
- In Hebrew, is the numerical value of each letter considered?
- In Hebrew, are letters chosen based upon sound or numerical value or a combination of both?

Oral Tradition

n wy t hd smthng s t wrt wtht ny vwls f y stdy n my clss y wll lrn t rd wht s wrttn knd f lk shrthnd

Translation:

One way to hide something is to write without any vowels. If you study in my class you will learn to read what is written kind of like a shorthand.

When oral tradition is gone, so is the pronunciation, words and meanings. For example hop and hope, can and cane, war and ware/wear are pairs and a triplet that have completely different meanings. One letter makes the difference. In the last example, ware and wear have the same vowels but the placement makes each word mean something entirely different. If they were all written as in the ***Torah***, you would read:

hp, hp

cn, cn

wr, wr, wr

The only way you would know the difference if is someone tells you or you can understand by the sentence.

The ***Torah*** has a specific number of letters written in a specific way for a specific reason. The ***Torah*** is written without any vowels or punctuation. One written error amongst the 304,805 letters invalidates the entire ***Torah*** scroll. The ***Torah*** is a code and this is part of understanding this code. Think about how many codes are embedded in this text.

Interestingly, I recently saw a math equation on social media that was written:

8 + 8 + 8 = 3 x 8 = 30

3 + 3 + 3 + 3 +3 +3 +3 x 8 = 30

I wondered how that teacher explained this to her students! If you know anything about math, you know that to get a correct answer the equation must be computed in a specific order. Most people do not dispute the fact that math is comprised of formulas. However, people are ignorant to the fact that letters and words are formulas that when used in specific ways create specific results. In the same way, words pronounced a specific way have specific meanings entirely different from each other. Without knowing English, if you said,

"I am sick…" every day, many times a day, you are going to create ill health somewhere in your life. This can be physical, mental, emotional, financial, relationships and/or all of these and more. Even with knowing the words, many people say, " I am sick (of hearing this, getting up early, going to work, hot weather, cold weather, rain, traffic, my boss/co-worker and so forth). Without awareness, each time you say "I am sick…" you are setting the stage for sickness to invade your life.

I have been around Hebrew enough years to know a little of the pronunciation. I have always liked the sound of the language and the music even if I can't understand it. When Stewart told me that he thought I should say the Ana Beko'ach prayer twice a day I didn't ask him why. I just said okay. The first time I was reading through the transliteration out loud, I was focusing on correct pronunciation. Suddenly, I had visions of the Earth. The continents were Medium Green, the oceans were all deep Medium Blue and there were pure white wispy clouds floating about in the atmosphere. I was taken aback because I was not looking for anything or asking any questions. I was only concentrating on the pronunciation. When I told Stewart he said that this is what the prayer is about: resetting and refocusing the Earth. Even though I did not have a conscious clue what I was doing, the words created the picture that I saw. Words and sounds are powerful.

- Do you need to know the meaning of words to make something happen?
- Do your words have more power when you know their meanings?
- Or, when you know the meaning do you try to make something happen rather than allow what is happening to come to you automatically?

- Does speaking words objectively allow the words to do what they are intended to do?
- Can negative energy change a neutral word to something negative?
- Can positive energy change a neutral word to something positive?
- Does giving your words to your Oversoul as you think and speak, give your Oversoul the opportunity to give them back to you infused with exactly what you need?
- If words in a book create pictures in your mind, does it make sense that words that you speak also create pictures?
- Can you speak something into existence?
- Do you speak your life into existence every day?
- Do you think your life into existence every day?
- Do words transmute and rearrange molecules and atoms?
- What do sound waves coming from your mouth look like?
- What do thought-forms emanating from your mind look like?
- If you calculate a math formula correctly, will you always get the same answer?
- If you calculate a word formula correctly, will you always get the same answer?
- If you continually say, "I am sick…" no matter who you are or what language you use, will something in your life always become sick?
- Do you have to understand the meaning of your words to get a result?
- How challenging would it be to read and write without vowels?
- Would you need an oral teacher of some kind?

Sound

The *Sefer Yetzirah*, the ***Book of Formation/Creation*** which was given before the *Torah*, places much emphasis on Sound. Each letter is placed in a category:

Gutterals:	אחהע	Aleph, Hey, Chet, Ayin (Throat)
Labials:	בומפ	Bet, Vav, Mem, Pey (lips)
Palatals:	גיכק	Gimel, Yod, Kaf, Kuf (palate/roof of mouth)
Linguals:	דטלנת	Dalet, Tet, Lamed, Nun, Tav (tongue)
Dentals:	זסצרש	Zayin, Samekh, Tzadi, Resh, Shin (teeth)

The text says:

> Engrave them with voice, carve them with breath, and set them in the mouth in five places.

Engrave them with voice = carefully pronounce each letter

Carve them with breath = concentrate on the breath that is exhaled as the letter is pronounced

Set them in the mouth = feel the place in the mouth from which the sound comes

Most likely when you studied sound in your science classes in school, sound waves were probably demonstrated by dropping a pebble in water and then watching the ripples emanate outwardly from the pebble. While this may give a general idea, what really happens is each sound carves something out of the air. When I used to teach my toning classes, I asked such questions as:

- What does the air feel when a bird flies through it?
- What does the air feel when a ball flies through the air?
- What does the air feel when rain is pouring down through it?
- What does the air feel when the leaves of the trees rustle?
- What does the air feel when you speak?

When I tone, I feel like a pipe in a pipe organ:

> A pipe organ feeds wind into pipes, causing the air to oscillate and produce a sound. The pipes stand in line above the box referred to as the wind-chest, with wind fed from below into the pipes the organist wishes to use to produce sound. https://www.yamaha.com/en/musical_instrument_guide/pipeorgan/mechanism/#:~:text=A%20pipe%20organ%20feeds%20wind,to%20use%20to%20produce%20sound.

Air comes up from my diaphragm and I control the air flow as well as my throat, lips, palate, tongue and teeth. This is a conscious and deliberate act to replicate a specific tone for a specific reason. The same thing happens when you speak, but most people do not pay attention to this process. Sound/words carve something out of the air which then creates something else. You look at words on a page but you do not focus on the empty space. In some of my classes, I have had people draw and create many things on paper. People focused on their creations. Then, when they were all done, we evaluated the "empty space" to see another perspective of their mind-pattern. While they focused "here" something else was going on "there". This is the same trick the global handlers use on you and why it is so easy for them to hide symbolism right in front of your eyes. Interestingly, Kabbalists say that the black letters in the ***Torah*** represent the physical world while the white space around the letters represents the nonphysical.

- Do you think about the space around physical objects?
- Are you so busy focusing "here" that you miss what is hidden "there"?
- Do you think about what happens in the air when you speak?
- Do you sing?
- Do you consciously think about the process of singing?
- Do you pay attention to the airflow and where the sounds emanate in your mouth?

- Or how the sounds bounce around in your mouth before leaving the opening?
- When you speak, do you think about where the word forms in your mouth?
- Can you feel the difference between the Gutterals, Labials, Palatals, Linguals, and Dentals when you pronounce the Hebrew letters?
- Why would it be important to be aware of where the sound comes from in your mouth?
- Is the human body a musical instrument?
- Can you feel the air flow from your diaphragm when you sing or speak?
- Can you answer the questions about how the air feels?
- Does this add another dimension to how you speak your life into existence?

Studying Kabbalah

Some people are upset that there are people teaching **Kabbalah** to those who do not know much about Judaism. Remember that **Kabbalah** is not a religion or meant to be a religion. **Kabbalah** is about instructing people about the *Torah*, which is also not meant to be a religion, but rather an instruction book to life. When I lived in New York all of this was challenging to comprehend. Many of the Jews I knew did not attend Temple services but did celebrate the Holidays and their children had Bar/Bat Mitzvahs. Often, they belonged to a Temple only so their children could have a place for their Bar/Bat Mitzvahs. Temple membership fees could be quite steep. Once the Bar/Bat Mitzvahs were over, the Temple memberships were often ended. The *Torah* portions were said in Hebrew, most people did not understand what was being said, but were proud of the child for his/her accomplishments.

I found the mix of following some Jewish rules and not following others strange. To me, I have always kind of been an all or nothing person. Either you are or you are not. For example, I attended many Passover Seders but when the **Haggadah** was read by the participants it often was done without respect. When the prayers were said I was told that it was more important to pronounce them correctly than to understand what they meant. Even those who had studied the **Torah** for their Bar/Bat Mitzvahs could not converse in Hebrew even if they could say the prayers of which they did not know the meaning. Then, I found out that there are many sects of Judaism, each with a wide range of religious tenets to be followed. The same thing can be said about any religion. There are so many offshoots that it is enough to make your head spin. I do not want to belong to any of these! This is why you study on your own, you connect to your own Source, and your explanations of what is or is not comes to you directly from All That Is. Your Soul is already connected. Your Soul can not be disconnected.

I always find interesting and useful information when I read about any religion. But ultimately I want and expect to get my own answers. I do not want someone else defining me for me. "Me" includes my Oversoul, God-Mind and more. I know what I know and what I know continues to deepen in various ways depending upon my studies. Right now, I am getting a lot out of my **Kabbalah** studies which I am sharing with you. I take nothing at face value. I question everything. I even explore the frequency of the authors via the Oversoul level as I read. I want to know who is writing what and what influences their opinions. I want to know what they are/were like as people. I need to read through their Color, Tone, and Archetypes embedded in their writings so I can sift through to the information/Truth vs. their opinion. I don't care how old the information is, how many years it has existed, and how many other people accept it as truth.

I AM an explorer of consciousness.

It is my duty to train my Self. You already unconsciously read and know frequency. I am showing you the best that I can how to do this for your Self. This way, you can do what you need to do to get the information that you need as well as acquire the wisdom to use it correctly.

- How important is it to study frequency?
- Is studying information different than studying frequency?
- Do you consider the source of your information?
- Do you think about how the information is literally colored/influenced by the person passing the information along?
- In *Decoding Your Life* do you remember the chapter that talks about how the forest can be peaceful to one person but scary to another?
- If information is old or many people agree on the information does this make the information correct?
- Is it easy to become enamored with fancy words and secrets to the point where information is secondary to the process?
- Have you been puzzled by people who are part of organized religion but they pick and choose which rules to follow or not follow?
- Do you want to define Self or do you want someone else telling you who and what you are?
- Can you use *Kabbalah* as part of your study of Self?
- Why does *Kabbalah* interest you?
- Do you need to understand Hebrew to understand the principles?
- Can *Kabbalah* give you a general direction and then you allow what is within you to rise up into your conscious mind?

- Do you need to have Hebrew genetics to get something out of **Kabbalah**?
- Knowing what you know now about the Lost Tribes of Israel are you surprised by how many people have Hebrew genetics?
- Do Hebrew genetics ensure that the information you garner from **Kabbalah** is used in the most correct and beneficial way?
- Why do you think the *Erev Rav* exist?
- Is it important to know the difference between Biblical Hebrew and the Hebrew language that is spoken today?

AFFIRMATIONS—MULTIDIMENSIONAL QUESTING

Using the *72 Names of God* and studying the Hebrew AlephBet, *Torah*, *Kabbalah*, and *Zohar* all help you dig through the layers of your Soul in both new and ancient ways; new to your conscious mind while awakening ancient genetics and memory. This is not a linear process; it is a multidimensional quest to access Soul layers at various depths that are unique to you.

I allow my ancient genetics and memories to awaken.

I give thanks that my ancient genetics and memories awaken in ways that I can handle.

I AM consistent in my inner work.

Consistency brings results.

I take careful notes of my personal progress.

I easily review where I was and where I AM.

My Spiritual tool bag grows.

I use my Spiritual tools with guidance and direction from Source.

I feel the various layers within my Soul.

I consciously know my Self, as appropriate.

Everything has a place and a time.
I actively but patiently pursue my quest.

I proactively change my mind-pattern.
My mind-pattern pulls deeper level knowledge to me.

That which is hidden is now revealed.
Knowledge comes to me with ease.

I have a firm foundation.
I AM prepared.

New knowledge stretches my inner boundaries.
My boundaries stretch multidimensionally.

I AM anchored within my Oversoul and God-Mind.
My logic and emotions are always in balance.

New doors of opportunity open.
I proactively walk through the doors.

I find the Truth of my Being.
The journey of my Soul opens before me.

Judgment falls away.
My observation skills expand.

Programming dissolves.
I AM whole and complete.

The meaning of life deepens.
Existence explains Itself.

I AM immersed in the frequency of All That Is.
I know by knowing.

I know greater peace and harmony.
I see the Souls around me with understanding and compassion.

Each person is on his/her own multidimensional quest.
Each person needs his/her own experience.

Resolving my own conundrums satisfies my Soul.
My own experiences are necessary.

Experience is my teacher.
Experiential learning is always the best.

My Hyperspace/Oversoul toolbox is my storehouse of knowledge.
Each layer of Self progressively unlocks as I go.

Physical reality provides my point of reference.
I AM a multidimensional Being.

My mind-pattern automatically releases what is no longer necessary.
My enhanced mind-pattern brings order and purpose to my life.

Correct people, places and things automatically flow to me.
I AM always exactly where I need to be.

I automatically know when and where to move.
My mental, emotional, spiritual and physical flexibility expands.

My energy on all levels of my Being increases.
My finances flow with ease.

My leadership abilities move to the forefront.
I AM the leader of My Self at all times.

I AM a follower of Spiritual Law.
I follow my Oversoul and God-Mind 24/7.

I AM always an example.

I choose to be an example of what is most correct and beneficial.

Book of Formation

K*abbalah* is only another tool that you can choose to use while focusing on your inner level work. One reason I chose to study this work is that I can feel the nonhuman frequency behind it. As I sort through the frequency I am doing my best to divest the information of the Color, Tone, and Archetype of human interpretation vs. that which is nonhuman. Nonhuman does not mean benevolent. This means I also need to search the frequency for malevolence. I have started some books with wonderful information. Then all of a sudden I run into information that makes me cringe. This is often done purposefully to engage you. Once engaged, you swallow everything when you are not consciously sensitive to the change of directions/frequency. In some of my **Kabbalah** research, I have found information that should not be public. Even reading the intros to some books felt evil and foreboding, definitely places I have no need to be.

Think about putting out a recipe for a nuclear bomb. Just because you have a recipe does not mean everyone should have access to it. Obviously, anyone who tries to make one will have disastrous consequences. I do not want to know how to make something like this. There is much evil in the world disguised in ways that tempt people to participate. Or people do not realize it is evil until they have immersed themselves in it. Extricating your Self from such situations can be challenging. Discernment is paramount. Trusting in Source is paramount. From ***The Red Sea Rules***, knowing that *the same God that led you in will lead you out* is paramount.

- When people hear the word **Kabbalah** do they automatically think "spiritual"?
- Do you realize that **Kabbalah** is not spiritual, but a set of how-to instructions for life?
- Do most people immediately think "good" when they think of the word "spiritual"?
- Do people consciously and/or unconsciously put something forward as spiritual/good when it can be the exact opposite?
- Do you sometimes automatically make assumptions without digging into the frequency behind your assumptions?
- Can communication of any kind, either inner or outer, be clear when it is based upon assumptions?
- How challenging is it for clear communication to happen?
- When you read, do the words clearly communicate?
- Can evil be clearly communicated?
- Can you always recognize evil?
- If you unwittingly experience something evil, does this teach you to not assume, question more, and force you to put more faith in Self and Source?
- What attracts you to study one body of work over another?
- What does human vs. nonhuman mean to you?

Long before I met Stewart I spoke to the Earth via my toning. I matched the Earth frequency, deep within its Being. I asked a lot of questions and received a lot of answers. Then, when I met Stewart and we were discussing what we knew about the Earth, it was interesting to me that his information matched what I had received. I did not need outer verification because I know what I know. If his information would have been different than mine I would not have changed my mind. I would have considered what he said and reviewed the frequency to see if his information was or was not valid.

Remember the example of the elephant in the room. Each person can describe it differently and each can be correct. Even if someone says the elephant is pink, perhaps the elephant opened its mouth and the person was looking inside. Rather than discredit the information that the elephant is pink, you must look at this frequency to see why the person said it. This is why I always listen carefully to comments written on my blogs. Notice I said "listen" not "read". The words on the page provide focus but as my eyes scan the comments I listen to the frequency of the words via my Oversoul. Then I listen to what my Oversoul tells me. I AM in the frequency.

When you are hungry, you know by knowing that you are hungry. Your body uses no words that say, "I am hungry, feed me". You know. You are not the body, you are not your stomach, but you are in the body/frequency. When you receive the message from your body, you start searching your cabinets and refrigerator for what to feed your body. You may ask your Self:

- Do I feel like eating vegetables?
- Do I feel like eating protein?
- Do I feel like eating pasta or rice?
- Do I want a meal or a snack?
- Do I want something to drink?

Technically, these are more accurate questions:

- Does my body need vegetables?
- Does my body need protein?

- Does my body need pasta or rice?
- Does my body need a meal or a snack?
- Does my body need something to drink?

You, the Soul-personality are communicating and having a complete conversation with your body. Your body is responding nonverbally. You are in the frequency of your body, you are nonverbally receiving frequency reports to your questions, you are interpreting the frequency, gaining knowledge, and responding accordingly.

- When your body is cold or hot, does it verbally tell you this?
- Does your body verbally tell you if your chair is too hard or soft?
- Do your feet verbally tell you if your shoes are comfortable or uncomfortable?
- Is the Soul-personality in the frequency of the body?
- Does the Soul-personality have matching Color, Tone, and Archetype with the body?
- Are you verbally asking the body questions and nonverbally receiving answers that you are interpreting?
- Do you know when your body is hungry?
- Do you have to ask someone else for outer verification to know that your body is hungry?
- Do you know by knowing when your body is hungry?
- If someone tells you that your body is not hungry when you know that it is, do you believe the other person over what you know?
- What are other examples of nonverbal communication that you are already doing?
- Do you know what you know regardless of what others say?

When you speak to other humans, you automatically match their tones and even mirror body language. Think about sports events where everyone wears the colors of their team and all say the same chants along with the cheerleaders/programmers. The wave was a popular archetype created by people in various seating sections standing up and sitting down in a group event, as directed. In plain sight, you have matching Color, Tone and Archetype. The arenas are generally in the shape of an oval. In Hyperspace an oval symbolizes time. Time is an illusion.

I have demonstrated this principle in many of my classes. People wearing the same colors sit together. I have put my hands in various positions and soon the entire class is mirroring whatever I am doing. You can try this your Self when you speak to anyone or a group. As the group mind comes into alignment with thoughts/mind-pattern the outer has to reflect it. This is Universal Spiritual Law. Observe in any group setting how people wearing the same colors gravitate to each other. Even in a crowded theater, observe how people who are in close proximity to each other wear the same colors. When you really stop to think about all of this, you understand that you are already matching Color, Tone and Archetype. This is what allows you to communicate and understand others. When you realize this, you take what you are already doing and apply this knowledge to all frequency. You understand the frequency by getting in the frequency via the Oversoul level, keeping in mind that your Oversoul is your Universal Translator.

One year I taught a 7-day Toning Intensive Seminar. It was in January, in Michigan in the middle of a blizzard. It was so cold and snowy that the outside wall of our seminar room had snow blowing in through the door with ice forming on the inside. The hotel was having heating issues so participants had to wear hats, coats, and gloves during the class. The room we were in had about 6 large framed prints, all containing the same image! The group was so intense and we were learning so much that when the hotel finally had the heating system repaired in another room, the group did not want to leave our freezing cold room! That room was so filled with our matching Color, Tone and Archetypes that the group chose their mental work over physical comfort. However, I did convince them to use the other room in the afternoon, but we then moved between the two rooms. Color, Tone and Archetype are your entry points into understanding any frequency. You are already doing this. Now, you need to observe and label your process so you can repeat it at will on the inner, deeper levels.

There is a famous story of a Rabbi who asked a family he was visiting for a sugar cube to sweeten his coffee. They gave him the sugar cube and he set it on the saucer of his cup. He took a sip of his coffee, shook his head, and then broke the sugar cube in half. He sipped his coffee again, shook his head, and broke the sugar cube once more. Then he sipped his coffee, smiled, and nodded that now, the coffee was perfect.

- How comfortable are you saying that you understand frequency?
- Do you observe when you match Color, Tone and/or Archetype?
- Do you observe body language?
- Is the position of your body an archetype?
- Does your body give off tones that perhaps you can only hear with your inner ear?
- Can you match the tone of your body with your voice?
- Do you think about the involuntary tones your body gives, such as burping, stomach growling, coughing, walking, and so forth?
- How does your body communicate to you without words?
- How do you communicate with others without words?
- How do others communicate with you without words?

- How do you get into the frequency of anything to understand it?
- Do you understand something by reading about it in a book?
- How do you know that you know something vs. repeat what you read in a book?
- Must you experience something to understand its frequency?
- Do you know anything without experiencing it?
- Are we are all connected on the inner levels as One Soul?
- If we are all One Soul, do you know what I know?
- Do you have to find the point where we are connected on the Oversoul level?
- Why do you need permission to communicate with others via the Oversoul level if ultimately everyone is One Soul?

There are thousands of books on **Kabbalah**. You can get lost trying to determine what to read. Then when you find books, you can spend eons of time studying them. This is why you need to understand frequency to direct your process. One book came to me in unexpected ways which led me to read a few more books by the author. He mentioned the **Book of Formation** which is older than the *Torah*. If I read Hebrew, I might want to study the *Torah*. Because I do not read Hebrew this means that I am not supposed to study the *Torah*. However, I have meditated upon it, entered its frequency, and learned many things that I can prove to no one except my Self. I know what I know. The Original *Torah* is said to be in the *Ark of the Covenant*.

Because the **Book of Formation** is said to have been given to Abraham 400 years before the *Torah* was given to Moses, I decided that I wanted to explore this approximately 4000 years old book. I decided upon 3 books with commentary on the **Book of Formation/ Sefer Yetzirah**. These books have kept my attention for several months.

The ***Sefer Yetzirah*** exists in multiple versions, including:

The Short Version, The Long Version, The Saadia Version, and The Gra Version, among others.[9] The differences among these versions tend to be minor.

The Short Version comprises about 1300 words while the Long Version about twice that. In the 13th century, Abraham Abulafia noted the existence of both of them.

In the 10th century, Saadia Gaon wrote his commentary based on a manuscript which was a reorganized copy of the Longer Version, now called the "Saadia Version".

In the 16th century, Isaac Luria redacted the Short Version to harmonize it with the Zohar, and then in the 18th century, the Vilna Gaon (known as "the Gra") further redacted it. This text is called the "Gra Version". https://en.wikipedia.org/wiki/Sefer_Yetzirah

The ***Book of Formation*** is a very short book It is interesting to me that something so short contains so much powerful information. This is why this book, if you want to call it that, has existed for 4000 years.

- How do you know what books to study?
- Is it important to put into practice what you read?
- Is reading only a way to direct your focus?
- Is reading a springboard into your own Deep State?
- What is the energy behind a book that can exist for 4000 years?
- What keeps the energy of the book alive/in continuation?
- Do you know that the original ***Torah*** is said to be in the *Ark of the Covenant*?
- If you do not read a language, can you still mediate on it/enter the frequency to learn something?

- What happens if you put the word *Torah* at your Pineal Gland?
- What happens if you put the word *Torah* in Hebrew letters תורה, at your Pineal Gland, remembering to observe it from right to left?

Anything that survives thousands of years survives for a reason. Generally, when something does not receive any energy, it falls apart For example, think of a building of any kind. The building must be maintained or it falls apart. There is so much hidden history buried in the ground that appears unattended, yet the history still survives. Think of artifacts hidden in caves. The Bosnian Pyramids were hidden in plain sight. The local people all know of these hidden histories. Someone somewhere holds these histories. I even know of Indigenous People in North America who sent messengers to other tribes in the South who hid secrets and artifacts. Some of the hidden histories are attributed to alien civilizations that do not show themselves to the average person.

Sometimes, history is hidden in other dimensions. Think of the stories that people tell of stopping at a restaurant or hotel to eat or sleep, but upon their return at another time, there is no sign that such a place ever existed. Even people come and go who appear to be from different time periods. But, just because something survives does not make it good or bad. It means that there is attention/energy that holds the information in this reality in some way for some reason. This includes all the **Kabbalah** work that has survived over time. Because it has survived, people pay attention to it, sometimes without coming to their own conclusions.

All of the **Kabbalah** work is full of commentary. The commentary has been written down, sometimes on the sides of handwritten manuscripts. Some of it has even been incorporated into the original work, which is why there are different versions of the same thing. But regardless of who has added what, the original is somewhere in the mix. Some people think because the information is old and survived, it must be true. One thing that I found curious was that many of the Kabbalist authors that I came across died relatively young. When I first started reading some of these books, I had a lot of questions.

- If the Kabbalist authors had the secrets to life, should they live longer than average?
- Or, were these ancient Souls that came for a specific reason to give specific information and when their work was done, they departed this reality?
- Why was there so much infighting amongst those studying **Kabbalah**?
- Why were there so many different schools of **Kabbalah**?
- Why was there more than one interpretation of the various tenents of **Kabbalah**?
- How many ways can history be hidden?
- Why is history such a mystery?
- How much history is hidden in the Earth?
- When you uncover your own inner Deep State, must it then follow that the inner Deep State of the Earth must be uncovered?
- In what ways can true history be revealed besides artifacts, books, and local folklore?

One of the first things I disagreed with when I read the Kabbalists' commentary was that when you want to elevate your Soul so you can merge into God, you need to loosen your Soul from your body. This is absolutely not correct! Hopefully, you have read **Hyperspace Plus** where you can visually see a 2 dimensional representation of the Oversoul Matrix. You do not loosen your Soul; you expand your focus. I thought no wonder they die young if this is what they are doing. Then, I read about what they call the *Kiss of God*. While this may sound lovely, I guess in this case "lovely" is a judgment call. The *Kiss of God* happens when you are meditating with God and you die! In their opinion, this happens because your Soul has elevated so high that you are kissed by/taken by God. No thank you!

I read some Kabbalist authors who I felt were promoting a type of New Age Judaism, where the goal is to feel good and get whatever you want by using specific formulas. There was nothing about taking responsibility or not judging God's world. The premise was always doing what you want, getting what you want, helping others get what they want. Anything you don't want is bad; anything you do want is good. There was no discussion of discernment or getting what God wants for you rather than what you want for you.

Keeping in mind that the **Torah** is a set of instructions about how life works and **Kabbalah** explains the **Torah** I realized that these ancient books were about helping people understand their lives and live in accordance with Spiritual Law. Spiritual Law is different than Religious Law.

Religious Law in Judaism tells Jewish women how to decide if they were clean or unclean and therefore could or could not have sex with their husbands. You would think that a woman could figure out if she was menstruating or not, but the rules are so detailed, that a woman must use a special white cloth that she wraps around her finger, inserts it into her vagina, and then looks to see if she is bleeding or not. If a woman is not sure, then she is to take her underwear and send it to her rabbi and let him make the determination. Read through the following to get an idea of what the commentary says a Jewish woman must do:

> Jewish law forbids sexual relations while a woman is a niddah and until she then immerses in the mikveh, or Jewish ritual bath, and the rabbis prescribe a number of additional regulations. The main ones are avoiding physical contact between spouses

and sleeping in separate beds while a woman is niddah. Many Orthodox couples also avoid passing objects directly to each other, seeing each other undress, or engaging in flirtatious conversation. According to halakhah, or Jewish law, a woman becomes a niddah, a menstruating woman, if she is experiencing the full flow of her period, or any time she sees red blood emerging from her body or on white underwear that she is wearing, unless she has good reason to believe that the bleeding is not uterine in origin. The **Torah** distinguishes between niddah, a woman having her regular menstrual period, yoledet, a woman giving birth (which includes a woman having a late miscarriage), and zavah, a woman experiencing an irregular flow of blood. According to the **Torah**, a niddah simply counts seven days from the first day of her period (including the first day) and then goes to the mikveh to purify herself on the night following the seventh day. Similarly, a yoledet simply counts seven days from the birth of a son or 14 days from the birth of a daughter before going to the mikveh. But a zavah must wait seven clean days after her blood flow has ended before undergoing purification. The **Torah's** description of the purification of the zavah serves as a guide to the details of niddah rituals:

When she becomes clean of her discharge, she shall count off seven days, and after that she shall be clean (Leviticus 15:18).

When she becomes clean of her discharge—the woman must establish that her bleeding has ended before beginning to count the seven clean days. She establishes this fact through an internal self-examination before sundown of the day before her seven clean days begin. This self-examination is called the hefsek tahara.

She shall count off seven days—the seven clean days are seven full days, from sundown to sundown. For example, if a woman starts her period on a Sunday, and does her hefsek tahara before sundown on Thursday, then the first of her seven clean days would be Friday, and the days would end on the following

Thursday at nightfall. During those days, all the restrictions of niddah still apply, and the woman is supposed to wear white underwear to make sure that she notices any bleeding. Also, part of the "counting" is performing more internal examinations (this process is called bedikah). The minimum number of internal examinations is one on the first clean day and one on the seventh (in addition to the hefsek tahara), but the Shulhan Arukh recommends two daily examinations on each of the seven days.

If blood appears on the woman's underwear, or as a result of the examinations, at any time during that week, she must perform a new hefsek tahara and start the seven days again from the next evening. However, some spotting may not be halakhically problematic if the color is not reddish. It is helpful for a woman to be familiar with the colors that are or are not halakhically problematic, since those distinctions can sometimes save her days of being a niddah.

And after that she shall be clean—once the seven clean days are over the woman may go to the mikveh. Mikvaot (plural of mikveh) are normally open every night of the year except for the nights of Yom Kippur and Tisha B'Av, so even if it is Shabbat or a holiday a woman may still go to the mikveh. A mikveh is halakhically defined as a pool of rainwater. However, modern mikvaot contain two pools, one of rainwater and one of (chlorinated and regularly cleaned and changed) tap water. The waters of the two pools are linked through one or two small openings so that the tap water pool takes on the halakhic status of rainwater. In this way, modern mikvaot are able to ensure that both halakhic and sanitary requirements are met. Some natural bodies of water may also be used as mikvaot.

Since another verse about using a mikveh requires that the entire body be immersed at once (Leviticus 15:16), people who immerse in a mikveh must rid themselves of any objects that interfere with the water touching all parts of the body.

This includes dirt, clothing, and jewelry, knots in the hair, or contact lenses. So before immersing, a woman washes herself thoroughly and inspects her body to make sure it is completely clean and free of interfering objects. Due to the same concern about making sure the whole body is in contact with the water, someone else must watch the woman immersing to make sure her whole body and hair go under the water and that she is not touching the walls or floor of the mikveh. When immersing, a woman recites the blessing: "Blessed are You, God, who sanctified us with Your mitzvot, and commanded us regarding immersion." Most Sephardic women recite the blessing before undressing and entering the water, but Ashkenazic women enter the water, dunk once, recite the blessing, and then dunk one or more additional times. After this immersion, the woman is no longer a niddah.

Behavior While Not a Niddah

When a woman is not a niddah, Jewish tradition encourages sexual relations and all other physical contact between a married couple. The couple is especially encouraged to have sex the night the woman returns from the mikveh, and on Friday nights. The only times sex is forbidden are on Yom Kippur, Tisha B'Av, during shiva, and on the days on which the woman anticipates her period's return.

https://www.myjewishlearning.com/article/the-laws-of-niddah/

Related Articles:

VIDEO: Ketamim (Stains)

Feminine Hygiene Pads

The Niddah Status

Sensation of Menses (Hargashah)

Stains (Ketamim)

Toilet Paper

Bleeding from Trauma (Dam Makkah)

Related Q&A

Staining from c-section scar

Light brown stains in early pregnancy

Light brown on sheet

Staining during active pills

Light brown stain on thigh

Cervical staining with Mirena

Hargashah and dark brown stains

Heavy staining around ovulation

Post-menstrual brown staining

Thyroid disease and spotting

(…there must be at least 100 more that I did not list here.)

Discovering an unexpected bloodstain can be stressful. Besides being suddenly required to separate from her husband, a woman is sometimes faced with the prospect that her normal menses will begin before she can go to the mikveh, prolonging the separation. Furthermore, she often wonders if there is something medically wrong. According to **Torah** law, a woman becomes niddah only when a bodily sensation (hargashah) accompanies her uterine bleeding. Our Sages, however, decreed that a bloodstain found on clothing or another object, unaccompanied by hargashah, can also render a woman niddah. However, they enacted several leniencies as part of this decree, to avoid overburdening women by causing them to become niddah frequently from extraneous stains. These leniencies are listed below.

Laws of Stains

Leniencies

    The size of the stain

    The type of surface on which the stain was found

    The color of the surface on which the stain was found

    The location of the stain

    A stain attributable to other causes

    The color of the stain

Precautions

    Staining or a Flow?

Leniencies

The first four leniencies listed here apply only when there has been no hargashah. Therefore, they do not apply to any discharge found on a bedikah cloth, or another item inserted internally such as a tampon or diaphragm, because the sensation of inserting or removing the item could have masked a hargashah.

The size of the stain

Only a stain larger than the size of a gris, roughly the area of a circle about 19 millimeters in diameter (approximately 280 mm2, about the area of a US dime or an Israeli shekel), renders a woman niddah. This measure is one of area, so a long narrow stain may still be smaller than a gris. When a woman is certain that a stain is smaller in area than a gris, she may be confident that it did not make her niddah.

When several smaller stains are found on the body, they render her niddah if the total surface area adds up to more than the size of a gris. When several smaller stains are found on a garment or other surface, the area of each stain is considered separately.

The type of surface on which the stain was found

The laws of niddah, and particularly the decree about stains, are closely associated with the laws of ritual impurity (tumah v'taharah). Accordingly, our Sages ruled that a stain would have halachic significance only if it could render the object on which it was found ritually impure. Thus, a stain found on an object that is not susceptible to ritual impurity (e.g., a plastic chair or toilet seat, or on the floor) does not render a woman niddah. There is a dispute among contemporary halachic decisors as to whether synthetic fabrics such as nylon are susceptible to ritual impurity; if a stain is found on a garment made from synthetic fabric, a specific halachic question should be asked.

Our site follows the halachic ruling that disposable pantiliners and pads are not susceptible to ritual impurity, so that a stain found on a disposable pantiliner or pad of any color does not make a woman niddah. If a woman uses a colored pantiliner, there are even more grounds for leniency. Please see our article on feminine hygiene pads for more information.

According to many authorities, a stain on toilet paper, a toilet seat or toilet water is treated as a stain on an object that is not susceptible to ritual impurity. But if blood is found on any of these within seconds of urinating, the leniencies of stains may not apply. Please see our article Toilet Paper for more information.

The color of the surface on which the stain was found

A stain found on a colored surface does not render a woman niddah. Therefore, it is highly recommended that women wear colored underwear (except during the seven clean days) and sleep on colored sheets, in order to avoid becoming niddah through staining.

This leniency applies to items of any color (except off-white and pale beige, which are considered shades of white). A woman can choose colors light enough that she will notice any staining, without the risk of a stain making her niddah.

The location of the stain

Only stains found where they could have come directly from vaginal bleeding can render a woman niddah. Thus stains found on the inner surface of the legs, or on the hands or feet, or on clothing from the hips down, pose halachic questions, but those on the upper body, or arms do not – unless a woman has done handstands or other acrobatics.

The following two leniencies apply to external stains, and may also apply to blood found internally (e.g., on a diaphragm) and to questionable bedikah cloths:

A stain attributable to other causes

If the stain could reasonably have come from another source, it does not make a woman niddah. For example:

If she has a wound on her body, to which the blood can reasonably be attributed (see Dam Makkah).

If she was working with blood, e.g., drawing blood in a laboratory, suturing a wound, or cleaning chickens.

If she can attribute the blood she found to someone else, e.g., she lifted a child with a nosebleed.

For women who fallow Ashkenazi rulings, the rules for attributing a stain to an external cause are more stringent during the first three of the seven blood-free days. Thus, if she is not absolutely sure that the blood is from an external source, she should consult a halachic authority.

The color of the stain

A flow or stain makes a woman niddah only if its color is one of those that halacha stipulates as niddah colors. Reds generally make a woman niddah; yellows or greens usually do not. Pink, brown, gold, orange, black or reddish shades should be evaluated by a halachic authority. Stains are best evaluated in natural sunlight (holding the cloth or stained item in the shade rather than in direct sunlight), as colors may appear different in artificial light.

Precautions for avoiding stains

It is completely legitimate, and halachically recommended, to rely on the leniencies built into the laws of stains. We recommend following the following precautions to avoid becoming niddah unnecessarily:

Wearing colored underwear or pantiliners (according to many opinions, including those followed by this website, disposable white pantiliners are also effective)

Not looking at toilet paper or taking care to wait fifteen seconds between urinating and wiping

Having relations on colored sheets, waiting a few minutes for both spouses to clean themselves afterwards, and using dark colored towels for cleaning. In any instance of finding bleeding immediately after relations, a halachic authority should be consulted as soon as possible

Not inserting tampons when not already in niddah

Not performing bedikot when there is no halachic requirement to do so

Staining or a Flow?

These leniencies above apply to the staining many women experience at various points during the reproductive life cycle (e.g., postpartum, perimenopause, while taking the active pills of hormonal contraceptives). They are not intended to prevent a woman from becoming niddah when she menstruates. A woman who feels a distinct hargashah or experiences a flow of blood becomes niddah even if she is wearing black underwear or disposable pantiliners or pads, and doesn't look at toilet paper.

There is no clearly defined halachic boundary between "staining" and a "flow." In practice, it is often relatively easy to distinguish. As a rule of thumb, bleeding that is too heavy to be contained by pantiliners, and would require a pad or tampon, is probably a flow. If she actually sees blood leaving her body, she is niddah. In doubtful situations, a specific halachic question should be asked. Close

Conduct while Staining

If a woman has spotting that does not meet the criteria for ketamim (and thus does not make her niddah), we usually recommend that she avoid actual relations until she has been clear of staining for about 24 hours. Other forms of physical affection continue as usual.

Refraining in this manner is a voluntary precaution against a flow beginning during relations, and also gives her time to evaluate the situation and determine whether the staining will develop into a real flow. It is not a halachic requirement, and does not indicate that she considers herself niddah.

Close https://www.yoatzot.org/becoming-niddah/522/

Sample question

My Hefsek Taharah was clean (after a few attempts) but I found a brown stain after performing the moch dachuk for about 30 minutes. Do I have to start over again with a new Hefsek Taharah tomorrow?

Answer:

If you found a small stain on your white underwear, check to see if it is smaller than a gris. A stain of any shape, whose area is less than that of a US dime or an Israeli shekel (a circle 19mm in diameter, or about 2.8 square cm), does not invalidate your clean days. If you're not sure of the area (e.g. it not perfectly round), or you found the brown spot on the moch itself or on a bedikah cloth, then the stain has to be shown to a rabbi in order to determine whether it invalidates your clean days. If it does, then you must do a new hefsek and start counting over again.

https://www.yoatzot.org/questions-and-answers/1158/

- How does reading these laws make you feel?
- Would you feel violated if you had to follow these laws?
- Would you feel worried and stress about correctly following these laws?
- Do you think the sages who interpreted the **Torah** were looking out for their flock or were they men who wanted to gain control over women?
- How would you feel about having to be watched to ensure you fully immersed in the mikveh bath?
- If you were raised this way, would this be normal?
- How do you feel knowing that this is only the tip of the iceberg of these kinds of laws for women?
- How many hours/days/years do you think the *sages* spent reaching all these conclusions?
- Does this commentary feel Spiritual?
- Do you think this is what the **Torah** is about?
- Do you think the *Kiss of God* should be a goal?
- Or that you should try to loosen your Soul from your body while meditating?
- Do you understand why it is wise to question everyone and everything?

Jews have a lot of laws to follow:

The Jewish tradition that there are 613 commandments (Hebrew: תרי"ג מצוות, romanized: taryag mitzvot) or mitzvot in the **Torah** (also known as the Law of Moses) is first recorded in the 3rd century CE, when Rabbi Simlai mentioned it in a sermon that is recorded in Talmud Makkot 23b. https://en.wikipedia.org/wiki/613_commandments#:~:text=The%20Jewish%20tradition%20that%20there,recorded%20in%20Talmud%20Makkot%2023b.

Most Jews keep Kosher households, meaning that they have two sets of kitchenware, one for dairy and one for meat and never the two shall touch. Kitchenware means pots, pans, serving utensils, silverware, plates, storage containers and more. Some Jewish homes have 2 complete kitchens, one for dairy and one for meat. And, most have 2 additional sets of kitchenware used only for Passover, so 4 sets of kitchenware total. And on the Sabbath, which is sundown Friday night to sunset Saturday night, they must rest which means even more strict laws that they must follow. These laws include everything from food to toilet paper to transportation and how far they can carry something from their home.

Here is one Rabbi's answer to the following question about the Sabbath:

> Rabbi, do you honestly believe that pressing a button to cross the road is considered doing work on the Sabbath? It doesn't seem so strenuous to me…
>
> Answer:
>
> It is not strenuous work that is forbidden on Shabbos, but rather creative work.
>
> During the working week we strive to make the world a better, safer and more comfortable place. We use our human ingenuity to invent, build, develop and improve the world around us. But on the seventh day we step back into ourselves. We take a break from trying to change the world and we appreciate the innate beauty of the world that Gd created. Instead of altering our surroundings we enjoy them. Rather than utilize the amenities that technology has given us we enjoy the blessings that Gd has

given us - love, family, friendship, meditation, and just being human.

Shabbos is a like a dream-world, and we enter this dream-world by leaving the mundane world behind. Even the smallest disturbance — like pressing a button — would bring us crashing back down to earth. And there's nothing worse than waking up from a dream before it's over.

https://www.chabad.org/library/article_cdo/aid/160977/jewish/Why-Is-Pressing-a-Button-Considered-Work-on-Shabbat.htm

There are thirty-nine general categories of labor that are forbidden on Shabbat. Each of these categories include a range of derivative laws and activities, some of which are described in *The Shabbat Laws*. The melachot are generally divided into six groups, classified according to the Mishkan's activities with which they are associated.

Read: An Introduction to the 39 Melachot

Field Work	Making Material Curtains	Making Leather Curtains	Making the Beams of the Mishkan	The Putting up and Taking down of the Mishkan	The Mishkan's Final Touches
Sowing Plowing Reaping Gathering and Binding Threshing Winnowing Selecting Grinding Sifting Kneading Baking	Shearing Wool Cleaning Combing Dyeing Spinning Stretching the Threads Making Loops Weaving Threads Separating the Threads Tying a Knot Untying a Knot Sewing Tearing	Trapping Slaughtering Skinning Tanning Smoothing Ruling Lines Cutting	Writing Erasing	Building Breaking Down	Extinguishing a Fire Kindling a Fire Striking the Final Hammer Blow Carrying

© Copyright, all rights reserved. If you enjoyed this article, we encourage you to distribute it further, provided that you comply with Chabad.org's copyright policy.

https://www.chabad.org/library/article_cdo/aid/102032/jewish/The-39-Melachot.htm

Kneading, the av melachah of losh, is forbidden on Shabbat. The melachah encompasses all activities which, like kneading, join small particles into one mass using liquid, and applies to both foods and non-foods. It also includes later treatment of dough, like basting or braiding.[1]

Kneading invariably involves two steps: a) Pouring the liquid into the flour; b) Mixing the flour and water together to make a dough. There is a Talmudic dispute regarding what exactly defines losh.[2] Rebbi says that just pouring the liquid over the flour is already losh, since the flour and water fuse on impact. Kneading them together is also Biblically forbidden, but as an independent, additional transgression. Rabbi Yosi Bar Yehuda, however, says that one only transgresses losh by mixing the ingredients together and not by merely pouring the liquid over the flour. While some halachic authorities, most notably Sefer Hateruma, follow Rebbi's interpretation, the vast majority side with Rabbi Yosi.[3]

There are a variety of substances that can be kneaded with liquid. Some, like fine flour, completely mix with water to the extent that the flour becomes a different entity—dough. These substances are halachically termed "bar gibul." There are other substances which are not kneadable, like oats or finely diced vegetables. When these are mixed with water they just clump together but don't transform into a new entity. These are called "lav bar gibul." It is apparent that Rabbi Yosi's ruling applies to bar gibul substances. The authorities debate, however,

---
1 Talmud Yerushalmi, Shabbat 50b.
2 Shabbat 18a.
3 Including Rif, Rambam and Rosh.

what he would say about kneading lav bar gibul substances.[4] Maimonides asserts that since one can't truly knead lav bar gibul ingredients, Rabbi Yosi would rule that one cannot Biblically transgress the melachah of losh with them, since the second step of kneading isn't done.[5] Accordingly, mixing them would only be rabbinically forbidden. Conversely, Tosafot maintains that since they are not kneadable, the second step is not applicable, and one Biblically transgresses losh simply by pouring liquids on them.[6]

Losh is only Biblically forbidden if done with a "belila ava" - a thick dough-like mixture which is not pourable. "Belila raka" - pourable mixtures, like dressings and dips, are only rabbinically forbidden.

It is extremely relevant whether a transgression is Biblical or rabbinic. One way to avoid a prohibition on Shabbat is to do the act in an unusual way. (Note: one cannot decide on one's own to do a forbidden act in an unusual way to avoid the issue. We follow the examples given by the sages.) If an act is only rabbinically forbidden, it is easier to apply the leniency. Also, a rabbinic prohibition will sometimes be waived in situations where the Sages felt it should not apply. For example, according to those who maintain that just pouring the liquid into the flour constitutes losh, there is no permissible way to make a belila ava on Shabbat, since there is no method of pouring unusual enough to permit a Biblical transgression.

Although most authorities follow Rav Yosi, the Rama[7] writes that one should be stringent and take into account those who follow Rebbi. Practically, this means that whenever possible one should prepare a belila ava before Shabbat regardless of whether

---

4 The Talmud (Shabbat 18a) records a disagreement between two sages. Rabbi Yosef says that Rabbi Yosi's opinion is that only kneadable ingredients are subject to losh. Abaye argues and says Rav Yosi would actually agree with Rebbi with regard to unkneadable ingredients, that one is liable for losh by just pouring liquid on them. Maimonides follows Rabbi Yosef, and Tosafot follows Abaye.
5 Hilchot Shabbat Chapter 21:33.
6 Shabbat 18a.
7 Orach Chayim 321:16.

it is bar gibul or not. If the food won't last when prepared the day before, in some cases one can be lenient and prepare them on Shabbat, provided it is done in an unusual way. For example, guacamole can be prepared on Shabbat but one should first put the lemon juice in the bowl before adding the avocado since this differs from the way it is normally done. Obviously, if one normally prepares it that way during the week he or she should do the opposite on Shabbat. One should also change the method of mixing, by using gloved hands or using a fork and making criss-cross movements. Note: there are many factors to consider and what is permissible with one food may not be by another, so each case should be treated individually.

If the mixture is a belila raka then one may always mix it using the same unusual methods described above. A useful tip suggested by the halachic authorities for one who wished to make a belila ava is to add extra liquid and make it a belila raka which allows for more leniencies.

If the mixture was kneaded already before Shabbat, one may add liquid on Shabbat and stir it gently. This is because the additional liquid actual makes the mixture less bonded together. Some authorities maintain that if the foods are cooked they are not subject to losh.[8]

Toladot

Mixing sand or earth with liquid.[9]

Losh in the Mishkan

Flour was kneaded with water to produce the showbread, the lechem hapanim.[10] Also, the dyes used in the mishkan were produced by mixing ground herbs with water and making it into a paste.[11]

---

8 Biur Halacha 321:14.
9 Eglai Tal Losh.
10 Rashi to Shabbat 73a.
11 Rav Hai Gaon.

Common activities to avoid

Making baby cereal or instant porridge in the usual way[12]

Making a thick salad dressing in the usual way

Mixing water and sand, and shaping sandcastles

By Menachem Mendel Wineberg

More from Menachem Mendel Wineberg | RSS

© Copyright, all rights reserved. If you enjoyed this article, we encourage you to distribute it further, provided that you comply with Chabad.org's copyright policy. © Copyright, all rights reserved. If you enjoyed this article, we encourage you to distribute it further, provided that you comply with Chabad.org's copyright policy.

https://www.chabad.org/library/article_cdo/aid/4819033/jewish/Losh-Kneading.htm

Cooking, the av melachah of bishul,[13] is forbidden on Shabbat. Although the word bishul means cooking, the melachah is better defined as enhancing a substance—food or non-food—by fire-generated heat. Enjoying hot food on Shabbat is a mitzvah, so it's important to understand the complexities of bishul to ensure that Shabbat is celebrated correctly.

One transgresses the melachah of bishul by heating liquids or solids to the point that they have significantly improved and are fit to consume. For food, this means cooking to the point of ma'achal ben druso'i,[14] which some authorities define as half cooked,[15] others as one-third cooked.[16] Liquids are considered cooked when they have reached the point of yad soledet bo

---

12 Making hot cereals can also involve the melachah of cooking.
13 The Mishnah (Shabbat 73a) calls this melacha "ofeh" - baking. As the Talmud explains there, this is because the first 11 melachot are presented in the order they would be done to bake bread.
14 Ben druso'ii was the name of a well-known robber who would eat his food par-cooked. Thus, foods cooked to that degree are called ma'achal ben druso'i - "the food of ben druso'i".
15 Mishnah Torah Hilchot Shabbat, chapter 9:5.
16 Rashi to Menachot 57a.

- the point at which one's hand would recoil because of the heat. The exact temperature of yad soledet bo is widely disputed, with some authorities putting it as low as 110 degrees Fahrenheit (43 degrees Celsius).[17] Speeding up the cooking process by stirring food that is hot but not yet cooked also falls under the prohibition of bishul, as does covering a steaming pot of uncooked food.

Reheating liquids that have already been cooked and fully cooled down falls under the Biblical prohibition.[18] Reheating cooked solid (dry) food, however, is permitted and is not considered bishul (see important caveats below). The reason for this distinction is that once a food is cooked it has already experienced a meaningful change. Heating it again doesn't really add anything. Cooked liquids, on the other hand, are rarely consumed in their cold state and need to be heated to be enjoyed. Therefore, just heating them up enhances them greatly, making one liable for bishul. Solid food, in this regard, refers to food that has no moisture, like bread. If the food is even slightly moist on the outside, like sauce on chicken, reheating it on Shabbat is forbidden.[19]

Heating food, using a medium that was heated by fire, toladot aish, is also Biblically prohibited on Shabbat. For example, adding cold food or liquid into hot food or liquid, such as adding cold water to thin out a thick soup that was just taken off the fire. In this scenario, we don't look at how hot the food is, but whether it is still in the same pot or pan in which it was cooked. Halachah considers the original receptacle to be the most problematic, since it has been on the fire and is more likely to retain heat and cause bishul. Putting bishul-susceptible food into a pot that was previously on the stove, with contents that are yad soledet bo, is a Biblical transgression. If the contents of the pot have been transferred into another container, called a kli sheni (second vessel), adding bishul-susceptible food is

---

17 Rabbi Moshe Feinstein in Igrot Moshe Orach Chayim 4:3.
18 Shulchan Aruch Harav 318:9.
19 Shulchan Aruch Harav ibid 11. As explained in Shabbat Kehalacha Vol.1 pg.144

definitely a rabbinic prohibition, and may also be Biblical.[20]

Some authorities maintain that bishul can also be transgressed by cooking something after it was already baked or roasted or baking or roasting something after it was cooked. For example, adding roasted meat into a steaming pot of cholent.[21]

Rabbinic Prohibitions

There are many rabbinic prohibitions connected to bishul. Here, we will focus on quite a common one, which restricts performing shehiya - leaving food on the stove before Shabbat to finish cooking automatically on Shabbat.

Biblically, there is no issue with putting food on a stove before Shabbat and allowing it to continue cooking on Shabbat itself.[22] The sages were concerned, however, that allowing one to do so might bring him or her to raise the heat on Shabbat to ensure that the food would be cooked in time, which breaches the melachah of mav'ir - burning, and can also involve bishul. Because one would only be tempted to speed up the cooking process if the dish still required a fair amount of cooking, the sages established a point at which a dish is considered sufficiently cooked that we needn't worry one will want to adjust the heat.[23] The sages ruled that one who wishes to put a dish that is not, at a minimum, ma'achal ben druso'i, on the stove, is required to turn off the fire[24] or cover it. By doing so he

---

20 Shulchan Aruch Harav ibid. 12.
21 This is the opinion of Rabbi Eliezer of Metz (Sefer Yereim #274).
22 See Shulchan Aruch Orach Chayim 352.
23 There is a dispute in the Talmud (Shabbat 36b) as to whether there is a concern that one will adjust the fire on the stove if the food has already been cooked to the point of ma'achal ben druso'i. The opinion of Chananya is to be lenient that one is only required to cover or remove the fire if he places a pot of food on the stove before Shabbat which is not ma'achal ben druso'i. Conversely, the sages argue that there is a real concern one might adjust the heat of the stove with certain foods even if they are already fully cooked. The Shulchan Aruch (Orach Chayim Siman 253) follows the opinion of the sages while the Rama (ibid.), a major halachic authority whom Ashkenasic Jewry typically follow, rules like Chananya. There are those (Mishnah Berurah Biur Halacha to Orach Chayim 253) who understand the Rama to mean that one can be lenient after the fact, but preferably one should endeavor to follow the view of the sages. The accepted practice is to be lenient even in the first instance.
24 Nowadays, if the fire is turned off, there is no point in putting something on the stove. However, the stoves of mishnaic times were made in such a way that even after the fire was no longer burning under the stove, it still retained some heat.

demonstrates that he isn't really interested in involving himself in the cooking process, so we aren't concerned he will adjust the heat of the fire. The way this is commonly done is to put a thin sheet of metal called a blech over the fire, and the food is placed on top of it. Some authorities also require one to cover the knobs of the stove. Although this method is fully permissible halachically, to avoid any issues that may arise, the authorities exhort one to try to have all food fully cooked before Shabbat, and put it on a blech simply to keep warm.[25]

Bishul in the Mishkan

Certain herbs and plants were cooked to produce dyes for the Mishkan.[26] Additionally, the lechem hapanim (showbread) was baked each Friday to be put on display in the Mishkan on Shabbat.[27]

Common Activities to Avoid

Pouring hot water straight from an urn onto coffee granules or a teabag. Seasoning cholent while it is still hot, in the pot in which it was cooked. Taking the cover off a pot of cholent if it is not yet fully cooked

By Menachem Mendel Wineberg

More from Menachem Mendel Wineberg | RSS

© Copyright, all rights reserved. If you enjoyed this article, we encourage you to distribute it further, provided that you comply with Chabad.org's copyright policy.

https://www.chabad.org/library/article_cdo/aid/4833881/jewish/Bishul-Cooking.htm

---

[25] This is to avoid other issues that can arise when putting foods which are not fully cooked on a fire. Stirring the pot, putting a cover on it, or moving it to a hotter area on the stove are all halachic issues at any stage of cooking, but they are far more problematic if done with foods that are not fully cooked.
[26] Rashi to Shabbat 73a.
[27] Rav Hai Gaon.

Passover Question:

Is it really necessary to have leaven "removed" from one's property during the eight days of Passover? My plan was to box it up and put it in my shed for the week. Is this acceptable according to **Torah**? If not, why?

Answer:

The prohibition against chametz is unique in that not only is its consumption forbidden (as is the case with most forbidden foods), and not only is it forbidden to derive any benefit from it (as is the rule regarding a select few forbidden food items), but we are actually prohibited from possessing any chametz for the duration of Passover. In the words of the **Torah**: "No leaven shall be seen of yours, and no leavening shall be seen of yours throughout all of your borders."[1]

According to the mystics, chametz is a metaphor for vanity and arrogance, substances which we must completely be rid of on Passover — the holiday when we embark on our journey to freedom, spirituality, and the **Torah**. Click here for more on this topic.

Ridding one's home of all chametz or leavened foods during Passover is not simple. Most of us have pantries and freezers which are full of items which are not kosher for Passover. In addition, eliminating all chametz would also include thoroughly scouring every utensil, pan and pot which were used together with chametz items, to rid them of chametz residue.

So the rabbis conceived a halachic device whereby all chametz foods are stored in a closet or room (or more than one), which are then closed and sealed for the duration of the eight days of the holiday. On the morning before Passover the chametz is sold, and the areas wherein they are stored are rented, to a non-Jew. In this manner, the chametz no longer belongs to us, until the end of Passover when the chametz is bought back from the non-Jew.

So your shed would work out just fine!

The procedure of selling and buying the chametz involves many legal intricacies, it is thus necessary to delegate a competent rabbi to perform the sale on our behalf. You can delegate your local rabbi or use an online form to perform the sale.

Incidentally you need to sell the chametz which may be in any properties you own or rent. This would also include your office or business premises. If you have a home on the beach or in the mountains, whether you use it or not, you still need to sell the chametz that is within it, too.

https://www.chabad.org/holidays/passover/pesach_cdo/aid/496883/jewish/Is-it-really-necessary-to-have-leaven-removed-from-ones-property.htm

The reason I included all of the previous commentaries is that I want you to understand how complex and in my opinion convoluted, religion can become. This is why I tell you that religion is entirely separate from Spirituality. You can spend a lifetime studying how to behave in daily life. You can spend another one reading the commentary of what has been written about how to behave in daily life. You can spend a lifetime trying to interpret how to behave in daily life for others as you try to answer their questions based upon what is already established. You can also see why Jews would view Gentiles who do not follow all these laws as lesser than they are. Because they do what they do, how they do, they can justify that they are holier than you. This does not make them better or worse; it explains what goes on behind the scenes that most people do not take the time to learn.

I have studied many, many religions through the years. They all fascinate me because human behavior fascinates me. But, I do not want to claim any of them as my own. There are reasons why I was not born into any of them. And, when you decide to study **Kabbalah**, you must also go in with eyes wide open. It is easy to become so enamored with various facets of anything that you become distracted from your quest for truth. I teach you how to pierce through the distractions into truth. As you are discovering, even simple questions are filled with distractions that can take you anywhere but the deepest truths that you seek.

- Do you always keep in mind that religion is separate from Spirituality?
- If you had 613 laws to follow, how would you feel if you broke even one of them?
- How many questions could you have about just one law?
- Could you spend your entire life trying to follow all 613 laws while wondering each step of the way if what you were doing was correct or incorrect?
- Can people with very good intentions spend lifetimes studying the 613 laws?
- Or trying to explain these 613 laws to others?
- Can you become so enamored in various facets of anything that you lose sight of the goal?
- Does human behavior fascinate you?
- When you read some of these questions and answers, do you read the frequency behind them?
- Can words on paper become your god?
- Would you have to trust your Rabbi over your Self?
- Would it be easy to leave a religion like this?
- Would it be easy to enter a religion like this, i.e., become a convert?
- Are all these laws another way to hide truth from people?
- Who gets to decide who has the truth vs. who does not?

My point is that it is very easy to become enamored with anything because you do not really understand what is going on. You fill in a lot of blanks in your head with what you know vs. reality. For example, most people equate holidays with fun, but the Jewish holidays are not fun. They are all about suffering. While resting on the Sabbath sounds like a nice way to relax and rejuvenate, the rules of what you can and cannot do are all about suffering. Even when reciting the prayers or reading the *Torah*, most people do not understand what is being said.

> Prior to the Holocaust, there were 11-13 million speakers of Yiddish among 17 million Jews worldwide.[10] 85% of the approximately 6 million Jews who died in the Holocaust were Yiddish speakers,[11] leading to a massive decline in the use of the language. Assimilation following World War II and aliyah, immigration to Israel, further decreased the use of Yiddish both among survivors and among Yiddish-speakers from other countries (such as in the Americas). However, the number of Yiddish-speakers is increasing in Hasidic communities.
>
> https://en.wikipedia.org/wiki/Yiddish

The language of the people was Yiddish, not Hebrew. As already discussed, Biblical Hebrew is different than Modern Hebrew. This means that understanding the *Torah* was left to the interpretation of the Rabbis; the same ones who want women to send them their underwear to decide if the women are clean or unclean; the same Rabbis who say you can't be trusted to fully immerse your Self in a ritual mikveh bath, you have to be observed; the same Rabbis who tell you how to heat your food so you don't work on the Sabbath and tell you what you can carry and how far on the Sabbath. Just because you are Jewish does not mean that you understand what Hebrew genetics are all about or understand your true history.

Similarly, most people would not be able to read Old English vs. today's spoken and written English. Here in the US every region has its own dialects, accents and colloquialisms. My paternal Grandfather always talked about one of my cousins who was in the *tar business*. My friend thought my cousin was in the tar business until I explained that *tar* is how my Grandfather said *tire*. We could fill an entire book about the clumsiness of languages which is why I tell you to speak, listen and learn via the Oversoul level. When you are in search of knowledge and truth, distractions are at every turn. You might be excited to study **Kabbalah**, but like any subject, you must proceed wisely based upon what you know by knowing. Without a clear understanding, you might decide that now you want to become a Jew without realizing what this means. So many times I have thought that I was onto some big secret of the universe only to be let down when I started digging. Simply because something is old or withstood the test of time does not mean that it is something to be revered and respected. This means that it needs to be observed and questioned to understand first, why, and second, if it is most correct and beneficial for you to explore it.

- Is it challenging to say that you know more than the experts?
- Is it challenging to say that you know the experts are incorrect, yet you may not be able to explain why other than your knowing by knowing?
- Have you been excited to explore a topic or body of information only to be let down when you discover that it isn't what you thought it was?
- Is it easier to leave the interpretations of your Spiritual Beliefs to others because then you think that as long as you follow what they say you are never incorrect?
- As a female, how would you like to contact your Rabbi to see if he would be available to examine your underwear right away?
- As a male, how would you like your wife to have to discuss such things with your Rabbi?
- Do you want others to explain to you what is and isn't work?

- If you do not agree with the group, are you therefore, declared not spiritual?
- How challenging is it to leave such a group?
- Are organized religions accepted societal cults?
- Do you equate holidays with fun?

While the **Book of Formation** is relatively short, the number of commentaries on it would fill volumes. Some of the interpretations left me a bit aghast at what you can do/should do. I already explained to you about the 3 Mother letters of Aleph, Mem and Shin. The **Book of Formation** further defines the Hebrew letters into 7 Doubles and 12 Elementals. The various rearrangements of these letters, called permutations, make various things happen, such as in the Original Creation. The commentaries then all give you a variety of formulas that you can say and do for other acts of creation. For example, there are *32 Paths of Wisdom*. There are also 221 Gates supposedly used to create the famous Golem in Prague.

Keeping in mind that I do not know Hebrew, going through the commentaries was a bit intimidating for me, but nevertheless, I persevered. When I came to the part about creating a Golem, I thought, "This is just wrong!". The majority of the formulas are time-consuming, detailed, and challenging to understand much less do. So again, I questioned if this information which is thousands of years old truly holds all the keys to this universe then why do the people who hold these keys not live forever in a paradise-type world. My answer is that they are not using or interpreting the information in the most correct and beneficial way.

I give you the example of a man who wanted to learn to walk on water. He went to his father and told him that he found a teacher who could show him how to do this, but it would take 7 years. After 7 years, the son returned and showed the father that he could walk on water. The father was unimpressed, telling the son that for 7 rupees he could hire a boatman to take him across. The moral of the story is to think about how you want to use your time and energy.

If you want to go from Los Angeles to New York you could walk. This would accomplish your goal but you would expend a lot of time and energy doing this. If someone told you about a mythical creature called a horse that you could ride across the land, you might decide to try this method instead. After finding a horse you would have to train it so you could ride upon it as well as learn about how to care for the horse. If you had a horse and someone told you about a car that could carry you even faster, you might be enthralled with that information. If that person gave you a book, described the car and told you how to build one, you would have another challenge, but it could be done. If someone showed up with an airplane and said you could arrive at your destination in a few hours you would think the plane was a miracle. All of these methodologies can get you from Point A to Point B. You could spend a great deal of time studying any one of them. You have to think about how you want to spend your time and resources. There are a lot of things that I do not want to study. I prefer to fold time and space, then step from Los Angeles to New York in an instant.

- If time is an illusion, is it possible to fold time and space, then step from one place to another in an instant?
- Would you prefer to walk from coast to coast, find a horse and train it to carry you, build a car to drive there, or fly in an airplane to your destination?
- If all of the above accomplishes your goal why choose one way over another?
- How do you choose how to accomplish your goal?
- If walking is the oldest known methodology, is that the best?
- Or is folding time and space older than all of the above?
- How could people misuse folding time and space?

- Just because you can do something, does this make it most correct and beneficial?
- What if you have the answer in your hands but do not interpret it correctly?
- Or what if you interpret one layer of information without considering other possibilities?
- Can one answer be the pathway to many doors?
- Does Creation have to be complex?
- Do you contemplate how to most wisely use your time and resources?

When you think about walking from Los Angeles to New York City vs. the various other types of transportation, the fastest recognized way to get there right now is to fly in an airplane. Every time you speed up how you get from Point A to Point B, you are folding time and space. To me, an airplane is like a time machine. If I was a settler crossing North America in a covered wagon and all of a sudden given the option of an airplane, I would think a miracle just happened. Mentally I would have been prepared for a long and arduous journey. Now, I arrive at my destination clean and comfortable, surpassing many dangers, within a few hours instead of months. I knew a woman born in the early 1900s. She told the story of the first time her mother rode in a car. She said that her mother hung on for dear life as the car sped on at 5 miles per hour! When I think of folding time and space, I think of the Oversoul Archetype, which is represented two-dimensionally by two ovals touching on one side. Time, or at least the illusion of time is represented by an Oval Archetype in Hyperspace.

When you study the **Book of Formation**, you learn about the *10 Sefirot*. The highest Sefirah closest to God is called Keter in classical **Kabbalah**. Keter is outside of time and space, so this is why the Rabbis talk about going up the Sefirot to reach Keter. In Keter where there is no time and space, all is possible. Because Keter exists outside of time and space it is here that changes can be made in this reality. To get to Keter, you must use the *32 Paths of Wisdom* which consist of the *10 Sefirot* and the 22 Hebrew Letters. This is called climbing the *Tree of Life*. There are many formulas and again, in my opinion, allegories of how to climb the *Tree of Life*. The goal is always to reach Keter. Classical **Kabbalah** teaches you to loosen your Soul from your body to do this. It is in Keter that the *Kiss of God* is possible. Above Keter is Ain Sof, or All That Is.

- Is an airplane a Time Machine?
- Does a telephone bend time and space so that you can speak to someone even though he/she is not physically present and perhaps not in your time zone?
- Does the Oversoul Archetype help you bend time and space?
- Do you think that you need to climb the *Tree of Life* to Keter to make changes in any reality?
- Could loosening your Soul from your body help you to reach a Higher state of consciousness?
- Is loosening your Soul from your body necessary to reach a Higher state of consciousness?
- Why does one Soul choose one path of study vs. another path?

Kabbalah also teaches that it is within the Sefirah of Keter that prophecy takes place. Because Keter is above time and space, you can see the *Eternal Now*. Kabbalists also call Keter the level of Nothingness. It is on this level that the Laws of Nature cease to exist and therefore can be altered. Some Rabbis are said to be Prophetic Rabbis. Most people worry relentlessly about the future so if someone can ally their fears, they feel at peace. If you know someone who can go to Keter, look in the *Eternal Now* and report back, then you think that you will feel better. However, if someone tells you something you do not want to hear, then you have other issues.

When I was 25 a psychic told me that I was going to get a divorce, have an operation, and die by the time I was 40. These words haunted me until I was well past 40. When you want to hear what the future holds, you want to hear what you want to hear in the way you want to hear it. Asking anyone to tell you your future opens you up to ugly and pretty lies as well as uncomfortable truth. When you read frequency, you can see the direction that a person's frequency is headed. Sometimes you are allowed to tell a person and sometimes you are not. The issue with knowing these things is that people with ill intentions then take advantage of others. Or, people are tempted to use this information to their own benefit instead of in ways that are most correct and beneficial.

When you use your Hyperspace/Oversoul techniques, you are stepping out of linear time. You can read your own frequency to determine which way you are headed so you can make more informed choices. Even your dreams are statements that tell you something profound. When you see your linear future, you can make bad things worse as well as sabotage good things. It is always best to stay in the *Eternal Now*, as challenging as that can be. Focus on this moment and then the next moment reveals itself.

- How tempting is it to want to know the linear future?
- In the *Eternal Now*, is everything already decided?
- Does it take a strong person to see what the linear future holds and allow what is most correct and beneficial to happen?
- Do you realize that your Hyperspace/Oversoul tools and techniques are teaching you to step outside of linear time and space?
- Using your Hyperspace/Oversoul tools and techniques are you more informed so you can make the most correct and beneficial choices?

- Do people who know the linear future appear wise to the uninformed?
- Do you have to be Spiritual to see the linear future or do you just need to know tools and techniques?
- Can you use knowledge of the linear future to control others?
- Or to control the outcomes of specific situations without regard to what is most correct and beneficial?
- As much as you might want to know the linear future, would you be able to handle the temptations and responsibility?
- Are you learning to be satisfied with your present moment?
- Is it easy to worry about the linear future?
- Does worrying take away your Present Moment peace?

10 Sefirot

The study of the Sefirot is another method of Self-correction as well as answering the questions why am I here, how did I get here, from where did I originate and where am I going

The *Tree of Life* has *10 Sefirot*, as discussed in **Template of God-Mind**. Sefirot is the pleural of Sefirah. Sefirah means counting. The Sefirot are the origin of All That Is based on the number 10. This includes everything from your 10 fingers and toes to the 10 sayings from which God created the world. The deeper you go into each Sefirah, the more you find. The names of the Sefirot come from the ***Torah***:

> God says I have filled him with the spirit of God, with Wisdom, with Understanding and with Knowledge Exodus 31:3

The ***Sefer Yetzirah*** states in Chapter 1:9 that the spirit of God referred to above refers to Keter (Crown) which is the first of the Sefirot.

Keter means Crown. This Sefirah sits above the other Sefirot and is the closest to Ain Sof. Ain Sof means the Infinite and is beyond comprehension of humankind. Keter is the Sefirah that funnels the Light of the Creator to the rest of the Tree. It is said that Keter contains the total inventory and potential of each Soul in the *Eternal Now*, and is the genesis of everything that you ever were, are or will be according to linear time.

- If you put the word "Keter" at your pineal gland, what comes into your mind?
- If you put the word "Keter" at your Crown Chakra, what comes into your mind?
- If your surname is "Keter" or a derivative thereof, what would this mean for that person/family?
- Is the *Tree of Life / 10 Sefirot* another way for you to dissect and look at the composition of your Soul?
- Can your personal study of the *Tree of Life* help you answer the questions why am I here, how did I get here, from where did I originate and where am I going?
- Can you use the *Tree of Life* as an extended method of Oversoul/God-Mind communication?
- Do you spin your Chakra Bands from the top down or the bottom up?
- While spinning your Charkas, do you see the *10 Sefirot* in each of the appropriate Chakra Bands as illustrated in **Template of God-Mind**?
- As you do this visualization, can it help you go deeper into your own Soul?

Wisdom and Understanding
> God says I have filled him with the spirit of God, with Wisdom, with Understanding and with Knowledge Exodus 31:3

After Keter/spirit of God, Wisdom refers to Chakhmah and Understanding refers to Binah, the next two Sefirot. Wisdom/Chakhmah and Understanding/Binah are the next two Sefirot again referenced in these verses from the ***Torah***:

> With Wisdom, God established the earth, and with Understanding, He established the heavens and with His Knowledge, the depths were broken up. Proverbs 3:19,20

> With Wisdom a house is built, with Understanding it is established and with Knokwledge its rooms are filled. Proverbs 24:3, 4

The following verse from the ***Torah*** names the next seven Sefirot:

> Yours O God are the Greatness (4), the Strength (5), the Beauty (6), the Victory (7) and the Spendor (8) for All (9) in heaven and earth; Yours O God is the Kingdom (10) Chronicles 29:11

Newer Kabbalistic texts call 4 Chesed/Love while older texts call 4 Gedulah/Greatness. Personally, I prefer Greatness. Newer Kabbalistic texts call 6 Yesod/Foundation while older Kabbalistic texts call 6 Yesod/Foundation/All. To me, it makes sense that All is the Foundation.

The *10 Sefirot* are said to parallel the 10 Hebrew vowels, so together with the 22 Hebrew letters the *Tree of Life* comprises the totality of the Hebrew language.

This is all interesting because this once again shows you how you can interpret whatever you have in front of you to teach you about you. The **Book of Formation** has remained relatively consistent through the years, which gives a constant for generations of people to use as a way to pass Understanding/Binah and Wisdom/Chakhmah with Knowledge/Daat to each other. Even when you do not agree on everything or each individual interpretation, you still have consistency.

Humanity looks for consistency and focus throughout history. When history is changed or rearranged people feel ungrounded and unsettled. People need to know who they are and where they came from, even if they may not like it or appreciate it in the moment. Family and culture is one way to maintain consistency. Deeply rooted histories and cultures are challenging to destroy. People who do not feel connected to any person, place or thing are easier to manipulate and control. This is why elders are no longer respected. They hold history and continuity. Without the mentoring and guidance of elders, youth lose the Understanding, Wisdom and Knowledge of experience. This makes the youth more manipulable and influenceable. You can see the attempts to sabotage humanity right now. The buzz words are "new normal" which the elder generations are fighting while the youth accept it even if they don't care for it. The elders fight the implications to preserve the old way for the youth.

- Are the old ways worth fighting for?
- Do youth understand the implications of change?
- Is change always seen as a positive?
- Is change inevitable?
- Are elders becoming a throwaway commodity, along with their life experience and potential for guidance and mentoring?
- Are elders a "planned obsolescence"?
- How easy is it to make people feel disconnected from each other?
- Is there a natural inner longing to belong somewhere?
- Can you use anything as an instruction manual to life?
- Why do some books/information/customs/cultures survive/thrive while others disappear?

God's Fingers

Chapter 1:3 in the ***Book of Formation*** says:

> Ten Sifirot of Nothingness
> in the number of ten fingers
> five opposite five
> with a singular covenant
> precisely in the middle
> in the circumcision of the tongue
> and in the circumcision of the membrum.

According to **Kabbalah**, Creation is said to have been accomplished with God's fingers. In many places in the **Bible** where God interferes directly with the physical world God's fingers or hands are referenced:

> When I see Your heavens, the work of Your fingers (Psalms 8:4). My left hand has founded the earth, and My right hand has spread out the heavens. (Isaiah 48:13).

To generate the tension and force of Divine Creation, all of the *10 Sefirot* had to be polarized to male and female sides. This is reflected in human procreation which must involve male and female, *five opposite five* as you shall see in the following information.

Generally the *10 Sefirot* are displayed in three columns. Moving the Sefirot of the central column to the right and left divides the Sefirot into two arrays to produce a powerful tension. In this configuration powerful spiritual forces can be directed and channeled.

In the following charts you can see the division of the *10 Sefirot* into Feminine and Masculine:

Five Feminine Strengths on the left side

Binah	Understanding (left thumb)	End
Gevurah	Strength (left pointer finger)	North
Hod	Splendor (left middle finger)	Down
Yesod	Foundation/All (left ring finger)	West
Malkhut	Kingship (left little finger)	Evil

Five Masculine Loves/Greatness on the right side

Keter	Crown (right thumb)	Good
Chakhmah	Wisdom (right pointer finger)	Beginning
Chesed	Love/Greatness (right middle finger)	South
Tiferet	Beauty (right ring finger)	East
Netzach	Victory (right little finger)	Up

The Feminine Sefirot include the three which are normally on the left as well as the two lower center Sefirot. The Five Feminine are on the side of Gevurah which is Strength, so they are called the Five Strengths. The Masculine Sefirot include the three normally on the left as well as the upper two center Sefirot. The Five Masculine Sefirot are called the Five Loves because they are on the side of Chesed which is Love. Again, referring to old Kabbalistic texts, this might be more accurately called Five Greatnesses.

There are a total of 14 bones in the 5 fingers of each hand. 1 + 4 = 5. In addition, this is the numerical value of Yad, the Hebrew word for hand.

Think of the use of the hands in healing work, such as the laying on of hands, blessing others, hands united in prayer. This is really a replication of the *five opposite five* Sefirot. In this way the Sefirot are polarized, creating spiritual tension that allows the powers of the Sefirot to be focused and used.

I have often taught people to feel this power of the hands. All you have to do is hold your hands about 12 inches apart from each other, palms facing each other with fingers pointing up and not touching each other. Mentally feel your fingers tingle. Gently pull your hands away from each other and then back towards each other. You can feel the energy moving back and forth. Take one finger from one hand, point it at the palm of the opposite hand. Still about 12 inches apart, use your pointer finger to draw a circle on the palm of the other hand. Draw the circle one direction and then the other direction. Make an

Oversoul Infinity Archetype. Now do the same with the opposite hand. You can also do this on the bottom of your feet which are another *five opposite five*.

I used to do hands-on healing of people. Two things happened. One, I found out that when the pain of others is taken away, so is their incentive for working on themselves. Pain is a powerful teacher and motivator. Two, by pulling the toxins out of people with my hands I was contaminating my Self on all levels with their personal energetic garbage. This is another example of just because you can do something does not mean that it is most correct and beneficial.

- Have you ever done or experienced hands-on healing?
- If so, what were the results?
- What were the results of doing the exercise above of moving currency through your hands?
- Does this add another layer of what you already know?
- Is it important to know the function of each of the *10 Sefirot*?
- Is this something that someone can explain to you, something that you must experience or a combination of both?
- Must Creation always take place with polarization, i.e., male/female?
- Is the human body designed to channel creative force?
- If you know what each Sefirot is designed to do, does this help focus your prayers?
- Can your physical body hold the power of the Sefirot?

Fluency of Speech

Circumcision of the tongue, as referred to in Chapter 1:3 denotes a fluency of speech. At one time, there was a saying regarding people who could not speak properly. They were said to have "uncircumcised lips".

In the ***Bible***, Moses said:

> How will Pharoah listen to me, when I have uncircumcised lips? Exodus 6:12

People are often seen raising their hands to give or receive blessings. Ideally, the hands should be at the level of the mouth for more powerful prayer. In addition, at one time, priests were expected to wash their hands and feet before worship as a way of cleansing these important parts of the body before bestowing any priestly blessings. Prophecy was considered the ultimate *circumcision of the tongue*.

God told Moses:

> I will commune with you, and I will speak to you from above the ark-cover, from between the two Cherubim, which are on the Ark of Testimony. Exodus 25:22

The ***Zohar*** says that the Cherubim represent the *10 Sefirot* divided into the Masculine and Feminine array. The Ark contains the original Tablets of the 10 Commandments, 5 Commandments on each Tablet. Thus the Tablets represent the same array as the Cherubim on top of the Ark. Now, a permanent state of tension is created through which the spiritual force of the *10 Sefirot* can be focused. This explains why the Ark is so powerful and so coveted.

The final line in Chapter 1:3 says:

> and in the circumcision of the membrum

Sexual organs between the legs represents the circumcision of the sexual organs. God gave Abraham and his descendants power over the transcendental plane, most obviously conception to bring a Soul down into this world. By concentrating your focus in your sexual area, you can bring down Souls of spiritual power. In addition, sexual/creative energy can be used for spiritual quest. The prophetic position favored by Elijah is thus explained:

> Elijah went up to the top of the Carmel, entranced himself on the ground, and placed his face between his knees. 1 Kings 18:42

This position allowed the intense concentration of spiritual energy. The tongue was in alignment with the sexual organs along with the hands. These body parts were closest to the toes. The 10 fingers, 10 toes, 1 tongue and 1 sexual organ parallel the 22 letters of the Hebrew AlephBet. In this way the body itself becomes the AlephBet, allowing the individual to write in the Spiritual Realm.

True Reality of Sexuality explains how the body forms archetypes during sexual activity. Be aware of all the movements of your body so you understand what you are archetypically creating as you move it. Dance is archetype in motion. You can especially see this in the cultural dances of the indigenous peoples. Every motion, no matter how slight, has a meaning. Labyrinths are created so you walk archetypes to imprint your Self, so be mindful if you choose to walk these. When I walk my dogs, I walk so that we create an Infinity Sign/Oversoul Archetype. When my boys were small, after dropping them off at school I stopped at an indoor pool where I swam archetypes in the water.

- Are you beginning to understand why the human body has the body parts that it has?
- Have you thought about why the human body is put together the way that it is, and the energetic and Spiritual principles behind it?
- Have you ever walked a Labyrinth?
- If so, did you know with what you were imprinting your Self?
- Have you created archetypes with your physical body?
- Or in any activity, such as walking or swimming?
- Do you think driving a vehicle on a specific road that is in a specific arrangement can affect you, even if you do not know what that archetype is or means?
- If you drive or are transported on the same path every day, does this imprint you with something?

- Have you thought about how every motion you make, no matter how slight, has a meaning on some level?
- Do you understand the importance of the *Ark of the Covenant*?
- Do you have a new appreciation for your fingers and toes?
- Do you understand now why hands are raised to give or receive blessings?
- Is it possible to become a living AlephBet and write in the Spiritual Realm?

God's Throne

The last line in the **Book of Formation**, Chapter 1:4 says:

And make the Creator sit on His base.

The **Bible** says:

He founded the earth on its base. Psalms 104:5

This means that everything in the physical world has a Spiritual counterpart and basis through which the physical can be elevated. There is a general rule in **Kabbalah** that every awakening from below motivates an awakening from above. When you do your Oversoul work, you send something up and you ask that something comes down to fill that empty space. The symbolism of God sitting means that He lowers His essence to be concerned with His creation. God's Throne is the vehicle through which He expresses such concern.

God is called the Yotzer in the ***Sefer Yetzirah***. Some people translate this as the Creator, but a more accurate translation is "the Former" or "the One who forms".

The 4 Universes

Atzilut is the highest universe and often referred to as "Nothingness". This is the domain of the Sefirot which because of where they are located. This is called the Sefirah of Nothingness.

Beriyah is the universe of Creation and the domain of the Throne. In Hebrew, Bara means to create and indicates to create something from nothing.

Yetzirah is the universe of Formation and the world of Angels. Yatzar means to form something from a substance that already exists, or something from something.

Asiyah is the universe of Making which consists of the physical world and its spiritual shadow. Asah means to make as in the completion of something. For example, when you make a sound, the sound is completed.

These **4 Universes** are alluded to in this ***Bible*** verse:

> All that is called in my Name, for My Glory (**Atzilut**) , I have created it (**Beriyah**) , I have formed it (**Yetzirah**) and I have made it (**Asiyah**). Isaiah 43:7

The ***Book of Formation*** along with the ***Bible***, is telling you how to create in this physical reality by explaining the various energetic levels that you must pass through, what each energetic level contains and how to best utilize each level. Everything is symbolic with many, many different layers. This is why you get different information each time you read the same book or contemplate information that you may have contemplated dozens of times before. As you change, whatever you are studying reveals more of what was once previously hidden to you. One of the biggest secrets hidden in plain sight is that your mind-pattern always pulls to you a reflection of what is going on inside. Most people, however reject the reflections rather than use them as tools of study. Or, you pick and choose what you like or do not like. What you like you accept; what you do not like you reject. The Truth is always the same.

But, like the elephant in the room, your interpretation of the elephant depends upon from which perspective you are looking. Change your location in the room and never before recognized information about the elephant reveals itself to you. The more you move around the same elephant, the more information you discover. If your path is always the same, you will only gather the same information. The more you expand your path around the elephant, the more you see. Each revolution around the elephant allows you to observe something you had not seen before because your perspective continues to change. The elephant is always the same; it is you who change and thus your discoveries are only new to you.

- Do you have a favorite book that you have read many times because you always find something new to discover?
- Or a favorite place to which you continue to return because it is familiar yet you still make new discoveries each time you visit?
- Or a favorite food that you enjoy eating in different variations?
- When you explore old favorite-anythings, do you continue to find new discoveries?
- Do you enjoy finding new levels of anything that you enjoy in life?
- Do you enjoy finding new levels of Being within your Self?
- Are some of the new levels challenging to face?
- Can you use your known tools and techniques but in new and different ways to help you face challenging new levels?
- If the *Torah/Bible* is a code that explains this reality, would everyone in existence know this on some level?
- Does Truth change?

32 Paths of Wisdom

These *32 Paths of Wisdom* consist of the 10 digits/fingers and toes plus the 22 letters of the Hebrew AlephBet. The *10 Sefirot*, the most basic concepts of existence, are a manifestation of the 10 digits.

The *32 Paths of Wisdom* parallel the human nervous system. There are 31 nerves that emanate from the spinal cord while the 32nd and highest path corresponds to the complex of cranial nerves, of which there are 12. Like the nerves, the *32 Paths of Wisdom* is a two-way street. Kabbalists say that to approach the Mind you must travel the 32 paths.

In Hebrew the number 32 is written לב which spells Lev, the Hebrew word for heart. The heart provides support to the brain and nervous system. Without the heart, the nervous system stops functioning as does the mind. The heart is called *the king over the soul* by the **Sefer Yetzirah**. The **Torah** is seen as the heart of creation. Interestingly, the first word of the **Torah** begins with a Bet. *Bereshit*, which is the first word of the **Torah**, translates to "In the beginning". The last letter of the **Torah** is the Lamed of Yisrael/Israel. Keep in mind that the Lamed and Bet together spell heart. The *32 Paths of Wisdom* are contained in the **Torah**. The **Torah** is therefore expounded upon in 32 different ways.

Chapter 1:1 of the **Book of Formation** says:

> With 32 mystical paths of Wisdom
> engraved Yah...
> And He created His universe
> with three books (Sepharim)
> with text (Sepher)
> with number (Sephar)
> and with communication (Sippur).

According to **Kabbalah**, the *32 Paths of Wisdom* are alluded to in the **Torah** by the 32 times that God's name Elohim is written in the first chapter of Genesis. The words "God said" are written 10 times. These are referred to the *10 Sayings* that created the world because the *10 Sayings* parallel the *10 Sefirot*.

In the beginning God created the Heaven and the Earth.
Genesis 1:1

God said is not in the above verse, but Kabbalists say that it is implied and understood, thus applying it to the *10 Sefirot* as follows:

In the beginning God Created	Keter
God said, let there be light	Chakhmah
God said, let there be a firmament	Binah
God said, let the waters be gathered	Chesed
God said, let the earth be vegetated	Gevurah
God said, let there be luminaries	Tiferet
God said, let the waters swarm	Netzach
God said, let the earth bring forth animals	Hod
God said, let us make man	Yesod
God said, be fruitful and multiply	Malkhut

As you can see, the number 10 continues to be an important factor throughout all of Creation. As you know from your Hyperspace/Oversoul work, the number 10 is the number of New Beginnings. I am always excited when my chronological age adds up to a 10 because I know New Beginnings are coming my way. Of course, you always have a choice to begin the old ways again and loop through the next 9 years until your next New Beginning cycle. Or, you can release the old and truly begin something New. The energies are there for you to move forward or to repeat old cycles. I do my best to release the old and build something New and better.

The metric system, based on the number 10 is used throughout the world except for 3 countries:

> That's right — the three countries which are not using the metric system are Liberia, Myanmar and of course... the United States of America. Why is the United States so keen on preserving the imperial system? In short, it's not because Americans hate the metric system — it's because they hate change, just like the rest of world. But in an ever-connected world, can the US afford not to line up to a standard that everybody else seems to adhere to? As we'll learn, this resistance to change comes at a cost but at the same time, change also has a cost.
>
> https://www.zmescience.com/other/map-of-countries-officially-not-using-the-metric-system/

- Are you aware of your own chronological age and what the number of each year means to you, personally?
- Do you use the number of your chronological age as a guidepost for the direction your Soul wants you to go?
- Do you know of life changes that happened when the numbers of your chronological age added up to 10?
- How many years before your chronological age adds up to 10?
- What does your current chronological age tell you about where you are in your cycle of learning, as interpreted for you in ***Healer's Handbook?***
- Why do you think the number 10 is so important throughout existence?
- Is the number 10 somehow a continual replication of the original creative forces here in this reality?
- Why do you think the USA does not use the metric system?
- Where else is the number 10 prominent in life?

Mother Letters

In *Kabbalah*, there are 3 Mother Letters in the Hebrew Alphabet:

Aleph, the first letter

Mem, the middle letter

Shin, the last letter

Technically, Tav is the last letter of the AlephBet, but it is considered one of the seven "Doubles" meaning that it has two sounds. Aleph, Mem and Shin are derived from Binah/Understanding, one of the *10 Sefirot*.

Proverbs 2:30 says, For you shall call Understanding a Mother.
Ezekiel 21:26 calls a crossroad "mother of a road."

Aleph, Mem and Shin form the horizontal links between the Sefirot in the *Tree of Life*.

God made is written 3 times and parallels the 3 Mothers as follows:

God made the firmament	א	Alef	Mother 1
God made two luminaries	מ	Mem	Mother 2
God made the beasts of the field	ש	Shin	Mother 3

Doubles

A Double is a Hebrew letter that has 2 sounds. *God saw* is written 7 times and parallels the 7 Doubles as follows:

God saw the light that it was good	ב	Bet
God saw that it was good	ג	Gimmel
God saw that it was good	ד	Dalet
God saw that it was good	כ	Kaf
God saw that it was good	פ	Peh
God saw that it was good	ר	Resh
God saw all that He had made	ת	Tav

Elementals

The remaining 12 Hebrew letters are called Elementals because they only have a single sound:

The spirit of God hovered	ה	Hey
God divided between the light and darkness	ו	Vav
God called the light day	ז	Zayin
God called the firmament	ח	Chet
God called the dry land earth	ט	Tet
God placed them in the firmament	י	Yud
God created great whales	ל	Lamed
God blessed them, be fruitful and multiply	נ	Nun
God created man	ס	Samekh
In the form of God He created him	ע	Ayin
God blessed them	צ	Tzadi
God said, behold I have given you	ק	Kuf

According to the *Sefer Yetzirah*, Chapter 5:1:
> their foundation is
>
> speech, thought, motion,
>
> sight, hearing, action,
>
> coition, smell, sleep,
>
> anger, taste, laughter.

These qualities parallel the 12 months, the 12 signs and 12 houses of the zodiac, 12 constellations in the Universe and the 12 tribes of Israel, the 12 permutations of the Tetragrammaton.

Chapter 5:2 says:
> Twelve Elementals
>
> Their foundation is the twelve diagonal boundaries:
>
> The east upper boundary
>
> The east northern boundary
>
> The east lower boundary
>
> The south upper boundary
>
> The south eastern boundary
>
> The south lower boundary
>
> The west upper boundary
>
> The west southern boundary
>
> The west lower boundary
>
> The north upper boundary
>
> The north western boundary
>
> The north lower boundary
>
> They extend continually until eternities of eternities
>
> And it is they that are the boundaries of the Universe.

These 12 boundaries correspond to the 12 edges of a cube. These 12 boundaries also relate to the 12 diagonal lines in the *Tree of Life*. The number 12 is also associated with the *twelve directors of the soul* in Chapter 5:6. As you can see, there are layers upon layers within layers of meaning in each and every one of these short verses and chapters.

Ain Sof

According to **Kabbalah**, the Creator is called Ain Sof, meaning the Infinite. There are other names for God which refer to the various ways through which God manifests in creation. For example, *Elohim*, refers to the manifestation of delineation and definition. Each of the *32 Paths of Wisdom* delineate and define a specific aspect of Creation. Because humans are a microcosm of the macrocosm as you learned in **Decoding Your Life**, the body symbolizes/represents/outpictures something in the forces of Creation.

The *6 Days of Creation* are represented in your 2 arms, 2 legs, torso and sexual organs. In Genesis 1:27 the **Torah** uses the word *Elohim* for God, which is generally translated to *God formed man in the image of God*.

Kabbalists actually interpret the first verse in Genesis to read,

> In the beginning He created Elohim, along with the heaven and the earth.

The name *Elohim*, is associated with the Constriction, or the Tzimtzum which you learned about in the **Template of God-Mind**.

Other designations for God include *Yah, the Lord of Hosts, God of Israel, the Living God/Elohim Chaim, King of the Universe, Almighty God/Omnipotent Almighty/El Shaddai*.

> God told Moses, I appeared to Abraham, Isaac and Jacob as El Shaddai. Exodus 6:3

I find it very interesting that the Hebrew ***Bible/Torah*** has many names for God but other organized religions do not. Translating from one language to another provides the opportunity for disinformation to become the accepted truth through widespread dissemination. The more people say something the more others accept it as the truth. Once this happens there is no need to look any further. Your fascinating introspections most likely fall on deaf ears. Mind-control at its finest.

Other cultures pay homage to the many displays and aspects of the One God/Creator. But often this is misinterpreted by conventional religion to say that the cultures pay homage to many gods. This is not true but because this has been stated as so, many people not only believe this but have forgotten that the One God/Creator is Within All. This means that everything in existence is Holy, all originating from the One Source. Instead of the One God/Creator being recognized as Within All, the One God/Creator is conventionally viewed as something outside of Self. In Catholicism, you cannot speak to God directly, but must use an outside intermediary like a priest. This is also why Catholics are supposed to go to daily Confession and also use a different version of the ***Bible*** than Protestants. While you know to go directly to your Oversoul daily/moment-by-moment, the Catholic must go to a Church to a priest. Catholicism teaches that the Pope is the Vicar of Christ with the only one true connection to God. In general, Catholics are not allowed to question any of the Catholic rules to which they are expected to adhere.

- Does the use of different languages promote confusion and miscommunication?
- Can the interpretation from the original to any language be used to purposefully distort information for control and manipulation?
- When people accept twisted truth as fact, is this the moment that brain-washing/mind-control starts?

- Once people accept twisted truth as fact, why is it so challenging to untwist these distorted facts?
- When you read the Kabbalists version of the first line in Genesis, how does this make you feel about the translation you were taught?
- Would you feel different about life if you were raised with the knowledge that each variation of God's name meant an aspect of God Itself?
- Is it important to honor all aspects of God the Creator?
- Is All That Exists Holy and therefore should be venerated as such?
- When you read about the Hebrew letters and their significance, do you understand why these letters are considered sacred emanations of Creation from the God-Mind Itself?
- Can this information survive because it is correct, incorrect, or because there is so much study of the *10 Sefirot* and the process of Creation?

Tree of Knowledge

The array of the *10 Sefirot* is known as the *Tree of Life*. **Kabbalah** calls the *Tree of Life* an energetic reality that lies beyond the recognized 5 senses. The center line comprised of Keter, Tiferet, Yesod and Malkhut when taken alone, is called the *Tree of Knowledge*. This is because it is on this line that good and evil come together. Daat, called a quasi-Sefirah of Knowledge located between Keter and Tifert, is the place where good and evil converge. The *Tree of Knowledge* refers to the physical world that is perceived with the recognized 5 senses. The *Tree of Knowledge* represents the Animal Mind that looks to the physical world to provide. The *Tree of Knowledge* is said to rise from imperfect human understanding.

This is the *Tree of Knowledge* of Good and Evil referred to in Genesis 2:9 from which Adam and Eve were forbidden to metaphorically eat.

The *Tree of Life* is the Spiritual Mind The *Tree of Life* recognizes chaos and disorder as an illusion. The *Tree of Life* provides the male/positive female/negative polarity necessary for Creation. These forces must be balanced to access the *Tree of Life* via the four actions of restriction, sharing, meditation and prayer. Restriction and sharing relate back to the Original Tzimtzum of Creation where first there was a restriction and then a release, or sharing. Meditation and prayer are important for Source communication and instruction to remove the cycle of negativity from your life.

From here, you can gain a deeper understanding of the Spiritual Mind vs. the Animal Mind. Humans continually choose the Animal Mind over the Spiritual Mind. Or they think they are choosing the Spiritual Mind over the Animal Mind. For some reason, the balance seems to escape almost everyone. Right now I am reading a book about toxic charity. This means that when you try to help others you often wind up harming them more than helping them. You foster dependence and take away human dignity. I have seen this happen in my own work when I have tried to help others, as I shared with you in **Heights of Wealth**. Via trial and error, as well as my own deep meditation and prayer, I am much better than I used to be when determining who to help and how. However, I was appalled to learn that:

> In the USA, total giving to charitable organizations was $410.02 billion in 2017.
>
> Historically, Religious groups have received the largest share of charitable donations. This remained true in 2016. With the 2.9% increase in donations this year, 31% of all donations, or $127.37 billion, went to Religious organizations. Much of these contributions can be attributed to people giving to their local

place of worship. All data is the property of Giving USA 2018, the Annual Report on Philanthropy.

https://www.charitynavigator.org/index.cfm?bay=content.view&cpid=42#:~:text=Total%20giving%20to%20charitable%20organizations,%3A%201987%2C%202008%20and%202009.

And that religious tourism is an USD$18 Billion Industry.

Religious tourism includes missionaries, pilgrimages, and any type of faith-based travel.

https://www.nomadafricamag.com/religious-tourism-an-usd18-billion-industry/

This means that a lot of people are making a lot of money off of poverty of Spirit. It is in the best interest of anyone only interested in profit to keep the poor, poor. The Animal Mind and the Spiritual Mind are always challenged to find a balance.

- Are you surprised to hear how much was given to charitable organizations in 2017?
- Do you think with this much money donated that poverty should be totally eradicated by now?
- Is there big business in keeping the poor, poor?
- Will poverty ever be eradicated if someone, somewhere can make money from poverty?
- Why is the mind-pattern of the poor never addressed?
- Why is there so much effort put into keeping the Animal Mind and Spiritual Mind separate?
- Can all of this be traced back to the *Tree of Knowledge* and the *Tree of Life*?
- Does humanity have a choice to align Animal Mind with Spiritual Mind?

- Can studying the *10 Sefirot* help you understand what you need to do to align with Spirit?
- Where do the donations go?

The 10 Directions/Depths

The ***Book of Formation*** Chapter 1:5 says:

> Ten Sefirot of Nothingness:
>
> Their measure is ten
>
> which have no end
>
> A depth of beginning
>
> A depth of end
>
> A depth of good
>
> A depth of evil
>
> A depth of above
>
> A depth of below
>
> A depth of east
>
> A depth of west
>
> A depth of north
>
> A depth of south
>
> The singular Master
>
> God faithful King
>
> dominates over them all
>
> from His holy dwelling
>
> until eternity of eternities.

Later Kabbalists say that these ten directions parallel the *10 Sefirot*:

	Ain Sof/Infinite Being
Beginning/Past	Chakhmah/Wisdom/Male
End/Future	Binah/Understanding/Female
Good	Keter/Crown
Evil	Malkhut/Kingship
Up	Netzach/Victory
Down	Hod/Splendor
North	Gevurah/Strength
South	Chesed/Love (Greatness)
East	Tiferet/Beauty
West	Yesod/Foundation/All

Each direction is said to extend without limit therefore each Sefirah shares a property with Ain Sof. Chahkmah gains Wisdom from the Past and influences the Future. Binah gains Understanding from the Past so the linear Future is impregnated by the Past. You cannot get to the Beginning or Infinity ago, and you cannot get to the End/Future Infinity. Keter is closest to God so it is said to denote the direction of Good. Malkhut is furthers from God so it denotes the direction of Evil. You cannot reach Infinite Good or Infinite Evil.

In addition, Keter is seen as the Cause. Malkhut is the archetype of Effect. A Cause cannot exist without an Effect, and an Effect cannot exist with a Cause. In this way, Keter and Malkhut are dependent upon each other.

According to the **Book of Formation** Chapter 1:7
Their end is imbedded in their beginning,
  and their beginning in their end

Up, Down, North, South, East, West have no end. You can never reach Infinite Up, no matter how far you go, Inifinite Down, Infinite North, Infinite South, Infinite East or Infinite West.

Depth indicates a great distance, physically, mentally, emotionally and Spiritually. Depth has no end.

Deep Study

The ***Book of Formation*** is an extremely deep study that has been pulled apart in a variety of ways to help you understand the energetic composition of your Soul. It presents another methodology to understand who you are, where you came from, where you are going and how you got to where you are now. Sometimes information like this is important to a person and sometimes not. You could spend your entire life studying any book because everything that comes into your life is a reflection of some part of you. Many years ago before the Internet, I had just a few books that I loved. I read each many times over the course of several years because each time I read them I gained something different. Now, with the Internet, there are so many books and subjects available that I am constantly adding to my personal library.

Every book, as a reflection of you, is a deep study. There is always going to be more. You have to decide how you want to use your time. You can study or you can live, or combine both aspects together. The more years you have, the deeper your personal Self-study becomes. Every decade, I think of how much more I know now. But a decade ago I thought I knew a lot. Now, I already know that as much as I know there is so much more to do, know and grow. The most important thing is to live your existence as a form of living prayer in conscious awareness. You are your own ***Book of Formation***. This information is already within. When the time is correct you always access what you need to know when you need to know it as well as the reason and the purpose. I enjoy getting to know my Self and appreciate the challenges along the way.

- Do you think people spend too much time in contemplation rather than in living?
- Or too much time in living and not enough time in contemplation?
- Is it challenging to find the balance of the two?
- Does the **Book of Formation** teach morality?
- Do people study it for formulas and information?
- Does having Truth mean that you use it morally and ethically?
- Do you behave only to avoid the consequences or because it is the correct thing to do?
- Does knowing the Spiritual Law provide guidance in what is correct?
- Can it sometimes be challenging to discern what is correct and incorrect?
- Can knowing the consequences be the nudge you may need to choose correctly?
- Does knowing the Spiritual Law help you understand consequences, even in hindsight?
- Are you surprised sometimes at your own personal depth?
- Or the depth of the subjects that you study?
- Could you spend your entire life studying just one book, if this was all that was available to you, and still grow?
- When you think of how much you know, is it overwhelming to think of what you do not know and how much more learning you will do during this lifeline?

AFFIRMATIONS—HEALING PAST SPIRITUALITY

You have a Spiritual Belief System genetically embedded within since childhood as well as via simultaneous existences. All of this influences your current Spiritual Belief System now. Removing, releasing and updating your relationship with your Creator is quite a feat that sometimes does not seem manageable. This set of affirmations helps guide you in the process.

My Spiritual Belief System challenges me.
I Self-evaluate where I was and where I AM.

I observe the origins of my Spiritual Belief System.
I contemplate the words of others during early childhood.

I observe my first impressions of what I was told.
I observe my first reactions to what I was told.

I observe my inner knowing as a child.
I question why I did or did not believe the words of others.

I evaluate the changes in my Spiritual Belief Systems through the years.
I observe specific incidents which contributed to Spiritual Belief changes.

I release via the Oversoul level those beliefs which were inaccurate.
I forgive those people who taught the inaccuracies.

I forgive my Self for believing the inaccuracies.
I had what I needed at the time for the experiences I needed.

I explore my Creator via experiential Self-exploration.
All my answers are inherently within.

I unlock who and what I AM one step at a time.
My Creator guides and directs every step of the way.

I AM in control of me.
I explore what I know to set the frequency of receiving verifiable answers.

I AM an explorer of consciousness.
I AM my own best teacher.

I explore my family's Spiritual Belief System.
There is a Spiritual Belief System embedded in my genetics.

I ask my ancestors via my Oversoul to show me their way.
Knowing their way shows me my way.

I research the Spiritual Belief System of my family.
I evaluate my mind-pattern that brought this system to me.

I research the Spiritual Belief Systems of the geographic location of my ancestors.

Hidden history reveals itself to me.

I ask my ancestors via my Oversoul to show me their way.

Knowing their way shows me my way.

I evaluate my genetics for embedded programming that affects my Spiritual Belief Systems.

I do my deprogramming exercises on a regular and consistent basis.

Genetic programming reveals false Spiritual Belief Systems.

I identify the frequency of false Spiritual Belief Systems.

I identify the frequency of false societal Spiritual Belief Systems.

I release the need to participate in false Spiritual Belief Systems.

I explore the Spiritual Belief Systems of my Simultaneous Existences.

My Simultaneous Existences reveal the patterns of my mind.

I allow the chaos that stirring and digging within my mind-pattern brings.

Proactive upheaval brings growth and change.

Deep within, all my questions are already answered.
I AM patient as I wade through my own inner process.

I allow the inner discomfort that comes with chaos.
I release what I no longer need to reveal what I do need.

I continue my forgiveness and release work on a consistent basis.
All that I find contributes to who I AM today.

I pay attention to and record my dreams.
Dreams are Self-messages to my conscious mind.

I AM a merger of my linear past, present and future Spiritual Belief Systems.
I now have the best and most accurate Spiritual Belief System.

I AM a living example of the best and most accurate Spiritual Belief Systems.
My thoughts, words, actions and reactions are my living testimony.

I inspire my Self to always grow more accurately.
I stay true to my known path.

I adjust my thoughts, words, actions and reactions according to my inner revelations.

Deep inner knowledge grows deeper.

God-Mind Wisdom guides my process.

Deep knowledge comes with deep wisdom.

Deep knowledge and deep wisdom come with deep responsibility.

I focus on correct thinking and action at all times.

My Spiritual Belief System guides my life.

My life is a prayer to my Creator.

AFFIRMATIONS—CREATING BY BREATHING

Your breath is the first and only thing that ties you into this reality; it is the last thing to leave when you exit. Nothing can exist without breath/vibration/frequency. Your breath is a statement that you are a Living Sentient Being who deserves respect.

I create with every breath I take.
My breath dictates my life.

Deep breathing allows deep thinking.
I breathe deeply.

Shallow breathe creates ill health.
I deepen my breaths.

I breathe in Medium Green to oxygenate.
My breath carries oxygen to all my cells.

My thoughts ride my breath throughout my body.
My physical cells respond to my thoughts. .

I breathe in Medium Green to emotionally heal.
Slow breathing calms my emotions.

My breath carries my words.
Words create.

I use my words wisely.
My words create my life.

My breath creates my sleep.
I follow my breath into deep and restful slumber.

My breath creates my posture.
Standing straight aligns my spine.

I breathe into my center aligned with my spine.
My breath creates the alignment which anchors me into Source.

I breathe my Self into my center.
I breathe all that I AM into my center.

I breathe all that I no longer need out the top of my head and into my Oversoul.
I breathe all that I need in through the top of my head from my Oversoul.

My breath upgrades and elevates all levels of my Being.
My breath focuses my thinking.

My breath represents my life force.
My breath aligns with the ebb and flow of my Creator.

Every cell in my body breathes.
I breathe in alignment with the breath of the Creator.

I AM synchronized with All That Is.
My breath is synchronized with All That Is.

I choose my words wisely.
My words transmute the air.

Time and space are manipulated through the air.
My words direct my time and space.

Words are sounds.
Sound needs air to carry it.

Sound creates.
I use sound to what is most correct and beneficial.

I hear the Sounds of Creation.
The Sounds of Creation direct my focus.

I AM one with the Sounds of Creation.
I AM one with a Universe of Harmony.

My breath brings Divine Order into my life.
My life is in Divine Harmony.

The Sounds of my life are in Divine Harmony.
I breathe in Divine Harmony.

I breathe out discord and chaos, up to My Oversoul.
My breath creates a vacuum to pull in what I need from my Oversoul.

I gratefully accept all that my Oversoul gives me.
My breath reminds me that I AM always connected.

My breath oxygenates each and every cell of my Being.
I AM the agelessness of my Soul.

My breath takes me deeper into the DNA of my Soul.
My breath harmonizes my inner and outer worlds.

Breath is sacred.
I AM a blessing to Self and others.

My breath creates my sacred space.
All space is sacred and I treat it as such.

Appendices

The 10 Sefirot

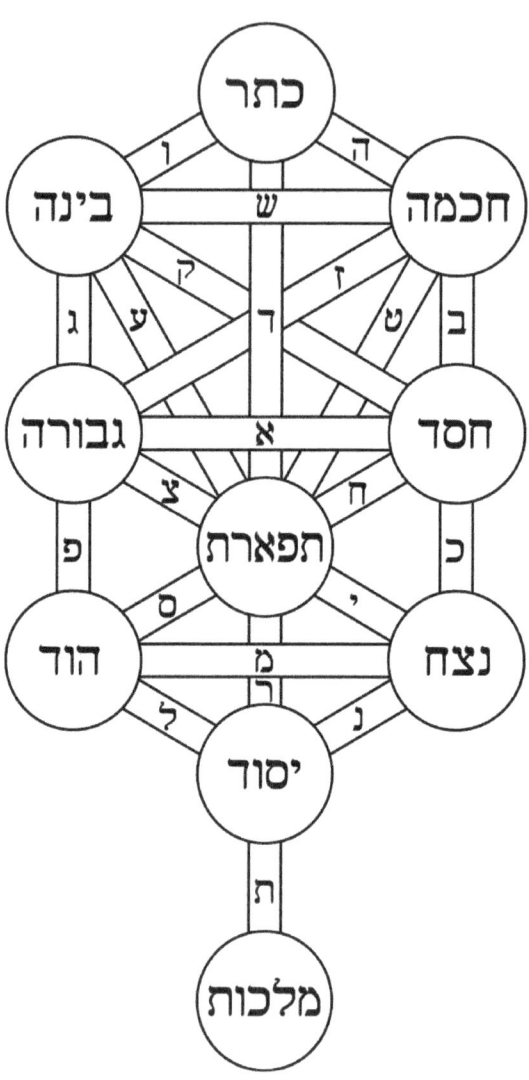

The 10 Sefirot Correlated to Hyperspace

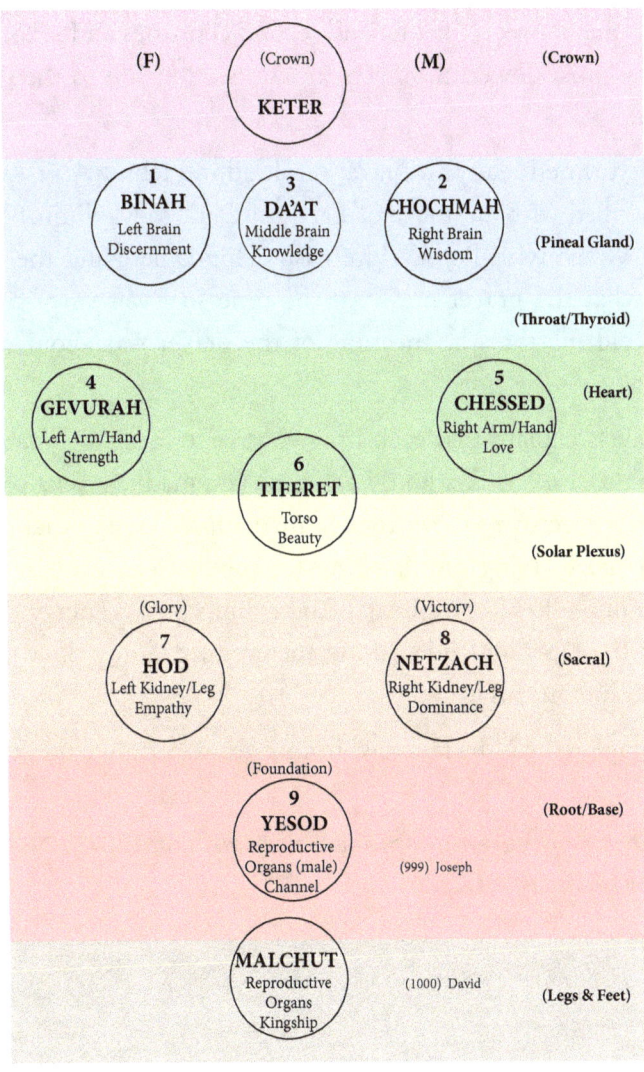

The Ana Beko'ach Prayer

42 Word Name of God

The *Ana Beko'ach Prayer* is a 42 word Name of God, 6 words on each of 7 lines, or 6 x 7 = 42. The prayer was formed by Rav Nehonia ben Ha Kana between the first and second centuries and is considered one of the most powerful prayers for connecting you to the Power of Creation.

The first time I read this prayer out loud in Hebrew, my vision was suddenly filled with an image of Earth in Dark to Medium Blues and Medium Green with Pure White wispy clouds here and there. I had no idea what the prayer meant at the time so I was surprised when Stewart told me that the meaning of the prayer was about resetting the world.

Kabbalists explain that each time you recite the *Ana Beko'ach*, you return to the time of Creation. Each time you meditate on a particular sequence, you return to the original uncorrupted energy that built the world. By performing the *Ana Beko'ach* meditation, you enrich your life with unadulterated Spiritual Light and cosmic energy. Say this prayer in the morning and again in the evening. Study the words and what each line means.

The prayer is read in Hebrew, from right to left. See the following page.

https://sorvete-de-morango.blogspot.com/2019/09/ana-bekoach-sheet-music.html

The Ana Beko'ach Prayer

#	Sefirah	Transliteration	Meaning
1	Chesed	ana b'koach g'dulat yeminecha tatir tzerurah	Removal of time, space and motion. Removing the negative influence of physical matter from our lives. Unconditional Love
2	Gevurah	kabel rinat amecha sagvenu taharenu nora	Restricting the reactive system. Closing the gates from Satan. Forgetting all limited thoughts
3	Tiferet	na gibor dorshei yichudecha k'vavat shamrem	Opening the channel of sustenance. Retrieving the Light from the Klipot. Removing hatred for no reason
4	Netzach	barchem taharem rachamei tzidkatecha tamid gamlem	The power to persevere
5	Hod	chasin kadosh b'rov tuvcha nahel adatecha	Clairvoyance – to be able to see the connection between cause and effect. To see the Big Picture
6	Yesod	yachid ge'eh l'am'cha p'neh zochrei kdushatecha	Spreading spirituality throughout the world, enlightening others particularly through Kabbalah
7	Malchut	shav'atenu kabel ush'ma tza'akatenu yodeh ta'alumot	The power to manifest things in the right way. Renewal and restoration
		baruch shem kevod malchuto le'olam va'ed (silently)	

I AM that I AM

The Hebrew text with niqqud

I am that I am is a common English translation of the Hebrew phrase אֶהְיֶה אֲשֶׁר אֶהְיֶה, 'ehyeh 'ăšer 'ehyeh ([ʔehˈje ʔaˈʃer ʔehˈje]) – also "I am who I am", "I will become what I choose to become",[citation needed] "I am what I am", "I will be what I will be", "I create what(ever) I create", or "I am the Existing One". [1] The traditional English translation within Judaism favors "I will be what I will be" because there is no present tense of the verb "to be" in the Hebrew language.

Its context is the encounter of the burning bush (Exodus 3:14): Moses asks what he is to say to the Israelites when they ask what God ['Elohiym] has sent him to them, and YHWH replies, "I am who I am", adding, "Say this to the people of Israel, 'I am has sent me to you.'"[2] 'Ehyeh is the first person form of hayah, "to be", and owing to the peculiarities of Hebrew grammar means "I am", "I was", and "I will be".[3] The meaning of the longer phrase 'ehyeh 'ăšer 'ehyeh is debated, and might be seen as a promise ("I will be with you") or as statement of incomparability ("I am without equal").[2]

https://en.wikipedia.org/wiki/I_Am_that_I_Am

What is a Mezuzah?

What is a Mezuzah?

The simple answer is: A Mezuzah is the small box you will often see on the right side of Jewish homes.

But what is inside the box?

Inside each Mezuzah box is a small parchment scroll which is the important part of the Mezuzah. It has two paragraphs from the **Torah** written on it by hand in special ancient Hebrew calligraphy

Why do Jewish people put a mezuzah on their doorposts?

In two places (Deut 6 and 11), the **Torah** (**Bible**) commands the People of Israel to inscribe words of the **Torah** upon their doors. The ancient Jewish tradition, recorded in the Talmud tells us that these verses command us to place a parchment scroll with these two paragraphs from the **Torah** on the upper third of the doors of our home.

Can I make my own Mezuzah?

You can certainly make the box for the Mezuzah. There are no laws regarding the box. It is only there to protect and beautify the scroll which is inside. You only have to make sure that it has enough room inside to insert the scroll without bending it or damaging it.

But making a mezuzah scroll is a different story. The ancient Jewish tradition gives very exact details regarding how this scroll is to be prepared and affixed. Here are some examples:

No two letters can touch

No letter can have any break in it

No letter can run off the edge of the page

There can be no spelling mistakes or missing words or letters.

Each letter must have a specific shape that doesn't look like any other letter

The ink must be jet black

The parchment must be made from the skin of a kosher animal and made with special intention to be used for mezuzahs.

The scribe must pronounce a formula, sanctifying the name of G-d before he writes a name of G-d in the mezuzah.

The mezuzah must be written in order. If a mistake is made, the scribe must erase back to the place where he made the mistake and continue from there.

These are just a few of the thousands of laws that apply to the writing of a mezuzah scroll. This means that the scribe who writes the mezuzah, must study these laws and practice for years before he can write proper, kosher mezuzahs.

Isn't the Mezuzah a kind of lucky charm?

Jewish people affix Mezuzahs because it is a Mitzvah (commandment) from the Torah not in order to receive any reward. But, the Torah does promise that when people are scrupulous in performance of the Mitzvahs, they will be blessed with good things.

There is also a tradition that G-d protects the home of one who is careful to affix kosher mezuzahs to all of the doors of their home. For this reason, it is customary to have the mezuzahs checked by a qualified Torah scribe whenever there is some unusual damage or illness in the home. We are concerned that letters may have cracked or been damaged by water and the mezuzah may be invalid.

https://mezuzahstore.com/pages/what-is-a-mezuzah

Glossary

A

ACTIVATION: When a program is brought to full function.

AFFIRMATION: A statement that defines a course of action, or a state of inner being; repeating words many times by thinking, speaking, or writing it to bring new avenues of action into your conscious mind.

AIN SOF: Without end; Infinite Being.

ANIMAL MIND: Located at the solar plexus and controlled by the Reptilian brainstem; controls the physical body; in charge of fight or flight.

AURA: Your personal energy field.

ALIEN: A physical being from another planet.

ALTER: Section or compartmentalized personality within a programming matrix.

ANDROGYNOUS: Male and female combined without sexual distinction.

ARCHETYPE: Symbol or glyph from hyperspace or mind-patterns.

ASTRAL PLANE: The border zone between physical reality and hyperspace.

B

BEAR FREQUENCY ARCHETYPE: Increases protective nature; enhances introversion for self-study; best for males.

BISEXUAL: Sexually desiring both males and females.

BREASTS ARCHETYPE: Enhances healthy breasts for Men and Women.

C

CANCELLATION ARCHETYPE: Removes anything unwanted.

CENTER: Your center is aligned along your spine, providing a safe space from which to work; you pull yourself into it by willing yourself into it.

CEREMONY: Gathering to celebrate or honor an entity or Illuminati holiday.

CHAKRA BAND: Energy center of the body and encompassing area.

CHAKRAS: Along the human spinal column there are main nerve bundles called ganglions, which are esoterically called "chakras," a word that means "wheels" in Sanskrit. They form along the "S" curve of the spine, which looks like a snake. For this reason the chakra system is referred to as "Kundalini," the Sanskrit word for snake.

COLLECTIVE CONSCIOUS MIND: The body of space that contains the accumulated known knowledge of humankind.

COLLECTIVE UNCONSCIOUS: The body of space that contains the accumulated thoughts of humankind; these established thought patterns directly affect what you move through today.

COMMUNICATION ARCHETYPE: Speaking up as appropriate.

CONSCIOUS MIND: Contains your present.

CONSTRUCT: Similar to a physical object created in the programming matrix to work with the alter in a specific function.

D

DEPROGRAMMING: Techniques to block and/or remove mind-control/programming.

DIRECT AWARENESS: To know by experiencing the knowledge.

DNA SEQUENCES: This refers to the DNA sequences opening up in the body, which is a form of Kundalini activation. DNA codes are the instructions that tell your body what to do and be. Some instructions you are running at birth. These dictate that you will have blue eyes, two legs, two arms, etc. Others activate later in life, such as health conditions, ability to play music, sing, etc.

DOLPHIN FREQUENCY ARCHETYPE: Eases mental shifting into hyperspace.

E

EMOTIONAL BALANCE ARCHETYPE: Obtains healthy emotional balance by balancing left and right hemispheres of the brain.

ENERGY: A physical substance consisting of shape, weight, consistency, and color.

ELF: Extra low frequency generally related to microwaves for mindcontrol purposes; energy.

ET (EXTRATERRESTRIAL): Borderline physical/non-physical beings not bound to our reality.

EXPANSION ARCHETYPE: Increases and expands goals and desires.

F

FEMALE ORGASM ARCHETYPE: Removes female frigidity; increase sexual responsiveness.

FREQUENCY: A rate of vibration that distinguishes one flow of energy from all other flows.

G

God-Mind: Neutral energy; All That Is.

Golem: Human animal created from mud; animated by a controller.

Group-Mind: Formed when vibrations band together.

H

Habit Response: An established pattern of behavior that allows you to react to any given situation without thinking, whether physical or mental. It can be positive, negative, or neutral.

Happiness Archetype: Establishes happiness.

Horizontal Experience: Pulls you out into similar growth.

Hyperspace: A region of consciousness that exists outside of linear space and time.

I

Illuminati: Member or associate of one of the 13 ruling families on Earth.

Illusion: The way you perceive things to be.

Individualized Consciousness Archetype: Helps you rise out of the Group-Mind into Your Own connection with Mind and Personal your Oversoul and God-Mind.

K

Kabbalah: Receiving.

Know by Knowing: To understand through direct awareness; to understand the feeling of an experience.

Knowledge: Information.

L

LANGUAGE OF HYPERSPACE: The Original Language that emanates from the Mind of God consisting of color, tone, and archetype (symbol).

LEADERSHIP ARCHETYPE: Installs Self-Leadership.

LION FREQUENCY ARCHETYPE: Increases your direct awareness to God-Mind power.

LOGOS CHRISTOS ARCHETYPE: Healing generator on specific body locations.

LOVE: Neutral energy that emanates from God-Mind that does not discriminate.

LYRAE: Star system in the Milky Way Galaxy that is the origin point for all humans.

M

MACROCOSM: God-Mind; All That Is; the larger picture of everything.

MALE ORGASM ARCHETYPE: Removes impotence; increases virility.

MATRIX PROGRAMMING: The structure in the mind that facilitates mind-control; 13 x 13 x 13, which equals 2,197 compartments.

MEDITATION: A process that moves you beyond words and connects you with silence, the level of feeling; the listening from which information is gathered; centered in the right brain.

MENTAL BALANCE ARCHETYPE: Creates mental balance in all areas.

MERGING WITH ASPECTS OF ALTERNATIVE SELVES ARCHETYPE: Bring current goals to fruition by merging with your Self in the *Eternal Now*.

MICROCOSM: You; a world in miniature.

MIND-PATTERN: Blueprint of a persons' thoughts.

N

NEGATIVE: Negative is not "bad," but merely a condition that exists; the opposite of positive, which explains another part of the same experience.

NEW BEGINNINGS ARCHETYPE: Start new projects, relationships, health, finances.

NEW WORLD RELIGION: Global religion.

NEW WORLD ORDER (NWO): Global government dictatorship being created by the Illuminati.

O

OBJECTIVE LISTENING: Listening and evaluating without judgment or criticism.

OBJECTIVE OBSERVING: Watching and evaluating without judgment or criticism.

OVERALL HEALING ARCHETYPE: Heals body, mind, and soul.

OVERSOUL: Neutral energy that comes out of God-Mind; your Oversoul is to you what your Earth parents are to your body. Your Oversoul is your point of origin out of God-Mind.

OVERSOUL ARCHETYPE: Your Point of Origin out of the God-Mind.

P

PINEAL GLAND: Organ at the center of the head.

POSITIVE: Positive is not better than negative, but is merely a condition that exists; the opposite of negative, which explains another part of the same experience.

POWER ARCHETYPE: Increases personal power via your mental abilities.

PRAYER: Request that affects the results of meditation; centered in the left-brain.

Pregnancy Archetype: Increases fertility; maintain healthy pregnancy.

Pregnancy Prevention Archetype: Cancels your fertility.

Proactive Learning: Active learning; gathering knowledge before an experience occurs.

Psychic Energy: Your personal energy; it flows back and forth, and is horizontal.

R

Reactive Learning: Passive learning; gathering knowledge after an experience occurs.

Reality: The way things really are; it may vary considerably from your perception of the way you think things are.

Rejuvenation Archetype: Enhances physical, mental, emotional, spiritual rejuvenation.

Release & Resolve Past Issues Archetype: Cleans out what you no longer need.

Relationships Archetype: Improves and enhances people connection.

Reptilian: A being with lizard-like characteristics from either the inner Earth or Draco star system; colonized Lemuria.

S

Self-Integration Archetype: Brown Merger Archetype; merges all parts of Self into one; great deprogramming aid.

Shapeshifter: A person who physically changes from one species to another.

Silence: The deepest level of inner awareness; the level of feeling; you connect with your Oversoul and God-Mind within silence.

SIMULTANEOUS EXISTENCE: All lifelines occurring at the same moment in the *Eternal Now*.

SPIRITUALITY: A state of inner being.

SPIRITUAL & INTUITION CONNECTION ARCHETYPE: Improves conscious connection with your Oversoul and God-Mind.

SOUL-PERSONALITY: Individual strand of an Oversoul.

SUBCONSCIOUS MIND: Contains your memories, moment-by-moment, lifeline-by-lifeline.

SUB-PERSONALITY: A group of similar emotions that becomes strong enough to develop its own consciousness; a sub-personality is not you, but it is a part of you.

SUPERCONSCIOUS MIND: Provides the direct link to your Oversoul and God-Mind.

T

T-BAR: Archetype emanating from the pineal gland relating to balance

TORAH: The *Five Books of Moses*; coded instructions for living; a code for life, instructions not a religion; given/revealed/transmitted to Moses approximately 3600 years ago.

TRIGGER: Sensory input that opens a program.

U

ULTIMATE PROTECTION ARCHETYPE: Protects whatever you desire.

UNIVERSAL ENERGY: Energy that is available to everyone; using it allows you to keep your psychic energy; it flows up and down, and is vertical.

UNIVERSAL LAW: Rules and regulations that pervade all creation; emanates from God-Mind.

V

VERTICAL EXPERIENCE: Pulls you up into new growth.

VIBRATION: Frequency rate of an energy.

VIBRATORY IMPRINT: Accumulated feelings of like experiences; they cause you to react to your experiences of today through your accumulated feelings of yesterday.

VISUALIZATION: Creating a mental scenario that can be manifested either mentally or physically; centered at the pineal gland.

W

WEALTH & PROSPERITY ARCHETYPE: Increases finances.

WISDOM: Knowledge applied.

WISDOM ARCHETYPE: Enhances your correct use of knowledge.

WOLF FREQUENCY ARCHETYPE: Enhances family relationships.

Y

YOU: Individualized neutral energy.

Z

ZOHAR/BOOK OF SPLENDOR: Soul of the *Bible/Torah*; the oral *Zohar/Book of Splendor* was revealed to a Rabbi approximately 2000 years ago.

Index

Symbols

3 Mother Letters 452
5 Books of Moses 355
6 Days of Creation 455
10 Commandments 444
10 Sefirot 444, 449
32 Paths of Wisdom 432, 435, 449
72 Names of God 11, 16, 33, 124, 353
72 Names of God Frequencies 74

A

Actualize Your Ideas 284
Addiction 145
Addictions 203, 336
Aleph 32
Alice in Wonderland 374
All of Existence 216
All That Exists 240, 264, 289
All That Is 435
Alternative Medical Apocrypha 147, 336
alternative realities 345
Alzheimer's Disease 193
Ana Beko'ach Prayer 480
Ancient Codes of Existence 12
Angels 103
Animal Mind 13, 19, 26, 34, 135, 138, 145, 173, 192, 203, 236, 248, 297, 377, 457
Appropriate Influence 316
Archetypes 60, 81, 355, 369

Ark 354
Ashkenazim 357
Asiyah 447
Atzilut 446

B

Beriyah 447
Bet 32
Bible 58
Biblical Hebrew 355
big picture 212
billionaires 162
Book of Formation 432, 446
Book of Formation/Creation 59
Book of Splendor 361
Brown Merger 205

C

Chakra Bands 137, 204
Chakra Band System 342
Chakra system 204
Cheereek 358
Cherubim 444
Chesed 17
Cholam 358
circumcision 444
Circumcision of the tongue 443
Collective Humanity 252
Color, Tone and Archetype 182, 268, 401
Completion 188
Conflict 123

Confronting Darkness 195
Conventional religions 291
Coronavirus 170

D

dark forces 170
death 279
Decoding Your Life 23, 59, 111, 115, 157, 186, 199, 207, 227, 287, 300, 374
depression 134
Divine Creation 441
Divine Energy 65
Divine Order 64, 116
DNA 24, 373
dream dictionary 90
Dream State 89

E

Earth 25, 85, 150, 159, 279, 298, 360, 398
Easter Massacre 95
Ego 200
energy field 107
Energy of Hebrew Letters 32
Eternal Now 42, 75, 162, 311, 313, 328, 342, 345, 361, 435, 438
Expansions 74, 174

F

Fear 207
fertility 137
Fertility Archetype 137
Five Greatnesses 442
Five Loves 442
Five Strengths 442
flow of consciousness 231
frequency 366
full spectrum frequency 166

G

Gematria 359
Genesis 359
genetic programming 135
Gevurah 17
Gimmel 32, 101, 102, 124, 372
global handler 94
Global Transformation 53, 120
God 37, 185
God-Mind 38, 51, 81, 97, 112, 138, 141, 142, 158, 166, 182, 216, 232, 243, 248, 280, 288, 294, 297, 316, 337, 342, 388

God of Israel 455
God's Throne 446
Gold 332
Green Psychic Flush 192, 204
Green Spiral Staircase 193

H

Haggadah 388
Happiness 261
hate 181
Healing 85
Healing Archetypes and Symbols 345
Hebrew 50, 58, 65, 94, 101, 102, 186, 369
Hebrew AlephBet 125
Hebrew genetics 16
Hebrew Letters 91, 101, 355
Heights of Relationships 115, 203, 204
Highest Good 297
holographic matrix 298
Holy Object 354
Hyperspace 34, 85, 97, 193, 208, 248, 291, 293, 401, 434
Hyperspace Archetype 32, 137, 139, 369, 373
Hyperspace/Oversoul 12, 24, 32, 34, 90, 97, 147, 193, 208, 248, 291, 293, 324, 337, 341, 450
Hyperspace Plus 292, 298, 406

I

illusion 291, 298, 315, 341
infighting 258
inner bridges 186
inner negativity 153
internal communication 186
Israelites 20, 31, 220

J

Jealousy 161
Judais 407
Judaism 53, 377, 387, 407

K

Kabbalah 11, 16, 49, 59, 65, 361, 377, 387, 405, 428
Kabbalists 95, 105
Keter 434, 438
King of the Universe 455
Kiss of God 435
Komatz 357
Kubutz 358

L

Labyrinth 445
Latin Alphabet 125
Laws of Nature 435
life force 231
Lime Green 162
limitations 263
Lord of Host 455

M

Maroon 196, 208
Maroon Frequency 166
Memory 191
Mezuzah 483
millionaires 162
Mind Over Matter 236
Mind-pattern 34, 41, 67, 99, 100, 102, 112, 119, 149, 154, 158, 169, 223, 229, 240, 243, 252, 263, 264, 323, 337, 447
Miracles 72
Montauk: Alien Connection 74
Moses 59, 220, 355, 375, 443
multidimensional 341
Muslims 54

N

Name Frequencies 51, 54, 97
Name Frequency 57, 71, 81, 112
Name of God Frequency 64
negative frequencies 162, 166
Negative memories 191
negativity 99, 109, 112
nekkudot 357
New Age Judaism 407

O

Objective Observing 315
One Source 116
Original Act of Creation 204
Original Creation 432
Oversoul 54, 59, 74, 81, 89, 97, 101, 104, 112, 116, 138, 141, 142, 158, 166, 181, 192, 193, 204, 212, 219, 224, 232, 240, 243, 248, 263, 264, 280, 293, 294, 297, 316, 342, 446
Oversoul Archetype 434
Oversoul dream 89
Oversoul Infinity Archetype 443
Oversoul level 124, 182, 186, 224, 240, 267, 288, 332, 346, 361, 401, 431
Oversoul Matrix 292, 298, 406
Oversoul Protection Techniques 34
Oversoul work 208

P

Pale Orange 332
Pale Orange Frequency 166
Pale Pink 288
Passover 388
Patach 357
Pedophilia 170, 204
personal transformation 119, 120
phallic symbols 23
Pineal Gland 51, 57, 87, 101
Plannedemic 13, 245
Power of Creation 480
Prayer 27
primordial 74, 86
programming 81, 89, 95, 112, 138, 142, 146, 204, 342
programming dreams 89
Prosperity 243
Protection 97
psychic energy 111, 231, 283

R

Rabbi 59
Red Frequency 287, 288
Red Sea Rules 11, 16
Reed Sea 20, 41, 58
Religious Law 407
Responsibility 3
Revelations 185
Revelations of Time & Space, History and God 16
Root Causes 150

S

Save The Children 123
Sefer Yetzirah 59, 124, 360, 385, 403, 437, 446, 449, 454
Sefirot 17, 375
Segol 358
Self-criticism 227
Self-deprecating 294, 295
Self-education 342
Self-empower 170
Self-esteem 199, 227, 228
Self-exploration 61

Self-fulfilling 74
Self-imposed 264
Self-judgment 227
Self-limit 265
Self-limitations 263
Self-pity 142
Self-protection 141
Self-punishment 146
Self-responsibility 299, 300
Self-responsible 142, 325
Self-Value 173, 199, 200, 227, 228
Self-Worth 161, 162, 165, 196, 199, 227, 228, 236
Sexual energy 203
Sheva 358
Shoorook 358
Silver 332
Simultaneity 342
Sleeping Beauty 374
Snow White 374
social media 123, 150, 251
Soul Growth 138, 154
Soul Mate 177
Soul-Personality 102, 276, 295, 341, 400
Sounds of Creation 355
Source 22, 138
Sparks of Light 68
Spiritual Belief System 345
Spiritual Direction 335
Spiritual High 261
Spiritual Law 60, 100, 103, 142, 173, 174, 374, 377, 401, 407
Spiritual Laws 38, 239, 316
Spiritual Mind 19, 26, 138, 174, 236, 248, 458
Stop the Conflict 123
Suicide Programming 166

T

Template of God-Mind 173, 185
Ten Commandments 375
Tetragrammaton 354
The Living God 455
The Power of Kabbalah 59
Tiferet 17
Time Travel 57
Tithing 173
Torah 11, 53, 58, 157, 354, 361, 382, 430, 449
Tree of Knowledge 457
Tree of Life 435, 437
Tribes of Israel 369

True Prosperity 244
True Reality 31
True Reality of Sexuality 445
Trusting Source 297
Truth 165
Tzayray 357
Tzimtzum of Creation 458

U

Unconditional Love 115, 288
Unconditional Love Frequency 117
Unconditional Sharing 275
Unity 260
Universal Law 126, 157
urgency of emergency 28

V

Victim mentality 252, 323
Viole 332

W

Waldensians 95
White energy fields 342
White Light 342
Wizard of Oz 374

Y

Yetzirah 447
Yiddish 430
Your Living Example 308

Z

Zohar 11, 18, 361, 444
Zohar/Book of Splendor 59

www.ingramcontent.com/pod-product-compliance
Lightning Source LLC
Chambersburg PA
CBHW060313230426
43663CB00009B/1688